CHRISTMAS 1955.

HELLO

SISTER

MARY

ELIZABETH!

HOLY,

HAPPY,

JOYOUS

CHRISTMAS

TO ALL MY CARMELITE SISTERS

IN NEW YORK CARMEL.

S.M.

SAINT BERNARD ON THE LOVE OF GOD

The Vision of Saint Bernard — Fra Lippo Lippi

SAINT BERNARD
ON THE
LOVE *of* GOD

. . . all can feel the God that smites,
But ah, how few the God that loves!

FRANCIS THOMPSON

TRANSLATED FROM THE LATIN
WITH SUPPLEMENTARY NOTES

BY

REV. TERENCE L. CONNOLLY, S.J., PH.D.,

LECTURER ON ENGLISH LITERATURE IN THE
GRADUATE SCHOOL OF BOSTON COLLEGE

Reprinted with permission of Spiritual Book Associates

THE NEWMAN PRESS
Westminster, Maryland
1951

Imprimi potest:
James T. McCormick, S.J.
PROVINCIAL, New England

Nihil obstat:
Arthur J. Scanlan, S. T. D.
CENSOR LIBRORUM.

Imprimatur:
✠ Patrick Cardinal Hayes
ARCHBISHOP, New York.

First Printing 1937
Reprinted by The Newman Press 1951

DESIGNED BY GEO. E. NEUHEDEL
PRINTED IN THE UNITED STATES OF AMERICA

TRANSLATOR'S NOTE

THIS TRANSLATION WAS originally made and privately printed to assist students of the poetry of Coventry Patmore who drew his inspiration largely from Saint Bernard's writings. Many of those who read and used the translation have convinced the translator that it has a more than academic appeal and that it should be given wider circulation. Obviously it is not meant for readers who can appreciate the original Latin. It is intended for those to whom Latin is a barrier. And it strives to present Saint Bernard's thought in a faithful rather than in an elegant English version. The Latin text used is chiefly that of Mabillon, with an occasional preference given the Rev. Mr. Williams' edition of *De Diligendo Deo*. In the selection of passages from the "Sermons on the *Canticle of Canticles*" the translator has limited himself to those found in the redaction begun by Patmore's second wife and continued by the poet himself after his wife's death and published under the title, "Fragments from a Fragment."

Today when mysticism and love are so frequently discussed and so seldom understood, and when the love of God is being treated by many incompetent writers, it is hoped that the following thoughts from Saint Bernard may be of some help to those who read them, whether they are souls who still have need of Christ the Physician, or those favored few who are already prepared for the embrace of Christ their Spouse.

TERENCE L. CONNOLLY, S.J., PH.D.

Feast of the Assumption, 1936.
Saint Mary's Hall,
Boston College,
Chestnut Hill, Mass.

TABLE OF CONTENTS

PART II.

Fragments from Saint Bernard's "Sermons on the *Canticle of Canticles.*"

PART I

THE BOOK OF SAINT BERNARD ON THE LOVE OF GOD

SAINT BERNARD ON THE LOVE OF GOD

PREFACE

TO THE ILLUSTRIOUS LORD AIMERIC, CARDINAL-DEACON AND CHANCELLOR OF THE CHURCH OF ROME, BERNARD, ABBOT OF CLAIRVAUX, WISHES LIFE UNTO THE LORD AND DEATH IN HIM

You were accustomed to ask prayers of me and not questions, and indeed I feel certain that I am equipped for neither. My professed vocation, it is true, imposes the former obligation upon me even if my way of acting does not, but in regard to the latter obligation (to speak the truth) I see that in me those qualifications are lacking which seem especially necessary to meet it—diligence and natural talent. Nevertheless it is pleasing, I admit, that in return for things of the body you ask those of the spirit, although to be sure, it would have been better if you had gone to one richer than I am. But since it is customary among the learned and unlearned alike to make excuses of this sort, and it is not easily known whether the excuse is really prompted by ignorance or by modesty unless the performance of the task enjoined makes it clear, accept of my poverty what I have, lest by keeping silence I should be looked upon as a philosopher. I do not, however, pledge myself to answer all your questions. To that, only, which you ask concerning the love of God I shall make answer as He Himself suggests. For, this tastes sweeter and is imparted more confidently and is heard with greater profit. Reserve the other questions for the more diligent.

CHAPTER I

WHY AND HOW GOD SHOULD BE LOVED

You wish, therefore, to hear from me why and how God should be loved? And I: the reason for loving God is God Himself; the way is to love Him beyond measure. Is this enough? It is, perchance, but only for one who is wise. But if *to the unwise I am debtor;*[1] where enough has been said to the wise I must also, as usual, administer to the needs of others. And so out of consideration for those who are slower to understand, I shall consider it no burden to repeat what I have said, more fully rather than more profoundly. There is a twofold reason, I should say, why God should be loved for His own sake: because nothing can be more justly, nothing more profitably loved. Indeed when the question is asked why God should be loved it may have one of two meanings. For the question may arise from the fact that a person does not clearly see what particularly constitutes the basis of his inquiry: whether it is God's title to our love or our own advantage in loving Him. To be sure, I would give the same answer to both of these questions: I find no other worthy reason for loving Him except Himself. And first let us examine the question of God's title to our love. A very special title to it is His who gave Himself to us despite the fact that we were so undeserving. For, what better than Himself could even He have given? If, then, in asking the reason why we should love God we seek to know His title to

[1] Romans, I, 14.

our love, it is chiefly this: *because He hath first loved us.*[2] He it is who is clearly deserving of being loved in return, especially if one considers who He is that loved, who they are whom He loved and how much He loved them. And who is He? Is He not the One to whom every spirit bears witness: *Thou art my God, for Thou hast no need of my goods?* [3] And the true love of this Sovereign One lies in this, that it does not seek its own interests. But to whom is such unmixed love shown? *When we were enemies,* it is said, *we were reconciled to God.*[4] God, therefore, has loved His enemies and that, *gratis.* But how much? As much as Saint John says: *God so loved the world as to give His only begotten Son.*[5] And Saint Paul adds: *He spared not even His own Son, but delivered Him up for us all.*[6] That very Son says of Himself: *Greater love than this no man hath, that a man lay down his life for his friends.*[7] Thus has the Just deserved from the ungodly, the Greatest from the least, the All-powerful from the weak. But some one may say: Yes, thus has He deserved of mankind, but of the Angels, not so. That is true, because the Angels had no need of it. Moreover, He who succored men in so great a necessity preserved the Angels from it, and He who by His love for men brought it about that they should no longer remain such as they were, the Same with equal love bestowed upon the Angels the grace of never becoming such as men once were.

[2] 1 St. John IV, 10.
[3] Psalm XV, 2.
[4] Romans V, 10.
[5] St. John III, 16.
[6] Romans VIII, 32
[7] St. John XV, 13.

CHAPTER II

HOW GREATLY GOD DESERVES TO BE LOVED BY MAN BECAUSE OF HIS GIFTS OF BODY AND SOUL. HOW THESE ARE TO BE KNOWN AND KEPT WITHOUT WRONG TO HIM WHO GAVE THEM

THOSE TO WHOM what I have said is plain will also, I think, plainly see why God should be loved: that is, whence He deserves to be loved. But if unbelievers blind themselves to these truths God is still ready to confound their ingratitude with His numberless benefits conferred for man's advantage and manifest to human sense. Who else, forsooth, supplies food to everyone who eats, light to everyone who sees, breath to everyone who breathes? But it is foolish to strive to enumerate what I have just spoken of as innumerable. It is enough, by way of example, to have mentioned the chief ones—bread, sun and air. The chief ones, I mean, not because they are superior but because they are more necessary since they pertain to the body. Let man seek his higher goods—dignity, knowledge and virtue—in that higher part of him which excels self, that is, in the soul. By man's dignity I mean his free will in which it is surely given him not only to excel other creatures but also to rule over all other [visible] living things. By knowledge I mean that by which he recognizes that his dignity is within himself but not from himself. By virtue I mean that by which he ardently seeks Him from whom he has his being and valiantly holds fast to Him when found.

Thus every one of these three goods presents a two-fold aspect.

Accordingly, human dignity appears not only as the prerogative of man naturally considered, but as the basis of his [moral] power of dominion which determines the fear which he commands in every other living creature on the face of the earth. Knowledge will likewise be of a double nature if we perceive that this same dignity as well as any other good that is in us dwells within us but is not from ourselves. Lastly, virtue, too, will be recognized as two-fold if it leads us to seek after Him to whom we owe our existence and when we have found Him, makes us cling to Him so that we shall never again be separated from Him. And so dignity without knowledge is of no avail; nay, it is even a hindrance if virtue be lacking, as the reasoning that follows makes clear. What glory can one have in possessing what he does not know that he possesses? Furthermore, to know what you have while not knowing that it does not come from yourself, begets glory but not in the sight of God. And to him who glories in himself the Apostle says: *What hast thou that thou hast not received? And if thou hast received, why dost thou glory as if thou hadst not received it?* [1] He does not say simply, *Why dost thou glory?* but he adds, *as if thou hadst not received it,* as if to declare that not he is blameworthy who glories in what he has, but he who glories in it as though he had not received it. Not without reason *vain* glory is the name given to glory of this sort for it lacks the solid foundation of truth [*i.e.,* is not in accordance with the facts of the case]. Indeed the Apostle draws a distinction between this and true glory when he says: *He that glorieth, may glory in the Lord.*[2] That is, in truth. For the Lord is truth.

It is necessary, therefore, that you know both what you are, and

[1] I Corinthians IV, 7. [2] I Corinthians I, 31.

that you are not such of yourself, lest you be altogether boastful [*i.e.* without any limitation], or vainly so [*i.e.* without any foundation in truth]. Finally it is said: *If thou know not thyself, . . . go forth and follow after the steps of the flocks . . . of thy companions.*[3] This is in truth what happens. When man fashioned in honor does not perceive the honor that is his, he is, by reason of such ignorance justly likened to the beasts of the field that share his present corruption and mortality. It happens, therefore, that a creature distinguished by the gift of reason, through not knowing itself begins to be herded with the droves of unthinking beasts. While ignorant of his own peculiar glory which is from within he is carried away by his own curiosity, determined upon fashioning himself conformably to things purely sensible and becomes one with the rest of visible creatures because he thinks that he has received nothing beyond the rest of them. And so we must be especially on our guard against this ignorance by which, perchance, we think of ourselves as being less than we really are. But no less, indeed much more, must we avoid that other ignorance by which we attribute to ourselves more than we possess. This is what happens when we deceive ourselves into thinking that any good whatever that we have comes from ourselves.[4] But besides both these kinds of ignorance you must shun and abhor that sort of presumption by which knowingly and of set purpose you may, perchance, dare to seek your own glory in goods that are not yours. Thus you would not fear to rob Another of the honor which comes from a good which you well know is in no way attributable to yourself. The former ignorance has no glory at all: the latter has, but not in God's sight. But this third evil, because it is now knowingly committed, usurps what belongs to

[3] Canticle I, 6-7.

[4] Cf. Galatians VI, 3.

God Himself. By comparison with that latter ignorance, this presumption is clearly more grievous and more dangerous in this, that in ignorance God is not known, but in presumption He is contemned. It is worse and more detestable than the former because while the former puts us in a class with the beasts of the field, this latter makes us the fellows of demons. Assuredly it is pride and the greatest offence of all to use the gifts we have received as if they were part of our very selves, and after having accepted favors to usurp the glory of the Bestower.

Thus it is that with these two, dignity and knowledge, there is also need of virtue which is the fruit of both. For it is through virtue that He is sought after and retained Who, as Author and Giver of all things, is deservedly glorified in everything. Otherwise, knowing and not doing what is worthy of him, a man *shall be beaten with many stripes.*[5] Why? Because *he would not understand that he might do well;*[6] rather, *he hath devised iniquity on his bed,*[7] while as a wicked servant he strives to arrogate to himself, nay, even to destroy the glory due his gracious Lord from those goods which, by the gift of intelligence, he knows for certain he has not of himself. It is evident, therefore, that dignity is altogether useless without knowledge, and knowledge without virtue is sinful. But the man of virtue to whom neither knowledge can be sinful nor dignity unfruitful, lifts up his voice to God and frankly confesses: *Not to us, O Lord, not to us; but to Thy name give glory.*[8] That is: We attribute to ourselves, O Lord, neither any knowledge nor any dignity; but to Thy name from whom all proceeds do we impute all.

But we have wandered rather far from our purpose while en-

[5] St. Luke XII, 47.
[6] Psalm XXXV, 4.
[7] *Ibid.* 5.
[8] Psalm CXIII, 9.

gaged in showing that those also who do not know Christ are sufficiently admonished by the natural law through the goods of body and soul which they perceive are theirs. How much they, too, should love God for God's own sake! For, to repeat briefly what has been said on this point, what infidel does not know that the necessities to which allusion has already been made—whence he derives life, whereby he sees, whereby he breathes—are administered to his body in this mortal life by no other than by Him *Who giveth food to all flesh,*[9] *Who maketh His sun to rise upon the good and the bad, and raineth upon the just and the unjust?*[10] What man is there, even though he be ungodly, who can think that the human dignity with which his soul is resplendent is attributable to any other than to Him who says in Genesis: *Let us make man to Our image and likeness?*[11] Who can deem any other the Bestower of knowledge save Him *that teacheth man knowledge?*[12] Who, again, can think that the gift of virtue has been bestowed in the past or hope for it to be given in the future, save from the hand, likewise, of the Lord of Hosts? God, then, deserves to be loved for His own sake even by the infidel who, although he knows not Christ, yet knows himself. Hence there is no excuse for any infidel, even, if he does not love the Lord his God with his whole heart, with his whole soul, and with all his strength.[13] For, that innate sense of justice which reason is not ignorant of, cries out to him from within that he is bound with his whole self to love Him to whom, he is not unaware, he owes all that he is. But it is difficult, nay impossible, for anyone with his powers of free will to render wholly to God's will the things

[9] Psalm CXXXV, 25.
[10] St. Matthew V, 45.
[11] Genesis I, 26.
[12] Psalm XCIII, 10.
[13] Cf. Deuteronomy VI, 5.

he once received from God, and not rather to twist them according to his own will and retain them as his own, according as it is written: *all seek the things that are their own;*[14] and again: *the imagination and thought of man's heart are prone to evil.*[15]

[14] Philippians II, 21.

[15] Genesis VIII, 21.

CHAPTER III

HOW MANY INCENTIVES CHRISTIANS HAVE, MORE THAN INFIDELS, FOR LOVING GOD

THE FAITHFUL, on the other hand, know well how complete is their need of Jesus and of Him crucified. While embracing in wonder *the charity* revealed in Him *which surpasseth all knowledge,*[1] they are filled with shame at not paying back even the very little which they are themselves, in return for love and condescension so great. Easily, therefore, do they grow in love who know that they themselves are more loved: for he to whom less has been given loves less.[2] The Jew or the Pagan, to be sure, can never be urged on by such spurs of love as the Church feels who says: I am wounded with charity;[3] and again: *Stay me up with flowers; compass me about with apples: because I languish with love.*[4] She sees *King Solomon in the diadem wherewith his mother crowned him;*[5] she sees the Only-begotten of the Father *bearing His own cross;*[6] she sees the Lord of Majesty struck and spat upon; she sees the Author of life and glory held fast with nails, pierced with a lance, overwhelmed with reproaches, finally laying down that precious Life of His for His friends. She sees all this and the sword of love pierces her soul the more and she says: *Stay me up with flowers, compass me about with apples: because I*

[1] Ephesians III, 19.
[2] Cf. St. Luke VII, 47.
[3] Cf. Canticle IV, 9.
[4] *Ibid.* II, 5.
[5] *Ibid.* III, 11.
[6] St. John XIX, 17.

languish with love.[7] These *apples,* to be sure, are the pomegranates which the bride led into the garden of her Beloved, plucks from the tree of life; they have borrowed their own peculiar savour from the Bread of Heaven, their color from the Blood of Christ. She [the Church] then sees death itself struck dead and the Author of death led in triumph. She sees captivity led captive[8] from hell [limbo] to earth, from earth to heaven, *that in the name of Jesus every knee should bow of those that are in heaven, on earth and under the earth.*[9] She perceives that the earth which under the ancient curse had brought forth thorns and thistles,[10] has sprung into blossom again at the grace of a new benediction. And in all this recalling that verse: *And my flesh hath flourished again, and with my will I will give praise to Him,*[11] she longs to add to the fruits of the Passion which she has plucked from the tree of the cross, some of the flowers of the resurrection whose fragrance especially allures the Beloved to visit her again and again.

At last she exclaims: *Behold Thou art fair, my Beloved, and comely; our bed is decked with flowers.*[12] In showing Him the bridal-couch she frankly makes known what she desires; and when she speaks of it as *decked with flowers,* she reveals whence she presumes to obtain the gratification of her desires. For it is not from her own merits but from the flowers gathered in a field which God has blessed.[13] Christ who willed to be conceived and reared in Nazareth finds his delight in flowers. The heavenly Bridegroom rejoices in such fragrance and freely enters often into the bridal-chamber of the heart which He has found filled with

[7] Canticle II, 5.
[8] Cf. Ephesians IV, 8.
[9] Philippians II, 10.
[10] Cf. Genesis III, 18.
[11] Psalm XXVII, 7.
[12] Canticle I, 15.
[13] Cf. Genesis XXVII, 27.

fruits of this sort and strewn with flowers. For where He perceives that the grace of His Passion or the glory of His Resurrection is pondered as the subject of diligent meditation, there straightway He is present with eagerness and joy. Know well that the memorials of the Passion are as the fruits of the past year and of all times past under the domination of sin and death, now at last in the fulness of time beginning to appear. But the signs of the Resurrection, mark you, are the new flowers of the season that follows and blooms forth, a new summer, under the influence of grace. Of these flowers the general resurrection which is to come will in the end of time bring forth the fruit which will remain forever. *For,* it is said, *winter is now past; the rain is over and gone. The flowers have appeared in our land;*[14] which means that summer has returned with Him who, released from the coldness of death, was restored to the mild Spring of a new life. *Behold,* He says, *I make all things new.*[15] He whose flesh was sown in death, bursts into blossom again in the resurrection, at the sweet odor whereof in the field of our valley, withered things straightway grow green once more, things that were cold grow warm again, and the dead pulse anew with life.

Because of the freshness of these flowers and fruits and because of the beauty of the field giving forth the sweetest fragrance, the Father Himself so delights in the Son that He says: *Behold the smell of my son is as the smell of a plentiful field which the Lord hath blessed.*[16] Plentiful indeed, *of* whose *fulness we all have received.*[17] But the bride, on terms of greater intimacy, gathers flowers and plucks fruit therefrom, with which to deck the innermost chamber of her own conscience so that the little bed of her

[14] Canticle II, 11-12.
[15] Apocalypse XXI, 5.
[16] Genesis XXVII, 27.
[17] St. John I, 16.

heart may give forth sweet odors to the Bridegroom at His coming. For if we wish to have Christ as a frequent guest, we must ever have our hearts fortified with unfailing testimonies both of His mercy in dying and of His power in rising from the dead. This is what David meant when he said: *These two things have I heard, that power belongeth to God, and mercy to Thee, O Lord.*[18] The testimonies concerning both of these truths have become credible in the highest degree,[19] for Christ died for our sins and rose from the dead for our justification and ascended [into Heaven] for our protection and sent the [Holy] Spirit for our consolation and will one day return for the consummation [of our souls' salvation]. Surely in death He showed mercy; power, in rising from the dead; and both in all the rest [of His life's mysteries].

These are the apples, these the flowers with which the bride prays that meanwhile she may be encompassed and sustained; feeling, I believe, that the power of love within her can in a measure become lukewarm and languid if it be not continually fostered by such helps, until, brought at last into the bridal-chamber she is caught in the long-desired embrace and exclaims: *His left hand is under my head, and His right hand shall embrace me.*[20] Then she will feel and judge how all the evidences of love which at His former coming she had received as if from the left hand of the Beloved are to be disdained in comparison with the surpassing sweetness of the right hand's embrace, and in time to come to be regarded as of a lower degree. She will feel what she has heard: *It is the spirit that quickeneth: the flesh profiteth nothing.*[21] She will know from experience what she had known from

[18] Psalm LXI, 12-13.
[19] Cf. Psalm XCII, 5.
[20] Canticle II, 6.
[21] St. John VI, 64.

hearsay: *my spirit is sweet above honey, and my inheritance above honey and honeycomb.*[22] In regard to what follows: *My memory is unto everlasting generations;*[23] this means that as long as the present age is seen to abide, in which a generation comes and a generation goes, the consolation which flows from the memory will not be lacking to the elect to whom, as yet, the full satisfaction of the presence [of the Bridegroom] is not granted. Hence it is written: *They shall publish the memory of the abundance of Thy sweetness.*[24] There can be no doubt that *they* are those of whom it had been said a little before: *Generation and generation shall praise Thy works.*[25] Memory, therefore, in a generation of time; presence, in the kingdom of heaven. By this latter the company of the elect already taken up into heaven is glorified: by the former, meanwhile, the generation of wayfarers is consoled.

[22] Ecclesiasticus XXIV, 27.
[23] *Ibid.* 28.
[24] Psalm CXLIV, 7.
[25] *Ibid.* 4.

CHAPTER IV

WHO THEY ARE WHO FIND CONSOLATION IN THE REMEMBRANCE OF GOD; AND WHO ARE MORE CAPABLE OF LOVING HIM

BUT IT IS important to consider what generation it is that finds comfort in the remembrance of God. Not *a perverse and exasperating generation,*[1] to which it is said: *Woe to you that are rich: for you have your consolation;*[2] but such as can say with truth: *My soul refused to be comforted.*[3] It is indeed right that those who do not find their delight in things present should here rejoice in the remembrance of things to come, and the remembrance of eternity should prove a source of delight to those who disdain to derive consolation from any of the things that pass away. And this is the generation of those who seek the Lord, seeking not *the things that are their own,*[4] but *the face of the God of Jacob.*[5] To those, therefore, who seek and sigh for the vision of God there is present, meanwhile, a sweet remembrance which, however, does not afford them complete satisfaction but makes them hunger the more for that which will satisfy them fully. To this, indeed, He Who is their Food bears witness in His own regard when He speaks thus: *They that eat Me, shall yet hunger;*[6] and he who is fed says, *I shall be satisfied when Thy glory shall*

[1] Psalm LXXVII, 8.
[2] St. Luke VI, 24.
[3] Psalm LXXVI, 3.
[4] Philippians II, 21.
[5] Psalm XXIII, 6.
[6] Ecclesiasticus XXIV, 29.

appear.[7] Yet, *blessed are they,* even now, *that hunger and thirst after justice, for,* one day, *they,* and not others, *shall have their fill.*[8] Woe to thee, *a wicked and perverse generation!*[9] Woe to thee, a people foolish and unwise who both loathes the remembrance of Him, and is terrified at the thought of His coming! Deservedly indeed, for neither now [on earth] would you be delivered *from the snare of the hunters,*[10] since *they that will become rich* in this world, *fall into . . . the snare of the devil;*[11] nor will you then [at the Last Judgment] be able to be *delivered . . . from the sharp word.*[12] O sharp word, O hard saying! *Depart from Me ye cursed into everlasting fire.*[13] Much harder, indeed, and sharper than that word which in the Church is repeated every day [at Mass] in remembrance of the Passion: *He that eateth My flesh and drinketh My blood, hath everlasting life.*[14] That is, he who recalls to mind My death and after My example mortifies his *members which are upon the earth,*[15] shall have life everlasting; that is, if you suffer with Him now you shall reign with Him hereafter.[16] And nevertheless, a very great number in these days also [as of old], recoiling from His voice, going back and walking no more with Him,[17] answers not by word but by deed: *This saying is hard, and who can hear it?*[18] And so, *A generation that set not their heart aright: and whose spirit was not faithful to God,*[19] but rather trusting *in the uncertainty of riches,*[20] is

[7] Psalm XVI, 15.
[8] St. Matthew V, 6.
[9] Deuteronomy XXXII, 5.
[10] Psalm XC, 3.
[11] 1 Timothy VI, 9.
[12] Psalm XC, 3.
[13] St. Matthew XXV, 41.
[14] St. John VI, 55.
[15] Colossians III, 5.
[16] Cf. Romans VIII, 17: 2 Timothy II, 12.
[17] Cf. St. John VI, 67.
[18] *Ibid.* 61.
[19] Psalm LXXVII, 8.
[20] 1 Timothy VI, 17.

weighed down at hearing even *the word of the cross,*[21] and looks upon any reminder of the Passion as burdensome. But in His presence how will that generation ever bear the weight of that other word: *Depart from Me, you cursed, into everlasting fire which was prepared for the devil and his angels.*[22] Assuredly *on whomsoever* this stone *shall fall, it shall grind him to powder.*[23] But *the generation of the righteous shall be blessed:*[24] they who with the Apostle, *whether absent or present,*[25] labor to please God. In the end they shall hear: *Come, ye blessed of My Father, possess you the kingdom prepared for you from the foundation of the world.*[26] Then that *generation that set not their heart aright,*[27] will too late, alas, come to know how sweet was the yoke of Christ,[28] in comparison with their anguish, and how light was His burden from which, in pride, they withdrew their stiff necks as from a weight bitter and crushing.[29] You cannot, O wretched slaves of Mammon,[30] you cannot at the same time glory *in the cross of Our Lord Jesus Christ,*[31] and place your trust in great hoards of money.[32] To go after gold is to prove how sweet is the Lord.[33] Hence He Whom you do not know in remembrance, as sweet, will prove bitter, no doubt, in His [actual] presence.

The faithful soul, on the other hand, longs eagerly for the presence [of God] and reposes sweetly in the remembrance [of Him], and until she is capable of *beholding the glory of the Lord*

[21] 1 Corinthians I, 18.
[22] St. Matthew XXV, 41.
[23] St. Matthew XXI, 44.
[24] Psalm CXI, 2.
[25] 2 Corinthians V, 9.
[26] St. Matthew XXV, 34.
[27] Psalm LXXVII, 8.
[28] Cf. St. Matthew XI, 30.
[29] Cf. Deuteronomy XXXI, 27.
[30] Cf. St. Matthew VI, 24.
[31] Galatians VI, 14.
[32] Cf. 1 Timothy VI, 17: Ecclesiasticus XXXI, 8.
[33] Cf. Psalm XXXIII, 9.

with open face,[34] she glories in the ignominy of the Cross.[35] Thus, truly, thus does the bride and dove of Christ[36] find rest meanwhile and sleep *among the midst of lots,*[37] having chosen for the present in remembrance of the abundance of Thy sweetness, Lord Jesus,[38] *wings . . . covered with silver,*[39] that is, the whiteness of innocence and purity; and hoping, besides, to be filled with joy at Thy countenance[40] where, also, *the hinder parts of her back* will be covered *with the paleness of gold.*[41] When with joy she has been brought into *the brightness of the saints,*[42] she will be more completely illumined by the light of Wisdom. With good reason, therefore, does she glory even now and say: *His left hand is under my head, and His right hand shall embrace me;*[43] reflecting that in His left hand is the remembrance of that love than which there is no greater, by which He laid down His life for His friends;[44] but in His right hand is the Beatific Vision which He has promised His friends and the joy [that flows] from the presence of Majesty itself. Justly is that vision of God,[45] that vision that makes us like unto God,[46] that inconceivable delight of the Divine presence, justly is it ascribed to the right hand concerning which it is joyously sung: *at Thy right hand are delights even to the end.*[47] Justly is it the left hand in which is placed that wonderful love which we have recalled to mind and which is ever to be remembered, for, *until iniquity pass away,*[48] it is upon this hand that the bride shall lay her head and rest.

[34] 2 Corinthians III, 18.
[35] Cf. Galatians VI, 14.
[36] Cf. Canticle V, 2.
[37] Psalm LXVII, 14.
[38] Cf. Psalm CXLIV, 7.
[39] Psalm LXVII, 14.
[40] Cf. Psalm XV, 11.
[41] Psalm LXVII, 14.
[42] Psalm CIX, 3.
[43] Canticle II, 6.
[44] Cf. St. John XV, 13.
[45] Cf. 1 St. John III, 2.
[46] Cf. 2 Corinthians III, 18.
[47] Psalm XV, 11.
[48] Psalm LVI, 2.

Justly, therefore, is the left hand of the Bridegroom under the head of the bride. Leaning back, it is upon it that she rests her head, that is, the intention of her mind, lest it should be inclined and bent toward fleshly and worldly desires; *For the corruptible body is a load upon the soul, and the earthly habitation presseth down the mind that museth upon many things.*[49] For when we come to consider it, what else is effected by compassion so great and so undeserved, by love so gratuitous and hence so amply proved, by esteem so unexpected, by meekness so invincible, by sweetness so wonderful? What, I ask, will all these effect when they are diligently pondered save that they will marvelously draw to themselves the soul of him who ponders them freed from every unworthy love; they will powerfully affect that soul and make it despise, as compared with themselves, whatever one cannot make the object of his desire save by contemning them [the aforesaid higher enjoyments]? Surely, then, the bride runs eagerly to the odor of their ointments,[50] loves ardently; and so loved, she seems to herself to love very little even when she has wholly bound herself first in love. Not without cause. For, what that is great can recompense a love so great shown by One who is Himself great; if a grain of dust[51] will have brought together its whole self to return the love of another, and that other—Majesty itself, forsooth—outstripping it in love,[52] is seen wholly bent upon its salvation? Finally, *God so loved the world, as to give His only Begotten Son.*[53] This, beyond doubt, is said of the Father. Again: *He hath delivered His soul unto death;*[54] nor is there any doubt that this is spoken of the Son. And it is said of the Holy Ghost:

[49] Wisdom IX, 15.
[50] Cf. Canticle I, 3.
[51] Cf. Isaias XL, 15.
[52] Cf. Psalm XX, 4.
[53] St. John III, 16.
[54] Isaias LIII, 12.

But the Paraclete, the Holy Ghost, whom the Father will send in My name, He will teach you all things, and bring all things to your mind, whatsoever I shall have said to you.[55] God therefore loves and loves with His whole Self because the whole Trinity loves, if, indeed, *the whole* can be said of the Infinite and Incomprehensible, or of what is simply One.

[55] St. John XIV, 26.

CHAPTER V

TO WHAT DEGREE THE OBLIGATION OF LOVE IS BINDING, ESPECIALLY UPON CHRISTIANS

One who knows these truths, I believe, realizes fully why God should be loved, that is by what title He deserves to be loved. But the infidel not having the Son, consequently has neither the Father nor the Holy Ghost.[1] For *He who honoreth not the Son, honoreth not the Father who hath sent Him,*[2] nor the Holy Ghost Whom He sent.[3] It is therefore no wonder if he has less love for Him Whom he knows less. Nevertheless even he [the infidel] is not unaware of the fact that he owes all that he is to Him Whom he recognizes as the Author of his whole being. What of me, then?—I who hold my God not only as the gratuitous Bestower of my life, most bountiful in His providence, a devoted Consoler, a solicitous Ruler, but a most abundant Redeemer as well, an eternal Conserver, One who enriches, One who gives glory. As it is written: *with Him* (*there is*) *plentiful redemption;*[4] and again: (*Christ*) *entered once into the holies, having obtained eternal redemption.*[5] Concerning His providence: (*The Lord*) *will not forsake His saints: they shall be preserved forever;*[6] and concerning His enriching [of us]: *good measure and pressed down and shaken together and running over shall they give into your*

[1] Cf. 1 St. John V, 12.
[2] St. John V, 23.
[3] Cf. *ibid.* XVI, 7.
[4] Psalm CXXIX, 7.
[5] Hebrews IX, 12.
[6] Psalm XXXVI, 28.

bosom.[7] And again: *eye hath not seen, nor ear heard, neither hath it entered into the heart of man, what things God hath prepared for them that love Him.*[8] And concerning His giving of glory: *we look for the Saviour, our Lord Jesus Christ, Who will reform the body of our lowness, made like to the body of His glory;*[9] and this: *the sufferings of this time are not worthy to be compared with the glory to come, that shall be revealed in us;*[10] and again: *For that which is at present momentary and light of our tribulation, worketh for us above measure exceedingly an eternal weight of glory, while we look not at the things which are seen, but at the things which are not seen.*[11]

What shall I render to the Lord for all these *things?*[12] *Reason* as well as natural justice impels that other [the infidel] to surrender his whole self to Him from Whom he has received all that he is, and reminds him that he is bound to love Him with his whole self. To me [a Christian], to be sure, faith reveals that He should be loved the more and to the degree that I understand He is to be esteemed above myself; I, forsooth, who hold that He is the Bestower not only of myself but even of His very Self as well. Finally (when the Psalmist asked, *what shall I render,* etc.) the time of [Christian] faith had not yet come, God had not yet become known in the Flesh, died upon the cross, come forth from the tomb, returned to the Father. Not as yet, I say, had He commended His great charity towards us[13]—that charity concerning which we have already spoken much—at the time when it was already commanded man to *love the Lord* his *God with*

[7] St. Luke VI, 38.
[8] I Corinthians II, 9.
[9] Philippians III, 20-21.
[10] Romans VIII, 18.
[11] 2 Corinthians IV, 17-18.
[12] Psalm CXV, 12.
[13] Cf. Romans V, 8.

his *whole heart, with* his *whole soul, with* his *whole strength,*[14] that is with all that he is, with all that he knows, and with every power that he has. Nor is God unjust in claiming as His own the work of His hands and His gifts.[15] For why should not a thing which has been made, love its Maker since it has the power of doing so? And why should it not do so as much as it can, since it has no power at all except as a gift from Him? In addition to this, the fact that it was made out of nothing, and that, gratuitously and in this present state of dignity, this fact makes the debt of love clearer and makes what is demanded of it appear more just. Moreover, how great do we consider that increase of His benefaction when He preserved *men and beasts,*[16] whereby God has multiplied His mercy![17] We, I say, who *changed* our *glory into the likeness of a calf that eateth grass,*[18] were by sinning *compared to senseless beasts.*[19] If I owe my whole self for being made, what more shall I give now in return for being re-made and re-made in such wise? For I was not re-made as easily as I was made, if, indeed, it is written not only of me but of every thing that was made: *He spoke, and they were made.*[20] But, in truth He Who made me so great, and that, by speaking once only, in re-making me, to be sure, spoke many times and worked wonders and endured hardships; not only hardships but things unworthy, even. *What shall I render to the Lord, for all the things that He hath rendered to me?*[21] In the first work He gave me myself; in the second, Himself: and when He gave me Himself, He restored me to myself again. Given, therefore, and restored, I

[14] Deuteronomy VI, 5.
[15] Cf. Hebrews VI, 10.
[16] Psalm XXXV, 7.
[17] Cf. *ibid.* 8.
[18] Psalm CV, 20.
[19] Psalm XLVIII, 13.
[20] Psalm CXLVIII, 5.
[21] Psalm CXV, 12.

owe myself in return for myself and I owe it as a twofold debt. What shall I render to God in return for Himself? For even if I were able to give myself back a thousand times, what am I in God's sight?

CHAPTER VI

A BRIEF RECAPITULATION AND SUMMARY OF WHAT HAS BEEN SAID

HERE FIRST SEE in what measure, yes, how beyond measure God has deserved to be loved by us; He who (if I may repeat in a few words what has been said) first loved us Himself[1]—He so great, yet He loved us greatly and *gratis;* we, so small and [sinners] such as we are.[2] Notice! I remember what I said in the beginning, that the way to love God is to love Him beyond measure. And since love which has God as its object, has as its object the Immeasurable and Infinite (for God is both Immeasurable and Infinite), what, I ask, ought to be the end or method of our love? What of the fact that our love itself is not given as a free gift but as the payment of a debt? Immeasurableness, therefore, loves, Eternity loves, *the charity . . . which surpasseth all knowledge*[3] loves, God loves of Whose *greatness there is no end,*[4] of Whose wisdom there is no measure, Whose *peace . . . surpasseth all understanding;*[5] and do we love Him in turn so much and no more? *I will love thee, O Lord, my strength . . . my firmament, my refuge, and my deliverer;*[6] and finally, [He is] whatever of mine that can be said to be the object of my desires and of my love. My God, my Help, I shall love Thee according to Your gift to me. And [this I shall do] after my own manner—which is less,

[1] Cf. 1 John IV, 19.
[2] Cf. Romans V, 8
[3] Ephesians III, 19.
[4] Psalm CXLIV, 3.
[5] Philippians IV, 7.
[6] Psalm XVII, 2-3.

to be sure, than justice demands but clearly not less than I am able to give; I, who although I cannot [give] as much as I owe, cannot, however, [give] beyond what I am able. I shall be able [to give] more when You deign to give me more: but never according to Your worth. *Thy eyes did see my imperfect being;*[7] but nevertheless, *in Thy book all shall be written*[8]—they who do what they are able to do, although they are not able to do what [in strict justice] they ought to do. It is clear enough, as far as I can judge, both how God should be loved and by what desert of his own. By *what* desert of His, I say, for to whom can its *greatness* be clearly manifest? Who can say? Who can know?

[7] Psalm CXXXVIII, 16. [8] *Ibid.*

CHAPTER VII

NOT WITHOUT FRUIT AND REWARD, IS GOD LOVED, AND EARTHLY THINGS CANNOT SATISFY THE LONGING OF THE HUMAN HEART

Now LET US see with what advantage to ourselves God is to be loved. But how little is our insight into this compared with what it really is! Nevertheless one ought not to remain silent about what is seen, even though it is not seen entirely as it is. Above, when it was asked why and how God should be loved, I said that the question *why* can be understood in two ways, so that it seems equally to ask, either by what desert of His or for what advantage of ours God should be loved. Then something having been said on the subject of God's desert—not in a manner worthy of Him but according to the power given me [*i.e.* to the best of my ability]—it remains that I should speak on the subject of reward in like manner, according as it is given me. For not without reward is God loved although He should be loved without thought of the reward. True charity cannot be unprofitable nor is it, however, mercenary; certainly it *seeketh not* its *own*.[1] It is a matter of affection, not a contract: it neither gains nor is gained by a compact. It exerts its influence freely and makes one free. True love finds satisfaction in itself [*i.e.* is its own satisfaction]. It has its reward but it is [the possession of] the object it loves. For whatever you seem to love because of something else, you clearly

[1] I Corinthians XIII, 5.

love that to which the end of love ultimately attains and not that [the means] by which it attains it. Paul does not preach the Gospel in order that he may eat but he eats in order that he may preach the Gospel: because he loves, not food, but the Gospel.[2] True love asks no reward but deserves one. It is when a man has not yet learned to love that a reward is set before him; it is due one who loves; it is awarded to him who perseveres. Finally in appealing [to a man] in matters of a lower order, it is the unwilling that we urge on with promises or rewards, but not the willing. For who is there who thinks that a man should be rewarded in order that he may do what he freely desires? No one, for instance, pays a hungry man to eat, or a thirsty man to drink, or a mother to give milk to the child of her womb.[3] Or who thinks that a man ought to be induced by a price or an entreaty to fence in his own vine, to dig about his own tree, or to erect the structure of his own home? How much less does the soul that loves God seek anything besides God as the reward of her love! If she seeks anything else, it is clearly something else and not God that she loves.

It is natural to everyone who uses his reason, to desire always according to his judgment and intention, what is more capable of satisfying him and to be content with nothing which is wanting in what he considers preferable. For he who has a good-looking wife, for instance, gazes with wanton eye and mind upon one more beautiful, and he who is dressed in costly attire desires something more costly, and one possessing much wealth envies the man who is wealthier. You may see those already abounding in farms and property, still, day by day adding field to field and with unlimited avarice extending their boundaries. You may see

[2] Cf. 1 Corinthians IX, 14-18. [3] Cf. Isaias XLIX, 15.

those, too, who dwell in the houses of kings and in spacious palaces, nevertheless joining house to house and with restless curiosity building up, tearing down, making the square round [*i.e.* turning everything upside down]. What do we see if not men elevated by honors? What do we see such men doing if not, with insatiable ambition straining more and more with all their might, toward higher things? And of all these there is no end because there is nothing found in these things that is absolutely the highest or best. And what wonder is it if that which is not able [by its very nature] to find rest anywhere short of the highest or best should not be really satisfied by things lower and worse? But this is foolish and [a sign] of utter madness always to be striving after those things which never, I do not say satisfy, but do not even moderate one's appetite, while whatever of such things you may chance to have, you none the less long for what you have not and ever restless pant after whatever may be wanting. Thus it happens that a vagabond mind running hither and thither among the varying and false delights of the world is tired out, not satisfied, by its vain exertion; while, starved, it counts as little whatever it gormandizes upon compared with what remains to be devoured and ever it craves the things removed from it, not less anxiously than it joyfully has and holds those that are at hand. For who is there who can gain the whole world? And although a man can never be certain when, with anguish, he may lose even the little which he has gained with toil, he is certain, nevertheless, that some time or other he will lose it.[4] Thus a perverted will strains eagerly after a direct short-cut to the *best* and hurries on to that whereby it may be filled. Yea, in truth, by such tortuous routes as these does vanity amuse itself, does iniquity de-

[4] Cf. Ecclesiastes V, 14.

ceive itself. So if you would attain to the fulfilment of what you wish for, that is if you would lay hold upon that which, once grasped, leaves no more to be desired—what is the necessity of putting the rest to the test? You run along by-paths and you will die long before you attain the object of your desires along this circuitous route.

Thus, then, *the wicked walk round about,*[5] desiring in a natural way that whereby they may put an end to desire, and foolishly rejecting the means by which they might approach their [true] end [*i.e.* God]: by *the end* I mean not *consumption* but consummation. Wherefore they make haste not to be consummated in a blessed end but to be consumed with empty toil—they who find their delight in the [external] appearance of things rather than in the Author of them, they who would run through everything to find out by experience concerning every individual thing before they trouble themselves about attaining to the Lord of the universe Himself. And indeed, they might reach their goal if at some time or other they might be made possessors of what they wish for, to wit, that one might possess everything except the Source of all things. For by the very law of his own cupidity, according to which in all other matters he is accustomed to hunger for what he has not rather than for what he has, and to loathe what he has because of what he has not; presently having obtained and having disdained everything in heaven and upon the earth, man would beyond the shadow of a doubt run at last to Him Who alone is lacking to him, the God of all. There henceforth, he would find rest; for as no rest restrains him, on one side; so now, no unrest moves him, on the other. He would for

[5] Psalm XI, 9.

certain say: *it is good for me to adhere to my God.*[6] He would say: *For what have I in heaven? and besides Thee what do I desire upon earth?*[7] And in similar strain: *Thou art the God of my heart, and the God that is my portion forever.*[8] Thus therefore (as has been said) a greedy man might ultimately attain to what is best if he could really attain the object of his desires [a false *best*] before he reached *the* Best.

Truly, since this is made absolutely impossible because life is too short, [man's] powers too weak, the number of his fellows too vast; they, assuredly, sweat along an endless road with futile toil who while they wish to get whatever they want refuse to attain to the end of all that is to be desired. And would that they wished to attain to an intellectual grasp of all things and not to an experimental knowledge of them! This, indeed, they could easily do and not in vain. For, the mind, as much quicker than bodily sense as it is more penetrating, has been given for this, that in all things it should anticipate sense, and that there is nothing that sense may dare to touch which the mind, preceding it, has not first proved useful. Hence I believe, the saying: *prove all things; hold fast that which is good;*[9] to the end, that is to say, that the former [the mind] may so provide for the latter [sense] that it may not attain its desire save only in accordance with the judgment of the former. Otherwise you shall not *ascend into the mountain of the Lord,* nor *stand in His holy place,*[10] because you have taken your soul in vain,[11] that is, your rational soul, while like the beasts of the field you follow sense,

[6] Psalm LXXII, 28.
[7] *Ibid.* 25.
[8] *Ibid.* 26.
[9] 1 Thessalonians V, 21.
[10] Psalm XXIII, 3.
[11] Cf. *ibid.* 4.

your reason unconcerned and offering no resistance in anything. Those therefore whose steps reason does not anticipate, run, but off the path,[12] and thus despising the counsel of the Apostle, *so run* not *that* they *may obtain*.[13] For when will they obtain Him Whom they refused to obtain save after all things else? It is a crooked road and an endless maze, to wish to attain all things first [*i.e.* before attaining God].

But not so the just man. Hearing, of course, the blame of the many tarrying in the maze (for many there are who eagerly pursue the broad way that leads to death),[14] he chooses for himself the king's highway, *neither turning to the right hand nor to the left*.[15] Finally the prophet bears witness to this: *The way of the just is right, the path of the just is right to walk in*.[16] These are they who by a salutary short way [17] are careful to avoid the roundabout way, dangerous and fruitless and choose the shortened and shortening word,[18] not to desire everything they see but rather to *sell what thou hast, and give to the poor*.[19] [Rev. Mr. Williams suggests that the *shortened word* may be: *One thing is wanting unto thee*.[20]] Clearly, *Blessed are the poor in spirit: for theirs is the kingdom of heaven*.[21] All indeed run; [22] but there is a distinction made among the runners. *For the Lord knoweth the way of the just: and the way of the wicked shall perish*.[23] Therefore, *Better is a little to the just, than the great riches of the wicked*,[24] since indeed, as the wise man says and the fool finds

[12] Cf. Isaias LIX, 8.
[13] 1 Corinthians IX, 24.
[14] Cf. St. Matthew VII, 13.
[15] Cf. Numbers XX, 17: XXI, 22.
[16] Isaias XXVI, 7.
[17] Cf. 2 Kings XVIII, 23.
[18] Cf. Romans IX, 28.
[19] St. Matthew XIX, 21.
[20] St. Mark X, 21.
[21] St. Matthew V, 3.
[22] Cf. 1 Corinthians IX, 24.
[23] Psalm I, 6.
[24] Psalm XXXVI, 16.

out from experience, *A covetous man shall not be satisfied with money;*[25] but *they that hunger and thirst after justice . . . shall have their fill.*[26] If indeed justice is the life-giving and natural food of the spirit that makes use of reason, money to be sure, no more lessens the hunger of the mind than air does that of the body. If then you should happen to see a starved man with mouth opened in the wind drinking in the air with puffed-out cheeks as if to satisfy his hunger thereby, would you not believe him mad? Thus it is not less madness if you think that a rational spirit is not more puffed up than satisfied by any bodily things whatever. For, what have bodies to do with spirits? Neither can bodies, surely, find refreshment in things spiritual nor can spirits find refreshment in bodily things. *Bless the Lord, O my soul . . . who satisfieth thy desire with good things.*[27] He satisfies us with good things, He incites us to good [*gratia praeveniente*], He preserves us in good [*gratia efficaci*], He prevents, He sustains, He fulfills. It is He who makes you desire; He is what you desire.

I said above: The cause of loving God is God. I spoke the truth, for He is both the efficient and final Cause. It is He who gives the occasion, it is He who creates the affection, He consummates the desire. It is He who wrought, or rather, was *made* [*i.e.* is what He is] in order that He might be loved; He it is hoped, will be so fruitfully loved as not to be loved in vain. His love makes our love ready and rewards it. He goes before more graciously than any other, He is repaid more justly, He is awaited more sweetly. He *is rich unto all who call upon Him;*[28] still He has nothing better than Himself to give. He gave Him-

[25] Ecclesiastes V, 9.
[26] St. Matthew V, 6.
[27] Psalm CII, 1, 5.
[28] Romans X, 12.

self to merit for us, He retains Himself to be our reward, He offers Himself as the food of saintly souls, He gives Himself as the price of the redemption of those [*i.e.* of every individual soul] in captivity. You are *good,* O Lord, *to the soul that seeketh* Thee:[29] what, then, to one who finds? But in this is the wonder that no one can seek Thee save him who first has found Thee. Therefore You wish to be found in order that You may be sought, to be sought in order that You may be found. You can, indeed, be sought and found but not prevented. For although we say, *in the morning my prayer shall prevent thee;*[30] there can be no doubt, however, that every prayer is lukewarm which inspiration has not prevented. We must now state whence our love has its beginning, since we have already told where it has its consummation.

[29] Lamentations III, 25.

[30] Psalm LXXXVII, 14.

CHAPTER VIII

THE FIRST DEGREE OF LOVE, WHEREBY A MAN LOVES HIMSELF FOR HIS OWN SAKE

LOVE IS A natural affection, one of four. They are well known; there is no need of mentioning them by name. [They are love, fear, joy and sorrow.] It would therefore be just that what is natural should serve its own Author before all others. Hence the first commandment is called the greatest: *Thou shalt love the Lord thy God,* etc.[1] But since nature is rather weak and feeble, it is impelled at the bidding of necessity to serve itself first. And there is carnal love by which before all other things man loves himself for his own sake, as it is written: *first . . . that which is natural; afterwards that which is spiritual.*[2] And it is not imposed by a command but implanted in nature; for who *ever hated his own flesh?*[3] But truly if this love, as is its wont, begins to be too precipitate or too lavish and is not at all satisfied with the river-bed of necessity, overflowing rather widely it will be seen to invade the fields of pleasure. At once its overflow is held in check by the commandment that opposes itself to it: *Thou shalt love thy neighbor as thyself.*[4] It happens, very justly indeed, that the sharer in nature should not be excluded from a part in grace as well, especially in that grace which is inborn in nature itself. If

[1] St. Matthew XXII, 37.
[2] I Corinthians XV, 46.
[3] Ephesians V, 29.
[4] St. Matthew XXII, 39.

man finds it a burden, I do not say to relieve his brother in matters of necessity but to administer to his pleasures, let him restrain his own unless he wishes to be a transgressor of the law. Let him be as indulgent as he likes to himself, so long as he is mindful to show the same degree of indulgence to his neighbor. The bridle of temperance is put upon you, O man, out of the law of life and of discipline lest you should go after your concupiscences and perish; lest in the goods of nature you become a slave to your soul's enemy, that is, to lust. How much more justly and honorably do you give such things to your fellow-sharer, that is, your neighbor rather than to your enemy! And if indeed, according to the advice of the wise man, you turn away from your own pleasures,[5] and according to the teaching of the Apostle, content with food and raiment,[6] you find it no burden to withhold your love for a little while *from carnal desires which war against the soul;*[7] surely, I think, what you take away from your soul's enemy you will find no burden to bestow upon the sharer of your nature. Your love will then be both temperate and just if what is taken from your own pleasures is not denied to your brother's needs. Thus carnal love is made to belong to our neighbor when it is extended to the common good.

But if, while you are sharing what you have with your neighbor, even the necessities of life should, perchance, be lacking to you, what will you do? What indeed, unless with all confidence you should *ask of* Him *Who giveth to all men abundantly, and upbraideth not;*[8] Who *openest thy hand, and fillest with blessing every living creature?*[9] There is no doubt, surely, that He who

[5] Cf. Ecclesiasticus XVIII, 30.
[6] Cf. 1 Timothy VI, 8.
[7] 1 St. Peter II, 11.
[8] St. James I, 5.
[9] Psalm CXLIV, 16.

is not absent in the midst of plenty will gladly be present in the time of need. He says, at length: *seek ye first the kingdom of God and His justice, and all these things shall be added to you.*[10] He promises that He will of His own accord give whatever is necessary to him who restricts himself in superfluities and loves his neighbor. This surely, is to seek first the kingdom of God and to implore help against the tyranny of sin, that you prefer to bear the yoke of modesty and restraint rather than endure that sin should reign in your mortal body. But this, too, is part of the righteousness in question, not to possess the gift of nature independently of him whose common nature you share.

Nevertheless, in order that it may be perfect justice to love one's neighbor, it is imperative that it be referred to God as its cause. Otherwise how can he love his neighbor without alloy who does not love him in God? He surely cannot love in God who does not love God. God must be loved first, in order that one's neighbor, too, may be loved in God. God, therefore, Who makes all else that is good, makes Himself to be loved. And He does it as follows. He who fashioned nature, it is He who shields it from harm as well. For it was so fashioned that it should have as a necessary Protector, Him whom it had as Maker, in order that what could not have come into being save through Him, should not be able to subsist at all without Him. And lest the creature might not know this about itself and consequently (which God forbid) in its pride arrogate to itself the benefits it had received from its Creator, the same Maker, in His high and salutary counsel wills that man should be harassed with troubles; so that when man has failed and God has come to his assistance, while man is being delivered by God, God, as is fitting, may be

[10] St. Luke XII, 31.

honored by man. For this is what He says: *call upon Me in the day of trouble: I will deliver thee, and thou shalt glorify Me.*[11] Thus it comes to pass in this wise that a man, an animal and carnal by nature, who knew how to love no one except himself may begin even for his own sake, to love God too, because in Him beyond a shadow of doubt, as he has often learned from experience, he can do all things—those, to be sure, which it is good to be able to do—and without Him he can do nothing.

[11] Psalm XLIX, 15.

CHAPTER IX

THE SECOND AND THIRD DEGREES OF LOVE

A MAN, THEREFORE, loves God but still for a while for his own sake, not for Himself. It is, however, a sort of prudence to know what you are able to do by yourself, what with God's help, and to preserve yourself guiltless for Him who keeps you unharmed. But if tribulation assails you again and again, and on this account there occurs an oft-repeated turning towards God; and as often, there follows deliverance obtained from God, is it not true that even though the breast were of steel or the heart of stone in one so many times rescued, it must of necessity be softened at the grace of the Rescuer so that man might love God not merely for his own sake but for God Himself. From the occasion that arises from frequent needs it is necessary that man should frequently, in repeated intercourse, go to God who in such intercourse is tasted, and it is by tasting that it is proved how sweet is the Lord.[1] Thus it happens that when once His sweetness has been tasted, it draws us to the pure love of God more than our need impels. Just as in the case of the Samaritans who said, speaking to the woman who had announced that the Lord was come: *We now believe, not for thy saying: for we ourselves have heard Him, and know that this is indeed the Savior of the world,*[2] similarly I say, we too, following their example, speaking to our flesh may justly

[1] Cf. Psalm XXXIII, 9. [2] St. John IV, 42.

say: We now love God, not for your necessity; for we ourselves have tasted and know how sweet is the Lord. For it is true that a need of the flesh is a sort of speech, and the benefits which it knows from experience it proclaims in transports of joy. And so for one who feels thus, it will not now be hard to fulfil the commandment in regard to loving his neighbor. For he truly loves God and in this way also loves the things which are God's. He loves purely and it is no burden for the pure to be obedient to a command; rather, *purifying* his heart, as it is written, *in* the obedience of *charity*.[3] He loves justly and gladly embraces a just command. This love is deservedly acceptable because it is disinterested [*i.e.* not offered with a view to obtaining future favors]. It is pure because it is paid neither by word nor tongue, but by deed and truth.[4] It is just, since it is paid back as it is received. For he who loves thus, to be sure, loves in no other wise than he is loved; seeking, in his turn, not the things that are his own but the things that are Jesus Christ's,[5] just as He sought the things that are ours, or rather ourselves and not His own. It is thus He loves who says: *Give praise to the Lord, for He is good*.[6] He who gives praise to the Lord not because He is good to him but because He is good, he truly loves God for God and not for his own sake. It is not thus that he loves of whom it is said: *he will praise thee when thou shalt do well to him*.[7] This is the third degree of love by which God is now loved for His very self.

[3] 1 St. Peter I, 22.
[4] Cf. 1 St. John III, 18.
[5] Cf. Philippians II, 21.
[6] Psalm CXVII, 1.
[7] Psalm XLVIII, 19.

CHAPTER X

THE FOURTH DEGREE OF LOVE, WHEN A MAN DOES NOT LOVE EVEN HIMSELF EXCEPT FOR THE SAKE OF GOD

HAPPY IS HE who has deserved to attain as high as the fourth degree where a man does not love even himself except for the sake of God. *Thy justice, (O Lord) is as the mountains of God.*[1] This love is a mountain and the high mountain of God. In truth, *a curdled mountain, a fat mountain.*[2] *Who shall ascend into the mountain of the Lord?*[3] *Who will give me wings like a dove, and I will fly and be at rest?*[4] This *place is in peace: and* this *abode in Sion.*[5] *Woe is me, that my sojourning is prolonged!*[6] Flesh and blood, vessel of clay, when will your earthly dwelling-place compass this? When will the mind experience such an affection as this so that inebriated with divine love, forgetful of self, and become in its own eyes like *a vessel that is destroyed,*[7] the whole of it may continue on to God and being joined to God, become one spirit with Him,[8] and say: *For Thee my flesh and my heart hath fainted away: thou art the God of my heart, and the God that is my portion forever?*[9] Blessed and holy, I would say, is he to whom it has been given to experience such a thing in

[1] Psalm XXXV, 7.
[2] Psalm LXVII, 16.
[3] Psalm XXIII, 3.
[4] Psalm LIV, 7.
[5] Psalm LXXV, 3.
[6] Psalm CXIX, 5.
[7] Psalm XXX, 13.
[8] Cf. 1 Corinthians VI, 17.
[9] Psalm LXXII, 26.

this mortal life at rare intervals or even once, and this suddenly and scarcely for the space of a single moment. In a certain manner to lose yourself as though you were not,[10] and to be utterly unconscious of yourself and to be emptied of yourself and, as it were, brought to nothing, this pertains to heavenly intercourse, not to human affection. And if indeed, anyone among mortals is suddenly from time to time (as has been said) even for the space of a moment admitted to this, straightway the wicked world grows envious, the evil of the day throws everything into confusion,[11] the body of death becomes a burden, the necessity of the flesh causes unrest, the fainting away of corruption [12] offers no support, and what is more vehement than these, fraternal charity [*i.e.* obligations to one's neighbor] recalls one [from the state of contemplation]. Alas! he is forced to return to himself, to fall back upon his own, and in his wretchedness to cry out: *Lord, I suffer violence, answer Thou for me;* [13] and this: *Unhappy man that I am, who shall deliver me from the body of this death?* [14]

Since however, Scripture says God *hath made all things for Himself;*[15] it will certainly come to pass that the creature will at one time or other conform itself to its Author and be of one mind with Him. We ought therefore be transformed into this same disposition of soul, so that as God has willed that everything should be for Himself, so we too may deliberately desire neither ourselves nor any other thing to have been in the past, or to be in the future, unless it be equally for His sake, to wit, for His sole will, not for our own pleasure. A need satisfied [calmed by satisfaction], or good fortune received will not delight us so much

[10] Cf. Galatians II, 20.
[11] Cf. St. Matthew VI, 34.
[12] Cf. Psalm LXXII, 26.
[13] Isaias XXXVIII, 14.
[14] Romans VII, 24.
[15] Proverbs XVI, 4.

as that His will is seen perfectly fulfilled in us and by us; which, too, is what we daily ask in prayer when we say: *Thy will be done on earth as it is in heaven.*[16] O love, holy and chaste! O sweet and pleasing affection! O pure and undefiled intention of the will! the more surely undefiled and purer, as there is mixed with it, now, nothing of its own; so much the sweeter and more pleasing, as its every feeling is wholly divine. To be thus affected is to become one with God. Just as a little drop of water mixed with a lot of wine seems entirely to lose its own identity, while it takes on the taste of wine and its color; just as iron, heated and glowing, looks very much like fire, having divested itself of its original and characteristic appearance; and just as air flooded with the light of the sun is transformed into the same splendor of light so that it appears not so much lighted up as to be light itself; so it will inevitably happen that in saints every human affection will then, in some ineffable manner melt away from self and be entirely transfused into the will of God. Otherwise how will *God . . . be all in all,*[17] if in man there is left anything at all of man himself. The substance, indeed, will remain, but in another *form,* another glory, and another power [*i.e.* a man's human nature and individual identity will remain, transfigured]. When will this be? Who will see this? Who will possess it? *When shall I come and appear before the face of God?*[18] O Lord, my God, *My heart hath said to Thee: my face hath sought Thee: Thy face, O Lord, will I still seek.*[19] Will I, do you think, see Thy holy temple?

As for me, I think that it will not have come to pass with perfect fulfilment that: *Thou shalt love the Lord thy God with thy*

[16] St. Matthew VI, 10.
[17] I Corinthians XV, 28.
[18] Psalm XLI, 3.
[19] Psalm XXVI, 8.

whole heart, and with thy whole soul, and with thy whole strength,[20] until the heart itself is no longer compelled to think about the body, and the soul ceases to have to attend to quickening the body and to providing it with sense-perception, and the body's strength freed from vexations is made strong in the power that is of God. For it is impossible wholly to concentrate all these [the heart, mind and virtue] upon God and to hold them fixed upon the Divine Countenance so long as it is necessary for them, absorbed and dissipated, to be subject to this frail and wretched body. And so, in a spiritual and immortal body,[21] in a body perfect, calm and acceptable, and in all things subject to the spirit, let the soul hope to *apprehend* the fourth degree of love, or, rather, to be *apprehended* in it;[22] for, in truth, it is within the power of God to give it to whomsoever He wishes, not for human diligence to procure by its own efforts. Then, I say, she will easily come into the possession of the highest degree, when, without the slightest delay, as she hastens most eagerly into the joy of her Lord,[23] no allurement of the flesh will now retard her progress, no vexation destroy her peace. Do we think, however, that the holy martyrs actually attained to this grace, even in part, while still detained in those victorious bodies of theirs? Great power of love, certainly, had caught up their souls, within, and thus they had strength so to expose their bodies, without, and contemn their tortures. But, assuredly, the sense of most bitter pain could not but disturb their calm, although it had no power to destroy their peace.

[20] Deuteronomy VI, 5.
[21] Cf. 1 Corinthians XV, 44.
[22] Cf. Philippians III, 12-13.
[23] Cf. St. Matthew XXV, 21, 23.

CHAPTER XI

THIS PERFECTION OF LOVE IS NOT POSSIBLE OF ATTAINMENT EVEN BY THE SOULS OF THE BLESSED SEPARATED FROM THEIR BODIES, BEFORE THE RESURRECTION

BUT WHAT, NOW, of souls separated from their bodies? We believe that they are completely immersed in that sea of eternal light and of eternity overflowing with light. But if (as is not denied) they would fain have received their bodies or, certainly long and hope to receive them; it is clear beyond a shadow of doubt that they are not yet completely changed from their former selves, for admittedly there is still something which they regard as their own, to which at least in small measure their attention returns. Therefore, until *death is swallowed up in victory,*[1] and until the very moment when perpetual light invades the boundaries of night on every side and holds them, until the heavenly glory shines forth even in bodies, until that moment souls cannot altogether set themselves aside as of no account and completely transformed pass over into God, since even then they are surely bound to their bodies, if not by life or sense, certainly by a natural affection [*i.e.* disembodied souls depend upon their bodies neither for life nor perception, yet they have a natural longing which will not be satisfied until they are again united with their bodies], so that without them they have neither the desire nor the

[1] 1 Corinthians XV, 54.

power to attain their [ultimate] consummation. And so, before the restoration of their bodies there will not be that complete absorption of souls in God [*i.e.* that fainting away, into God],[2] which is their perfect and highest state; nor would the spirit now seek again for the fellowship of the flesh if it could attain to its perfect consummation without it. In truth, not without progress for the soul is the body laid down or taken up again. *Precious,* indeed, *in the sight of the Lord is the death of His saints.*[3] But if death is precious, what is life, and *that* life? Nor is it any wonder if the body, now glorified, seems to confer something upon the spirit, since even when weak and mortal it is manifest that it was of no little help to it. O how truly did he speak who said: *to them that love God, all things work together unto good.*[4] To the soul that loves God the body avails in its weakness, it avails in its death, it avails in its restoration: in the first instance, forsooth, for the fruit of penitence; in the second, for rest; in the last, for consummation. Rightly she does not wish to be made perfect without that which she feels helps her to what is good for her in every state.

Clearly a good and faithful companion to a good spirit is the flesh which if it is a burden, is a source of delight; or, certainly is a source of delight and hardly a burden at all. The first state is full of toil but abounding in fruit; the second is one of complete repose but in no wise wearisome; the third abounds in glory, as well. Listen to the Bridegroom in the Canticle inviting to this three-fold progress: *Eat,* He says, *O friends, and drink, and be inebriated, my dearly beloved.*[5] Those still toiling in the body He calls to food; those who have laid down the body and are enjoy-

[2] Cf. Psalm LXXII, 26.
[3] Psalm CXIV, 15.
[4] Romans VIII, 28.
[5] Canticle V, 1.

ing complete repose, He invites to drink; those who again take their bodies up He urges even to inebriation, and these He calls His most beloved ones because they most abound in charity. For, in the case of all others whom He calls not *most beloved,* but *friends,* there is a difference. As a result, those, to be sure, who groan, still weighed down in the flesh,[6] are held dear in return for the love that they have. But those who are already freed from the fetters of the flesh are dearer according as they are made more ready and become less incumbered for loving. Rightly, then, beyond both others are they called *most beloved* and are so, who having now received a second garment in bodies which they have resumed with glory, are borne along in the love of God more freely and more swiftly according as there is nothing of their own left in them to cause them the slightest anxiety or to retard their progress. This distinction neither of the other states can claim since in the first the body is carried along with labor; and in the second it is awaited not without a certain peculiar quality of desire for something that is absent.

First, then, the faithful soul eats her bread but alas! in the sweat of her brow.[7] Still, in fact, remaining in the flesh she still walks by faith,[8] which, to be sure, must be reduced to action through love because if it be not expressed in works it is dead.[9] This very work itself is food, as the Lord says: *My meat is to do the will of* My Father.[10] Henceforth, having divested herself of the flesh she no longer eats the bread of sorrow but it is allowed her to drink more abundantly, as if after meat, of the wine of love not unmixed however, but as is read in the Canticle as

[6] Cf. 2 Corinthians V, 4.
[7] Cf. Genesis III, 19.
[8] 2 Corinthians V, 7.
[9] St. James II, 17.
[10] St. John IV, 34.

spoken by the Bridegroom: *I have drunk my wine with my milk*.[11] For the soul even then, mixes with the wine of divine love the sweetness of natural affection with which she longs to resume her body and that, glorified. She glows [with love], therefore, having already drunk of the wine of holy charity but clearly not as yet to the point of inebriation; for, in the meanwhile, the admixture of this milk tempers that ardor. Finally, inebriation is wont to upset the mind and to render it altogether forgetful of itself. But she has not entirely forgotten self who still dwells upon her own body that is to be raised from the dead. But when this has been attained which alone was lacking, what is there now that hinders her from leaving self, in a way, wholly to go to God to become completely unlike herself [as she was before assuming her glorified body], to the degree in which it is granted her to be made most like unto God? Then, at last, admitted to the cup of wisdom concerning which it is read: *my chalice which inebriateth me, how goodly it is!*[12]—what wonder is it if now she becomes inebriated with the plenty of the house of God,[13] when, vexed with no anxiety for what is her own and free from care she drinks that wine pure and new, with Christ in the kingdom of His Father.[14]

Wisdom, in truth, gives a triple banquet and from a single love [her own] she supplies the fare,—she herself feeding those who labor, she herself giving drink to those who rest, she herself inebriating those who reign as kings.[15] But just as in a banquet for the body food is served before drink, since nature prescribes such an order, so too here. First, indeed, before death we *eat the*

[11] Canticle V, 1.
[12] Psalm XXII, 5.
[13] Cf. Psalm XXXV, 9.
[14] Cf. St. Matthew XXVI, 29.
[15] Cf. St. Matthew XIX, 28.

labors of our *hands,*[16] with labor masticating what is to be swallowed. But after death, in the spiritual life, we drink, clarifying what is perceived by a very pleasing sort of facility. Finally, our bodies living once again in immortal life, we become inebriated, abounding in wondrous plenty. This is the meaning of what the Spouse says in the Canticle: *eat, O friends, and drink, and be inebriated, my dearly beloved.*[17] Eat before death, drink after death, become inebriated after the resurrection. Justly now are they *most beloved* who are inebriated with love, and justly are they inebriated who have deserved to be brought into the wedding-feast of the Lamb,[18] eating and drinking at His table in His kingdom,[19] when He now presents *to Himself a glorious church, not having spot or wrinkle, or any such thing.*[20] Then straightway He inebriates His most beloved, then does He *make them drink of the torrent of* His *pleasures;*[21] since, indeed, in that close and pure embrace of Bridegroom and bride, *the stream of the river maketh the city of God joyful.*[22] This I think is nothing else than the Son of God Who *passing will minister unto them as* He Himself promised,[23] so that from this source *the just feast and rejoice before God: and be delighted with gladness.*[24] Hence that satiety without weariness; hence that insatiable desire of knowledge, without restlessness; hence that longing never satisfied [*inexplebile*] yet never knowing want; hence, finally, that inebriation without drunkenness, filled with truth, not with strong drink, not drenched with wine, but on fire with God. Thus that fourth degree of love is now possessed forever when

[16] Psalm CXXVII, 2.
[17] Canticle V, 1.
[18] Cf. Apocalypse XIX, 9.
[19] Cf. St. Luke XXII, 30.
[20] Ephesians V, 27.
[21] Psalm XXXV, 9.
[22] Psalm XLV, 5.
[23] Cf. St. Luke XII, 37.
[24] Psalm LXVII, 4.

God alone is loved in the highest possible degree; because, now, we do not even love ourselves save for His sake, so that He Himself is the reward of those who love Him, the reward eternal of those who love for all eternity.

CHAPTER XII

CHARITY, AS TREATED IN A LETTER TO THE CARTHUSIANS

I REMEMBER WELL that a while ago I wrote a letter to the holy Carthusian brethren and in it, among other matters, I discussed these very grades of love. But, perchance, I there said other things though not foreign to the matter, on the subject of charity, and for this reason certain of those remarks I do not consider it useless to add to this discourse as well, especially since it is easier to transcribe what has already been written than to write something new.[1] That, I say, is true and genuine charity and must be admitted as proceeding entirely from *a pure heart, a good conscience and a faith unfeigned,*[2] by which we love the good of our neighbor as well as our own. For he who loves only what is his, or loves it more, stands convicted of loving good unchastely, since he loves for his own and not for His sake. And such a one cannot obey the prophet who says: *Give praise to the Lord for He is good.*[3] He gives praise, to be sure, because, perhaps, He is good to him but not because He is good in Himself. Therefore let him understand that it is against him that that reproach was directed by the same prophet: *he will praise thee when thou shalt do well to him.*[4] There is a man who gives praise to the Lord because He is powerful, and there is a man who gives praise to Him because He is good to him, and, again, there is a man who gives

[1] Cf. Letter XI No. 3, *etc.*
[2] I Timothy I, 5.
[3] Psalm CXVII, 1.
[4] Psalm XLVIII, 19.

praise to Him because He is simply good. The first is a servant and fears for himself; the second, a hireling, desires things for his own sake; the third, a son, gives honor to the Father. And so he who is afraid and he who desires things for his own sake, both act for themselves. Only the charity which is found in a son, *seeketh not her own.*[5] For this reason I think that it was of charity that it was said: *The law of the Lord is unspotted, converting souls;*[6] for it is she [Charity] alone which is strong enough to *convert* a soul from love of self and of the world, and direct it to God. For, neither fear nor love of one's self converts the soul. At times they change an expression of countenance or an external act, but an affection, never. Even a servant, to be sure, sometimes does the work of God but because he does not do it freely he is known still to remain in his hardness. Even the hireling does the work of God but because he does not do it without recompense he is convicted of being carried along by his own cupidity. Truly, where there is something of one's own there is a distinction between one person and another; where there is a distinction between one person and another there is a corner [reserved for one's self]; and where, to be sure, there is a corner there without doubt there is dirt and mouldiness. And so, may that very fear by which he is restrained be his law for the servant; may his cupidity by which he, too, is circumscribed be the hireling's law, since by it he *is tempted . . . being drawn away and allured.*[7] But neither one of these two can be unspotted, or can convert souls. But charity converts souls whom she makes free agents.

Again, I would call her unspotted because she has accustomed

[5] 1 Corinthians XIII, 5.
[6] Psalm XVIII, 8.
[7] St. James I, 14.

herself to retain for herself nothing of her own. Certainly, in the case of one who has nothing of his own, all that he has is assuredly God's, but what is God's cannot be unclean. Therefore the unspotted law of the Lord is charity, which seeks not what is useful for itself but what is of use to many. For it is called the law of the Lord either because He Himself lives by it or because no one possesses it except as a gift from Him. Nor let it seem absurd that I have said that even God lives by law, since I said by no other law save charity. What in that supreme and blessed Trinity preserves that supreme and unspeakable unity, save charity? It is law, then, and charity the law of the Lord which in a certain way holds the Trinity together in unity and binds it *in the bond of peace.*[8] Let no one think, however, that I am here taking charity as a quality or as a sort of accident (otherwise I should be saying, which Heaven forbid, that there is in God something which is not God), but as that divine substance which, surely, is neither new nor unusual because John says: *God is charity.*[9] Therefore charity is rightly called both God and the gift of God. And so charity gives charity, the substantial gives what is an accident. Where it means the Giver it is the name of substance, where it means the gift it is the name of a quality. This is the eternal law, the Creator and Ruler of the universe. Indeed, *all things* have been made by *her in measure, and number and weight,*[10] and nothing is left without a law, since even the very law of all [charity] is not without a law, not however any other than itself, by which, although it did not create itself nevertheless it is its own rule.

[8] Ephesians IV, 3.
[9] 1 John IV, 8.
[10] Wisdom XI, 21.

CHAPTER XIII

THE LAW OF SELF-WILL AND CUPIDITY: THE LAW OF SERVANTS AND HIRELINGS

BUT THE SERVANT and the hireling have a law, not from the Lord, but which they themselves have made for themselves:—the former by not loving God; the latter by loving something else, more. They have, I say, a law; not the Lord's but their own; nevertheless it is subject to the law which is the Lord's. And indeed each one of them could make a law for himself, but he could not withdraw it from [subjection to] the unchangeable order of the law eternal. Then, I should say, each one made a law unto himself when he preferred his own will to the universal and eternal law, perversely, to be sure, wishing to imitate the Creator, so that just as He is a law unto Himself and this of His own right, so, man also would rule himself and make his own will his own law. Heavy and insupportable yoke upon all the children of Adam alas! bending down our necks and bowing [our heads], so that our *life hath drawn nigh to hell.*[1] *Unhappy man that I am, who shall deliver me from the body of this death?* [2] by which, surely, I am pressed down and almost crushed so that *unless the Lord had been my Helper, my soul had almost dwelt in hell.*[3] Weighed

[1] Psalm LXXXVII, 4.
[2] Romans VII, 24.
[3] Psalm XCIII, 17.

down under this burden was he groaning who said: *Why hast Thou set me opposite to Thee, and I am become burdensome to myself?* [4] Where he said, *I am become burdensome to myself,* he shows that he himself was a law unto himself and that no other had done this [*i.e.* made this law] save himself for himself, But what, speaking to God, he first said—thou hast *set me opposite to Thee*—indicated, nevertheless, that he had not escaped the law of God. This, to be sure, pertained to the eternal and just law of God, that he who would refuse to be ruled sweetly by God should be ruled by himself as a criminal, and he who of his own accord cast off the sweet yoke and light burden of charity [5] should unwillingly carry the insupportable burden of his own will. Thus in a wonderful and just way the eternal law both set its fugitive opposite to Himself and kept him subject, for while he did not elude the law of justice which judges according to every man's deserts, he did not, however, remain with God in His light, in His rest, in His glory, but was subject to His power and excluded from His felicity. O Lord my God, *why dost Thou not remove my sin, and why dost Thou not take away my iniquity?*[6] so that having cast away the heavy load of my own will I may breathe under the light burden of charity, that now I may not be encompassed with servile fear nor seduced by mercenary cupidity, but that I may be led by Thy spirit, the spirit of liberty by which Thy sons are led and may it give testimony to my spirit that I am one of Thy sons [7] since the same law is mine as is Thine, and as Thou art so may I also be in this world. These, indeed, are they who do what the Apostle says: *Owe no man*

[4] Job VII, 20.
[5] Cf. St. Matthew XI, 30.
[6] Job VII, 21.
[7] Cf. Romans VIII, 14-16.

anything, but love one another;[8] without any doubt as God is, so too are they in this world. They are neither servants nor hirelings, but sons.

[8] Romans XIII, 8.

CHAPTER XIV

THE LAW GOVERNING THE CHARITY OF SONS

THUS NEITHER ARE sons without law unless perchance someone should think otherwise because of this which has been written: *the law is not made for the just.*[1] But it ought to be known that the law promulgated in fear by a spirit of servitude is one thing; it is quite another, given in sweetness by a spirit of liberty.[2] Sons are neither constrained to be under the former, nor do they suffer themselves to be without the latter. Do you wish to hear why the law is not made for the just? *You have not received,* he says, *the spirit of bondage again in fear.*[3] Do you wish to hear how, nevertheless, they are not without the law of charity? *But you have received,* he adds, *the spirit of adoption of sons.*[4] Then, hear the just man confessing how he is not under the law nor yet without law. *I became,* he says, . . . *to them that are under the law, as if I were under the law* (*whereas myself was not under the law*), . . . *To them that were without the law, as if I were without the law,* (*whereas I was not without the law of God, but was in the law of Christ*).[5] Hence it is not rightly said that the just have no law, or that the just are without the law, but *the law is not made for the just;*[6] that is, it is not imposed upon them as upon

[1] I Timothy I, 9.
[2] Cf. Romans VIII, 15.
[3] *Ibid.*
[4] *Ibid.*
[5] I Corinthians IX, 20-21.
[6] I Timothy I, 9.

unwilling subjects but it is given them as to willing subjects, with a freedom equal to the sweetness with which it is breathed into them. Hence, also, the Lord says beautifully: *Take up My yoke upon you;*[7] as if He would say: I do not place it upon the unwilling, but you, if you are willing, take it up; otherwise you will find not rest but labor for your souls.

The law of charity, therefore, is good and sweet. It is not only lightly and sweetly borne but renders the laws even of servants and hirelings bearable and light. It does not destroy these laws, to be sure, but it brings about their fulfilment in accordance with Our Lord's words when He said: *I am not come to destroy (the law) but to fulfil* it.[8] It modifies the one, it puts order into the other, and it lightens both of them. Never will charity be without fear, but chaste fear; never will it be without its desire of personal gratification, but kept within bounds. Charity, therefore, perfects the law of the servant when it imparts devotion, and that of the hireling when it directs aright his desire of reward. Surely devotion mingled with fear does not annihilate those last but purifies them. Dread of punishment, only, is taken away, without which fear can not exist so long as it is servile; and this fear is pure and filial, *enduring for ever and ever.*[9] For, the text which reads, *perfect charity casteth out fear,*[10] is to be understood of a dread of punishment which (as we have said) is never wanting to servile fear. This (we said) making use of that sort of speech in which, often, the cause is put for the effect. As for a desire for personal gratification, it is then kept within bounds by the charity which is joined to it, when evil is completely rejected, better things are preferred to the good, nor are good things desired save

[7] St. Matthew XI, 29.
[8] St. Matthew V, 17.
[9] Psalm XVIII, 10.
[10] 1 St. John IV, 18.

on account of those which are better. When the complete fulfilment of this will have been attained through God's grace, the body and every good that pertains to the body will be loved only for the sake of the soul; the soul for the sake of God; but God for His own sake.

CHAPTER XV

THE FOUR DEGREES OF LOVE, AND THE HAPPY STATE OF THE HEAVENLY COUNTRY

NEVERTHELESS, BECAUSE WE are carnal [1] and are born of the concupiscence of the flesh,[2] it follows as a necessary consequence that our desire for personal gratification, or our love should have its source in the flesh. But if it is directed according to the right order of things, advancing by its several degrees under the guidance of grace, it will at last be consummated by the spirit because: *that was not first which is spiritual, but that which is natural; afterwards that which is spiritual.*[3] First, therefore, man loves himself for his own sake; for, he is flesh and he can have no taste for anything except in relation to himself. And when he sees that he cannot subsist of himself he begins to seek God through faith as something, as it were, necessary for him,[4] and to love Him. Thus he loves God according to the second degree, but for his own sake, not for Himself. But when, in truth, on account of his own necessity he has begun to worship and come to Him again and again by meditating, by reading, by prayer and by being obedient, little by little God becomes known to him through experience, in a sort of familiarity, and consequently He grows sweet; and thus by tasting how sweet is the Lord [5] he

[1] Cf. Romans VII, 14.
[2] Cf. 1 St. John II, 16.
[3] 1 Corinthians XV, 46.
[4] Cf. Hebrews XI, 6.
[5] Cf. Psalm XXXIII, 9.

passes to the third degree so that he loves God now, not for his own sake but for Himself. Yes, in this degree he stands still for a very long time and I know not if the fourth degree is attained in its perfection by any man in this life so that forsooth, a man loves himself only for the sake of God. If there are any who have experience of this let them declare it; to me, I confess, it seems impossible. But it will be so, beyond a doubt, when the good and faithful servant has been brought into the joy of his Lord[6] and *inebriated with the plenty of* God's *house.*[7] For, forgetful of himself in a wonderful way, as it were, and as if entirely freed of self he will continue on, wholly, into God, and thereafter being joined to Him he will be one spirit with Him.[8] I am of the opinion that this is what the prophet meant when he said: *I will enter into the powers of the Lord: O Lord I will be mindful of Thy justice alone.*[9] He felt, certainly, that when he entered into the spiritual powers of the Lord he would have laid aside self in all that concerns the infirmities of the flesh, so that he would have to give no thought to the flesh, but his whole being would in the spirit, be mindful of the justice of the Lord alone.[10]

Then, for certain, the several individual members of Christ will be able to say, everyone concerning himself, what Paul said of the Head: *And if we have known Christ according to the flesh; but now we know Him so no longer.*[11] No one, there, will know himself according to the flesh because flesh and blood shall not possess the kingdom of God.[12] Not that the substance of flesh will not be there, but that every carnal necessity will be

[6] Cf. St. Matthew XXV, 21.
[7] Cf. Psalm XXXV, 9.
[8] Cf. 1 Corinthians VI, 17.
[9] Psalm LXX, 16.
[10] Cf. *ibid.*
[11] 2 Corinthians V, 16.
[12] Cf. 1 Corinthians XV, 50.

wanting and the love of the flesh will be absorbed in the love of the spirit, and human affections, weak as they now are, shall be changed into those which are divine. Then the net of charity which now, drawn through this great and vast sea does not cease to gather together fish of every kind, when brought at last to the shore, casting forth the bad, will retain only the good.[13] Indeed in this life the net of charity includes fish of every kind within its vast folds, where, fashioning itself to suit all according to the time [14] and taking over the good and evil fortunes of all and, in a sense, making them its own, it is wont not only to *rejoice with them that rejoice,* but also to *weep with them that weep.*[15] But when it shall have reached the shore [eternity] casting away as bad fishes everything that it suffered in sadness, it will retain those only which can give it pleasure and be to it a source of gladness. For can it be that Paul, for instance, will then be weak with the weak or be on fire for those who are scandalized,[16] where scandals and weakness will be far away? Or will he, surely, mourn for those who have not done penance,[17] where it is certain there will be no one either sinning or doing penance? Far be it from us to think that he will lament and weep over those who are to be condemned to everlasting fire together with the devil and his angels,[18] in that *city* [*of God*] which *the stream of the river maketh . . . joyful,*[19] and whose gates *the Lord loveth . . . above all the tabernacles of Jacob;* [20] because in the tabernacles although the joy of victory is sometimes felt, there is, nevertheless, the anxiety of combat and often danger to life itself, but in that native land no suffering or sadness will be al-

[13] Cf. St. Matthew XIII, 47-48.
[14] Cf. 1 Corinthians IX, 19.
[15] Romans XII, 15.
[16] Cf. 2 Corinthians XI, 29.
[17] Cf. *ibid.* XII, 21.
[18] Cf. St. Matthew XXV, 41.
[19] Psalm XLV, 5.
[20] Psalm LXXXVI, 2.

lowed to enter in, even as it is sung thereof: *The dwelling in thee is as it were of all rejoicing;*[21] and again: *everlasting joy shall be unto them.*[22] Finally, how shall one be mindful of mercy where the justice of God alone will be remembered?[23] Just so, where now there will be no place for misery or occasion for pity, surely there can be no feeling of compassion.

[21] Psalm LXXXVI, 7.
[22] Isaias LXI, 7.
[23] Cf. Psalm LXX, 16.

THE END OF THE BOOK ON THE LOVE OF GOD

PART II

FRAGMENTS FROM SAINT BERNARD'S "SERMONS ON THE *CANTICLE OF CANTICLES*"

CHAPTER I

THE SIGNIFICANCE OF THE TITLE OF SOLOMON'S "CANTICLE OF CANTICLES"

YOU MUST NOT think that there is no significance in the fact that the title of this Book is not simply a "Canticle", but the "Canticle of Canticles". Many, indeed, are the canticles which I have read in Holy Scripture and no one of them do I remember as being called by such a title. Israel sang a song to the Lord because it had escaped both the sword and the yoke of Pharaoh, by the two-fold service of the sea, marvellously delivered and at the same time avenged.[1] Yet what it sang was not called the "Canticle of Canticles", but, if I remember rightly, *Israel,* says the Scripture, *sang this* CANTICLE *to the Lord.*[2] Debbora also sang a song,[3] and Judith sang a song,[4] and the mother of Samuel sang a song,[5] some of the prophets also sang a song, and no one of these, as we read, called his song the "Canticle of Canticles". . . . But that famous king, Solomon, singular in wisdom, exalted in fame, having an abundance of material things, secure in peace, is known to have had need of nothing such as, received, would have led him to repeat that song of his. Nor does his own writing seem anywhere to suggest any such thing. (Sermon I, §7.) And so it was under divine inspiration that he sang the praises

[1] Cf. Exodus XIV.
[2] *Ibid.* XV, 1.
[3] Cf. Judges V.
[4] Cf. Judith XVI.
[5] Cf. 1 Kings II.

of Christ and the Church, the grace of holy love, and the mysteries of marriage eternal. At the same time he expressed the longing of a saintly soul and composed a nuptial song exulting in spirit, in delightful but figurative language. . . . Therefore, I believe, it is because of its very excellence that this nuptial song is distinguished beyond all others by the title, "Canticle of Canticles", just as He to whom that song is sung is alone called, *King of kings and Lord of lords.*[6] (*Ibid.* § 8.)

It is a canticle that is itself the fruit of all the rest. The anointing of grace alone can teach a canticle of this sort; experience only, can unfold its meaning. Let those who have had experience of it recognize it; let those inexperienced in it burn with a longing not so much of knowing as of actually experiencing it. For, it is not a noise of the mouth, but a shout of the heart; not a sound of the lips, but a tumult of internal delights; a harmony of wills, not of voices. It is not heard outside, for it does not cry out in public. Only the one who sings hears it, and the one to whom it is sung, that is, the Bridegroom and the bride. For it is a nuptial song expressing the chaste and joyous embrace of souls, the harmony of their behavior, the blending of their affections in mutual charity. (*Ibid.* § 11.)

[6] 1 Timothy VI, 15.

CHAPTER II

THE INCARNATION, ANNOUNCED BY PATRIARCHS AND PROPHETS

VERY OFTEN WHEN I reflect upon the eager yearning with which the men of old sighed for the presence of Christ in the flesh, I am filled with remorse and confusion on my own account. Even now I can scarcely restrain my tears, so great is the shame I feel for the tepidity and sloth of these wretched times. For, to what one of us has the actual conferring of this grace brought joy as great as the longing with which the promise of it consumed the saints of old?

Speaking therefore out of their very souls' desire they said: *Let Him kiss me with the kiss of His mouth;*[1] passionately desiring not to be deprived of sweetness so great. (Sermon II, §1.) In truth, any perfect soul under the old dispensation would, as it were, say: "To what end, in my regard, those babbling lips of the prophets? . . . I do not now hear Moses. For me he has become a man of a stammering tongue.[2] Isaias is *a man of unclean lips.*[3] Jeremias *cannot speak, for* he is *a child.*[4] And all the prophets lack real power of utterance. . . . No longer in them or through them let Him speak to me, for *dark* are *waters in the clouds of the air.*[5] But let Him in His own Person, *kiss me with the kiss of His mouth,* He whose presence is full of grace and the

[1] Canticle I, 1.
[2] Cf. Exodus IV, 10.
[3] Isaias VI, 5.
[4] Jeremias I, 6.
[5] Psalm XVII, 12.

waters of whose wonderful teaching I pray may become in me *a fountain of water, springing up into life everlasting*".[6] . . . Not that I am so presumptuous as to expect to be kissed with His *mouth.* That is the singular prerogative of the happiness that pertains to the particular human nature which He assumed, and to no other. But more humbly I pray to be kissed with the *kiss* of His mouth. This, to be sure, is common to the many who can say: *And of His fulness we all have received.*[7] (*Ibid.* § 2.) Pay close attention, now, to what I am going to say. Let the mouth that gives the kiss be the Word becoming Flesh. Let the Flesh [Human Nature] which is assumed be the mouth that receives the kiss—a kiss, in truth, perfected equally by Him who gives and Him who receives it,—a single Person subsisting in two natures, the Mediator between God and men, the Man, Christ Jesus. In this sense none of the saints would ever presume to say, *Let Him kiss me with His* MOUTH, but only *with the* KISS *of His mouth.* They reserved the former prerogative for the Nature upon which, alone, and once only, the mouth of the Word impressed a kiss when the whole fulness of Divinity poured Itself into that Nature in the flesh. Happy kiss! . . . in which God is united to Man. . . . This union of natures joins things human with those that are divine, *making peace . . . both as to the things that are on earth, and the things that are in heaven.*[8] *For He is our peace Who hath made both one.*[9] (*Ibid.* § 3.)

[6] St. John IV, 14.
[7] St. John I, 16.
[8] Colossians I, 20.
[9] Ephesians II, 14.

CHAPTER III

WHAT IT IS TO KISS THE FEET, THE HAND, AND THE LIPS OF THE LORD

I SHOULD LIKE to discover if to any one of you it has ever been given to say with sincerity: *Let Him kiss me with the kiss of His mouth.* For it is not the privilege of every man to speak these words out of a real desire of heart. But if anyone has even once received this spiritual kiss from the mouth of Christ, that personal experience stirs him to his soul's depths and filled with delight he eagerly prays that the favor may again be granted him. It is my opinion that there is no one who can even know what it is, except him who experiences it. It is, as it were, a hidden manna and only he who has eaten still hungers for it. It is *a fountain sealed up,*[1] of which no stranger can partake; but he alone who drinks, still thirsts for it. Hear him who has had this experience, how earnestly he prays! *Restore unto me,* are his words, *the joy of Thy salvation.*[2] Far be it, then, from a soul like mine to lay claim to this grace—a soul weighed down with sins, still subject to the passions of flesh which has never yet felt the sweetness of the spirit, ignorant of and inexperienced in the delights which are internal. (Sermon III, §1.)

Nevertheless, to a soul who has been thus favored I shall indicate the position it becomes her to occupy in the service of her Beloved. Let her not rashly raise herself up to the lips of the

[1] Canticle IV, 12.

[2] Psalm L, 14.

Fairest of Bridegrooms, but let her, with me, cast herself at the feet of a most austere Lord, and with the Publican, trembling with fear let her *not so much as lift up* her *eyes towards heaven,*[3] lest dazzled by its light, eyes accustomed to darkness should be blinded by glory, and stricken by the unwonted splendors of Majesty, should be overwhelmed anew with the darkness of a still denser cloud. Let it not seem to you—O whoever you may be, if you are such a soul—let it not seem to you that that place is vile and contemptible where the holy woman who had been a sinner divested herself of sin and put on the garment of sanctity. . . . Therefore after the example of the holy Penitent do you also prostrate yourself before Him, O wretched that you are, that your wretchedness may cease. Bow down to the very earth. Embrace His feet. Appease Him with kisses. Bathe Him with tears which do not cleanse Him but you, and you will become as one of the *sheep that are shorn, which come up from the washing.*[4] Thus, to be sure, you will be so overwhelmed with shame and grief that you will not dare to lift up your face until you hear those same words, *Thy sins are forgiven thee,*[5] until you hear: *Arise, Arise . . . O Captive daughter of Sion; . . . arise, shake from thee the dust.*[6] (*Ibid.* §2.)

Even after you have imprinted the first kiss upon the feet, you must not presume immediately to raise yourself up to the *kiss of the mouth.* But there will be a step midway for you before you can attain to this—an intervening kiss, as it were, when you take His hand and kiss it. Let the explanation of all this run somewhat as follows. If Jesus has said to me, *thy sins are forgiven thee,* what will it avail unless I give up sin? If after washing my

[3] St. Luke XVIII, 13.
[4] Canticle IV, 2.
[5] St. Luke VII, 48.
[6] Isaias LII, 1-2.

feet I soil them again, will it be of any advantage to have washed them? Defiled with every sort of sin I long lay in *the mire of dregs;*[7] but to fall back again now, will without doubt be worse than to have continued to lie there. Finally I remember that He who healed me said to me: *Behold thou art made whole: sin no more lest some worse thing happen to thee.*[8] But He who gave the will to repent must of necessity bestow the strength to remain sinless, so that I may not again and again commit the sins I now repent of, and make my *last state . . . worse than the first.*[9] Woe to me even as I do penance, if straightway He were to withdraw His hand, He, without Whom I can do nothing. Nothing, I repeat, neither repent nor continue in the state of grace. Hence I hear the counsel which the Wise Man gives: *repeat not the word in thy prayer.*[10] I tremble, too, at the threat which the judge directs towards the *tree that doth not yield good fruit.*[11] I confess that for such reasons as these I am not altogether content with the former grace by which I have repented of evil, unless I shall have received a second, also, so that I may *bring forth fruit worthy of penance,*[12] and thenceforth may not return to my *vomit.*[13] (*Ibid.* §3.)

This, therefore, it remains for me to ask for and to receive before I shall presume to aspire to higher and holier things. I do not want suddenly to attain the loftiest heights of sanctity. I desire to progress gradually. To the degree that the boldness of a sinner is displeasing to God, is the timidity of a penitent pleasing to Him. . . . What! still stained with dust will you touch those sacred lips? Only yesterday drawn out of the mire will you today

[7] Psalm XXXIX, 3.
[8] St. John V, 14.
[9] St. Luke XI, 26.
[10] Ecclesiasticus VII, 15.
[11] St. Matthew III, 10.
[12] St. Matthew III, 8.
[13] Proverbs XXVI, 11.

be admitted to the glory of His countenance? For you there must be a transition effected by way of His hand. It must first cleanse you: it must first raise you up. How will it raise you up? By giving you that whence you will derive confidence. What is that? The beauty of sinlessness and the worthy fruits of penance, which are works of devotion. These will lift you up from the dunghill to the hope of hazarding stronger deeds. To be sure, as you receive the gift, kiss the hand; that is, not to yourself, but to His name give the glory. Give Him this glory once for offences pardoned; give it again for virtues conferred. Otherwise, certainly, you must see to it that you protect yourself against such thrusts as these: *What hast thou that thou hast not received? And if thou hast received, why dost thou glory, as if thou hadst not received it?*[14] (*Ibid.* §4.)

Having finally in these two kisses experimental proof of divine condescension, perhaps you will not feel it presumptuous to attempt things holier still. For in proportion as you grow in grace, will your confidence increase. Hence it happens that you love more ardently and knock more confidently for that which you feel you need. For now, *to him that knocketh, it shall be opened.*[15] That final good, the kiss containing in itself whatever there is of highest condescension and marvelous sweetness, will not be denied, I believe, to one with such a disposition of soul . . . Uniting ourselves to Christ our Lord in this holy kiss, we are, through His condescension made one spirit with Him. (*Ibid.* §5.)

[14] I Corinthians IV, 7.

[15] St. Luke XI, 10.

CHAPTER IV

THE ARDENT LOVE OF THE SOUL FOR GOD

Let Him kiss me with the kiss of His mouth.[1] Who speaks? The bride. Who is she? The soul thirsting for God. I now put before you various dispositions of soul so that the one that is especially suited to a bride may shine forth more clearly. If one is a servant he is in dread of his lord's face. If one is a hireling he hopes for pay from his lord's hand. If one is a disciple he gives ear to his teacher. If one is a son he honors his father. But the soul who begs a kiss, is in love. Among the gifts of nature this affection of love holds first place, especially when it makes haste to return to its Origin, which is God. Words cannot be found so sweet as to express the sweet affections of the Word and the soul for each other, except *bride* and *Bridegroom*. For persons so related, all things are held in common. There is nothing that one can appropriate as his own, nothing that one can divide so that the other is excluded from a share. Both have one inheritance, one home, one table, even one flesh. On this account, *a man shall leave father and mother, and cleave to his wife: and they shall be two in one flesh.*[2] The woman, likewise, is commanded none the less, to *forget* her *people and* her *father's house,* so that the man may *greatly desire* her *beauty.*[3] If, therefore, to love is the special

[1] Canticle I, 1.
[2] Genesis II, 24.
[3] Psalm XLIV, 11-12.

and chief prerogative of those espoused, not inappropriately, the soul who loves may be called by the name of spouse or bride. The soul who loves asks a kiss. It does not ask liberty nor reward, nor heritage, nor finally, even knowledge, but a kiss—clearly after the manner of the chastest spouse burning with a holy love and altogether powerless to conceal the flame that consumes her. See how abruptly she dispenses with an introduction in what she has to say. Being about to ask something great of one who is great, she nevertheless uses no pretence of flatteries, as is so often done. With no circumvolutions does she make a round-about approach to that which she desires. She makes no exordium. She does not strive to render her hearer kindly disposed. But out of the abundance of her heart suddenly bursting forth, simply and, as it were, boldly, *Let Him kiss me,* she says, *with the kiss of His mouth.* (Sermon VII, §2.)

Does it not clearly seem to you as if she would say, *What have I in heaven? And besides Thee what do I desire upon earth?*[4] She loves chastely, beyond a doubt, who seeks him himself whom she loves, not anything else whatever, that he has. She loves holily because she loves not in the concupiscence of flesh, but in the purity of spirit. She loves intensely who is so intoxicated with her own love that she does not think upon the majesty of him whom she loves. What! *He looketh upon the earth, and maketh it tremble.*[5] . . . But what can be plainer than that *perfect charity casteth out fear?*[6] (*Ibid.* §3.)

[4] Psalm LXXII, 25.
[5] Psalm CIII, 32.
[6] 1 St. John IV, 18.

CHAPTER V

BY THE KISS OF THE MOUTH OF GOD IS MEANT THE HOLY SPIRIT. THE CHURCH ASKS THAT THIS KISS BE GIVEN HER SO THAT SHE MAY HAVE KNOWLEDGE OF THE HOLY TRINITY

IT SEEMS TO ME (if I may begin on a higher plane than usual) that a certain ineffable kiss which no creature had ever received was meant by Him who said: *No one knoweth the Son but the Father: neither doth any one know the Father, but the Son, and he to whom it shall please the Son to reveal* HIM.[1] For the Father loves the Son and embraces Him with a singular love. The Most High embraces His Equal; the Eternal, His Co-Eternal; the One, His Only-Begotten . . . (Sermon VIII, §1.)

I hold for certain that to so great and so holy an *arcanum* of divine love not even the angelic creation is admitted. . . . See the new Spouse [the Church] receiving the new kiss, not, however, from the *mouth* but from *the* KISS *of His mouth.* He breathed on them, it is said. There can be no doubt that Jesus breathed upon the Apostles, that is, upon the primitive Church, and said: *Receive ye the Holy Ghost.*[2] That was, assuredly, a kiss. What? —the physical breath? No, but the invisible Spirit.

He was communicated by the Lord's breathing so that by this it should be understood that He proceeds from the Son equally as from the Father after the manner of a real kiss which is equal-

[1] St. Matthew XI, 27.

[2] St. John XX, 22.

ly his who gives and his who receives it. And so it is enough for the bride if she is kissed with the *kiss* of the Bridegroom, even if she is not kissed with His *mouth.* Nor does she think it a slight thing or a thing to be despised that she is kissed with a *kiss,* which is nothing else than to be filled with the Holy Ghost. Certainly if the Father is rightly interpreted as giving the kiss and the Son as receiving it, it will not be very far from the fact to understand the kiss itself as the Holy Ghost who is the unalterable peace, the indissoluble bond, the indivisible love, the inviolable unity between the Father and the Son. (*Ibid.* §2.)

It is, therefore, through His inspiration that the bride grows bold and confidently asks under the name of a kiss, that the inpouring of the Holy Ghost be granted her. She holds in memory something which cannot cease to be a motive of confidence. For when the Son said, *no one knoweth the Son, but the Father: neither doth any one know the Father, but the Son,* He added, *and he to whom it shall please the Son to reveal* HIM.[3] Now, when the Father and the Son are perfectly known to anyone, how can he be ignorant of the Goodness of the Two? And that Goodness is the Holy Spirit. (*Ibid.* §§3, 4.)

Therefore when the bride asks a kiss she begs for the grace to be the recipient of this three-fold knowledge, as far as it can be acquired in this mortal flesh. But she asks it of the Son to whom it pertains to reveal things to whomsoever He will. The Son, then, reveals Himself to whomsoever He will and He reveals the Father. But this revelation, beyond a doubt, is made by a kiss, that is, by the Holy Spirit. To this the Apostle is witness who says: *To us God hath revealed Them by His spirit.*[4] . . . Further-

[3] St. Matthew XI, 27. [4] 1 Corinthians II, 10.

more, the revelation which is made through the Holy Spirit not only enlightens the soul to knowledge but also enkindles it to love. As St. Paul says: *The charity of God is poured forth in our hearts by the Holy Ghost Who is given to us.*[5] (*Ibid.* §5.)

[5] Romans V, 5.

CHAPTER VI

THE DESOLATION AND CONSOLATION OF THE BRIDE

LET US RETURN now to the text and give the reason for the bride's words as well as for what follows from them. . . . Let us suppose, then, that those whom we have called the Bridegroom's companions come once again to the bride to visit and to greet her. When they have found her weary and softly moaning, wondering what can be the reason for this, they speak, let us say, in some such manner as this: "What has happened? Why do we find you sadder than is your wont? What is the reason for this unexpected moaning? . . . Come, tell us how we can help you." (Sermon IX, §1.)

"I cannot rest," she says, "unless He *kiss me with the kiss of His mouth.*[1] I am thankful for kissing His feet and I am thankful for kissing His hands. But if He has any regard for me, *Let Him kiss me with the kiss of His mouth.*[2] I am not ungrateful, but I am in love. I have received favors, I confess, beyond my deserts, but they are far short of my desires. I am impelled by desire, not by reason. Do not, I beg of you, blame presumption, where affection urges me on. A sense of modesty, it is true, protests. But love conquers. I am not unmindful of the fact that *the king's honor loveth judgment.*[3] But intense love does not wait upon the judgment. It is not restrained by counsel. It is not

[1] Canticle I, 1.
[2] *Ibid.*
[3] Psalm XCVIII, 4.

checked by a sense of false modesty. It is not subject to reason. I ask, I implore, I entreat with all my heart: *Let Him kiss me with the kiss of His mouth.* Lo! for His sake, these many years I have been at pains to live in chastity and restraint. . . . I resist my evil passions. I apply myself to prayer with constancy. I am on the watch against temptations. *I recount . . . my years in the bitterness of my soul.*[4] . . . I do not desire what does not belong to me. Rather I have given away myself and what is mine, with equal largess. *In the sweat of* my *face* I *eat* my *bread.*[5] But for the rest—in all these, everything is a matter of routine; nothing of sweetness. What am I, unless, according to the Prophet, *Ephraim, . . . a heifer taught to love to tread out corn?*[6] And in the Gospel he who does only what he is obliged to do, is considered an unprofitable servant.[7] I am in some way, perhaps, performing my duties. But my soul is as earth without water. In order, therefore, that my holocaust may be made fat, *Let Him kiss me,* I implore, *with the kiss of His mouth.*" (*Ibid.* §2.)

Many of you in your manifestations of conscience are wont to complain of just this sort of languor of an arid soul and dulness of a stolid mind which cannot attain to exalted and subtle truths because they know little or nothing of the sweetness of the spirit. What is it that such souls long for, unless it be for *the kiss of His mouth?* Clearly they are longing and sighing for the Spirit of wisdom and of understanding—of understanding by which they may satisfy their quest for knowledge; of wisdom by which they may come to enjoy the full savor of what their intellects have grasped. It is my belief that it was with these very sentiments that the Prophet prayed when he said: *Let my soul be*

[4] Isaias XXXVIII, 15.
[5] Genesis III, 19.
[6] Osee X, 11.
[7] Cf. St. Luke XVII, 10.

filled as with marrow and fatness: and my mouth shall praise Thee with joyful lips.[8] (*Ibid.* §3.)

While the bride is speaking of the Bridegroom, suddenly He is at her side—He grants her wish, He gives the kiss and in her regard fulfils the word which is written: *Thou hast given him his heart's desire; and hast not withholden from him the will of his lips.*[9] . . . Those whose ardent desire is to pray often, know from experience the truth of what I am saying. Frequently we approach the altar with a lukewarm and arid heart, and give ourselves to prayer. But suddenly the waters of grace pour in upon those who persevere; the heart becomes fertile, and the whole interior is filled with a flood of devotion. (*Ibid.* §7.)

[8] Psalm LXII, 6.

[9] Psalm XX, 3.

CHAPTER VII

THE PATIENCE OF CHRIST WITH SINNERS AND HIS MILDNESS TOWARDS PENITENTS. THE PRACTICE OF THESE VIRTUES BY THOSE WHO ARE HIS MINISTERS

In Christ there are two proofs of the gentleness of His nature. He patiently awaits the return of the sinner and He gently receives the penitent. This twofold sweetness of delicious savor abounds in the breast of the Lord Jesus—his long-suffering in waiting for the sinner and his readiness in granting him pardon. But listen! This is not an original thought of mine. For you read in regard to long-suffering: *Despisest thou the riches of his goodness and patience and long-suffering?* And again: *Knowest thou not that the benignity of God leadeth thee to penance?*[1] . . . And concerning readiness to forgive you read: *In whatever hour the sinner shall repent, his sin shall be forgiven him.*[2] You read: *Let the wicked forsake his way and the unjust man his thoughts, and let him return to the Lord, and He will have mercy on him, and to our God: for He is bountiful to forgive.*[3] Beautifully does David sum up both these attributes in a few words, when he says: *The Lord is . . . long-suffering and plenteous in mercy.*[4] It is because the spouse has had experience of this twofold goodness that her confidence increased, as she confesses, so that she dared ask a kiss. (Sermon IX, §5.)

[1] Romans II, 4.
[2] Ezechiel XXXIII, 11-12.
[3] Isaias LV, 7.
[4] Psalm CII, 8.

CHAPTER VIII

THE VIRTUES OF CHRIST IN HIS CHURCH AND IN ITS MINISTERS

IT IS WITH the Church, our spiritual mother, as it is with Christ. For example, if perchance she notices any one of those whom she has begotten in the Gospel, shaken by some violent temptation and hence troubled and sad and made to waver, not being able to withstand the force of the temptation, how she sympathises with him, how she caresses him! How she grieves for him, how she comforts him! How many pious reasons she discovers, presently, to raise him up from the depths of desolation. On the contrary, if she perceives that a soul is ready, quick, and making fair progress, she is happy. She approaches him with helpful advice. She incites him to further efforts. She instructs him in what is required to persevere and exhorts him to continue on to greater and greater perfection. She becomes all to all. She makes the feelings of all, her feelings. Finally, she proves herself the mother no less of those who falter, than of those who steadily advance.

How many individuals there are today who reveal themselves otherwise affected! I speak of those who have undertaken the care of souls. It is a fact that cannot be mentioned without a groan that springs from wretchedness of soul—the opprobrium of Christ, the spittings, the scourges, the nails, the lance, the cross, even His death itself—all these they melt down in the furnace of avarice and squander in the acquisition of shameful gain, and hasten to thrust into their own purses the price of the Redemption of the world. (Sermon X, §§2-3.)

CHAPTER IX

THE VIRTUES CHARACTERISTIC OF THE BRIDES OF CHRIST

THERE ARE CHARACTERISTICS of the Bridegroom and other characteristics of the bride which we may call ointments. . . . Let us select those especially appropriate for the bride. There is the ointment of contrition, and there is the ointment of devotion, and that of piety. The first is pungent, causing pain. The second is soothing and relieves pain. The third is healing, and cures the disease itself. Let us discuss these separately and more in detail. (Sermon X, §4.)

There is, then, the ointment which the soul entangled with many offences makes for herself, if, when she begins to ponder her ways, she gathers together, piles up, and grinds in the mortar of conscience her many and different kinds of sins, and within the crucible of a burning breast melts them all down, as it were, over the fire of repentance and sorrow so that she can say with the Psalmist: *My heart grew hot within me: and in my meditation a fire shall flame out.*[1] Behold this is one ointment with which the sinful soul ought to make fragrant the beginning of her conversion, and apply it to her still fresh wounds. For, the first *sacrifice* that must be offered *to God is an afflicted spirit.*[2] So long, therefore, as a soul, like one who is poor and needy, has nothing wherewith to compound for herself a better and more

[1] Psalm XXXVIII, 4. [2] Psalm L, 19.

precious ointment, let her not neglect, meanwhile, to prepare this, even though it be made of stuff apparently of no value, because, *a contrite and humble heart, O God, Thou wilt not despise.*[3] For, the soul will be less contemptible in the eyes of God, the more contemptible she becomes in her own eyes when she remembers her sins. (*Ibid.* §5.)

Yet if we say that this invisible and spiritual ointment was typified by that visible ointment with which, according to the Gospel, the feet of God-made-Man were anointed by a sinful woman, we cannot then consider such ointment worthless. For what is it we read concerning it? *And the house was filled with the odor of the ointment.*[4] . . . If we realize what fragrance is diffused throughout the Church by the repentance of one sinner, and how strong an odor of life unto life any penitent becomes if his repentance is public and perfect, surely of him also we shall say with equal confidence, *the house was filled with the odor of the ointment.* Finally the sweet odor of penitence reaches even to the mansions of the blessed above, so that on the authority of Truth Itself, *there shall be joy before the angels of God upon one sinner doing penance.*[5] Rejoice, penitents! Take courage, you who are weak! . . . Let your hands with confidence distill the bitterness of myrrh into this ointment, for, a contrite and humble heart God will not despise. That anointing must not be looked upon with scorn, nor must it be counted worthless, the odor of which not only stimulates men to repentance but moves even the angels to joy. (*Ibid.* §6.)

But there is an ointment as much more precious than this, as its ingredients are more excellent. The ingredients of the former

[3] Psalm L, 19.
[4] St. John XII, 3.
[5] St. Luke XV, 10.

are not far to seek. We find them within our very selves and that, without difficulty. Out of our own little gardens we very easily gather an abundance of these as often as necessity requires. For who is there who has not at hand enough offences and sins of his very own, if he does not deliberately conceal the truth? These are, as you realise, the ingredients of the first ointment which we have already described. But the sweet spices of the second, this earth of ours nowhere brings forth, but *far and from the uttermost coasts,*[6] must we seek them. For, *every best gift and every perfect gift is from above, coming down from the Father of lights.*[7] This ointment, in fact, is made of the divine favors bestowed upon the human race. . . . Assuredly when these, in the mortar of the breast, have been crushed and pounded with the pestle of frequent meditation, then all fused together by the fire of holy desire and finally enriched with the oil of gladness, there will be an ointment far more precious and more excellent than the former. To prove this it is sufficient to cite the testimony of Him who says; *The sacrifice of praise shall glorify Me.*[8] There can be no doubt that a remembrance of favors moves one to praise his benefactor. (*Ibid.* §7.)

Moreover since Scripture bearing witness concerning the former ointment says only that it is in no wise despised,[9] it is clear that the latter is more highly commended in that it is said to give glory. Besides, the first is applied to the feet, the second to the head. For if in Christ the head is to be referred to the Divinity when Saint Paul says, *the Head of Christ is God,*[10] without doubt he anoints the Head who gives thanks, for this attains to God,

[6] Proverbs XXXI, 10.
[7] St. James I, 17.
[8] Psalm XLIX, 23.
[9] Cf. Psalm L, 19.
[10] 1 Corinthians XI, 3.

not man. Not that He who is God is not Man, since God and Man is one Christ, but because every good, even that which is administered through man, is from God, not man. For, *it is the spirit that quickeneth: the flesh profiteth nothing.*[11] And therefore, *cursed be the man that trusteth in man.*[12] For although all our hope hangs upon the God-Man, it is not, however, because He is Man, but because He is God. Consequently, the former ointment is applied to the feet, the latter to the head, since the humility of a contrite heart accords well with the Flesh [*i.e.* Christ's Human Nature], and the giving of glory is in keeping with Majesty [*i.e.* His Divinity]. (*Ibid.* §8.)

A penitent newly converted is humiliated and cast down in conscience and disquieted when he feels that because of the short time since his conversion, his old passions are not yet dead within him. Hence the necessity he has of occupying himself with again uprooting from the garden of his heart the thorns of disquiet and the briars of evil desire, a work which does not suffer him to stray beyond himself. What then? One who groans under the burden of such a task, will he be able at the same time to exult in the praises of God? How can the mouth of one who is groaning and lamenting, give forth, as did the mouth of Isaias, the sound of *thanksgiving and the voice of praise?*[13] For as we learn from the Wise Man, *A tale out of time is like music in mourning.*[14] Moreover, the giving of thanks follows, not precedes a favor. Furthermore a soul that is still in sadness does not rejoice in a favor received, but stands in need of one. She has incentives to offer prayers, but not to return thanks. For how can one recall a favor which he has not received? With reason, therefore, I have

[11] St. John VI, 64.
[12] Jeremias XVII, 5.
[13] Isaias LI, 3.
[14] Ecclesiasticus XXII, 6.

said that it does not pertain to a soul in the state of spiritual poverty to produce this ointment which ought to be made of divine favors remembered. A soul cannot see the light so long as she fixes her gaze upon the darkness. She is plunged into bitterness, to be sure, and the sad remembrance of sins fills her memory, nor will it permit anything whatever of a joyous nature to enter in. . . . The second ointment, therefore, is not for those who are in a state of spiritual poverty. (*Ibid.* §9.)

But see who they are who not without cause glory in an abundance of it. *And they* (the Apostles) *indeed went from the presence of the council, rejoicing that they were accounted worthy to suffer reproach for the name of Jesus.*[15] They had thoroughly anointed themselves, to be sure, with unction of the Spirit, these men whose mildness did not desert them, I do not say because of words, but not even because of stripes. They were, indeed, rich in charity which no expenditures can exhaust and from it they were easily enabled to offer up *holocausts full of marrow.*[16] Their brimming hearts poured out everywhere the holy unction with which they had been filled beyond measure, when, *they began to speak* (the wonderful works of God) *with divers tongues, according as the Holy Ghost gave them to speak.*[17] Nor can there be any doubt that it was they who were rich in those same ointments, they to whom the Apostle bore witness, saying: *I give thanks to my God always for you, for the grace of God that is given you in Christ Jesus, that in all things you are made rich in Him, in all utterance, and in all knowledge; as the testimony of Christ was confirmed in you, so that nothing is wanting to you in any grace.*[18] O that I may be able to give just such thanks as

[15] Acts, V, 41.
[16] Psalm LXV, 15.
[17] Acts II, 4.
[18] 1 Corinthians I, 4-7.

this on your account, that I may see you rich in virtues, prompt in the praises of God, and more plenteously abounding in this spiritual wealth in Christ Jesus Our Lord. (*Ibid.* §10.)

CHAPTER X

TWO FACTS PERTAINING TO THE WORK OF MAN'S REDEMPTION: THE WAY IN WHICH IT IS ACCOMPLISHED, AND ITS FRUIT

I SAID AT the end of my last talk and I feel no reluctance in repeating it, that I desire every one of you to become a partaker of that sacred unction in which holy devotion recalls God's favors with joy and the giving of thanks. This is good for two reasons. First, it lightens the hardships of the present life and certainly they become easier to bear for us who rejoice in the praises of God. Secondly, because nothing so perfectly manifests on earth the state of those who dwell in Heaven, as the joy of those praising God. As Scripture says, *Blessed are they that dwell in Thy house, O Lord: they shall praise Thee for ever and ever.*[1] . . . (Sermon XI, §1.)

For this reason I counsel you, my friends, to turn your steps aside now and then from the sad and disquieting remembrance of your past ways, and to set forth upon the smoother paths of the more peaceful remembrance of God's benefits, so that you who are thrown into a state of confusion at the sight of self may find relief in a glance at Him. I desire you to make trial of what the holy Prophet counsels, saying: *Delight in the Lord, and He will give thee the requests of thy heart.*[2] And indeed sorrow for sins is necessary, but it should not be continual. It should be in-

[1] Psalm LXXXIII, 5. [2] Psalm XXXVI, 4.

terspersed with the more cheerful remembrance of Divine clemency lest, perchance, the heart be hardened by sadness and perish through despair. . . . If Cain had been held in check by this rein he would never have cried out in despair: *My iniquity is greater than that I may deserve pardon.*[3] God forbid! God forbid! His fatherly love of us is greater than any injustice whatsoever.

. . . The repeated, rather, the continuous remembrance of divine munificence will easily convince you of this. Otherwise, how will that precept of the Apostle be fulfilled, *in all things give thanks,*[4] if the things for which thanks is due are allowed to fade from the heart? I would not that you should be branded with the reproach addressed to the Jews concerning whom Scripture bears witness that *they forgot His benefits, and His wonders that He had shewn them.*[5] (*Ibid.* §2.)

. . . At least that benefit which is the chief and greatest, namely, the work of our Redemption, ought not, even for a moment, fade from the memory of the redeemed. And in this work there are two things of greatest importance which occur to me, which I shall take care to suggest for your consideration. And this I shall do in as few words as possible, being mindful of the saying: *Give an occasion to a wise man, and wisdom shall be added to him.*[6] The two things, therefore, are the way in which the Redemption was accomplished, and its fruit. The way, to be sure, was the emptying-out of God's own Self:[7] the fruit is that we are filled with Him. To meditate on the latter is the seed-plot of hope: the former is an incentive for the highest reaches of love. Each is necessary for our progress lest our hope should be mer-

[3] Genesis IV, 13.
[4] 1 Thessalonians V, 18.
[5] Psalm LXXVII, 11.
[6] Proverbs IX, 9.
[7] Cf. Philippians II, 7.

cenary if it be not accomplished by love, or love grow lukewarm if considered productive of no fruit. (*Ibid.* §3.)

Besides, we await such fruit of our love as He whom we love has promised: *good measure and pressed down and shaken together and running over shall* be given *into your bosom.*[8] That measure, I hear, will be without measure. But I would like to know what that is which will be measured, or rather, what that immeasurable thing is which is promised us: *the eye hath not seen, O God, besides Thee, what things Thou hast prepared for them that wait for Thee.*[9] Tell us, You who are making the preparation, what is it that You are preparing? We believe. We are confident that in truth, as You promise: *We shall be filled with the good things of Thy house.*[10] But with what good things, I pray, or of what sort? Perchance with corn, with wine and with oil, with gold and silver and precious stones? But these we have known and have seen; yes, have seen and have despised. This we seek—what *eye hath not seen nor ear heard* and what has not *entered into the heart of man.*[11] This it is that gives satisfaction. It is this that tastes sweet. This it is that gives us delight as we inquire into the nature of it, whatever it may be. *And they shall all be taught of God,*[12] it is said, and *God* shall be *all in all.*[13] As I understand it, the plenitude [of blessedness] which we await from God is nothing else than a plenitude of God Himself. (*Ibid.* §4.)

But who can comprehend *how great is the multitude of . . . sweetness*[14] comprehended in that brief saying, *God* shall be *all*

[8] St. Luke VI, 38.
[9] Isaias LXIV, 4.
[10] Psalm LXIV, 5.
[11] 1 Corinthians II, 9.
[12] St. John VI, 45.
[13] 1 Corinthians XV, 28.
[14] Psalm, XXX, 20.

in all?[15] Not to speak of the body, I observe three powers in the soul—reason, will, memory—and these three powers are the very soul itself. How much is wanting to their completeness and perfection in this life, everyone who walks in the Spirit, feels. Why this, unless that God is not yet *all in all?* Hence it is that very often the reason errs in its judgments, the will is shaken by a fourfold passion, and the memory is confused by a manifold forgetfulness. *To* this triple *vanity* a noble *creature was made subject, . . . not willingly, . . . but in hope.*[16] For He *Who satisfieth* the soul's *desire with good things,*[17] He it is who will be to the reason a fulness of light, to the will an abundance of peace, to the memory the abiding presence of eternity. O Truth, O Love, O Eternity! O blessed Trinity, Source of blessedness! It is for you that my wretched trinity [the three powers of soul] sighs in its wretchedness, since it is unhappily an exile. Departing from You, it has entangled itself in what errors, what sorrows, what fears! Ah, me! What a trinity it is that we have exchanged for You! *My heart is troubled,*[18] and hence my sorrow. *My strength hath left me,*[19] and hence my terror. *The light of my eyes itself is not with me,*[20] and hence my error. O trinity of my soul, how different a trinity [from the Divine] have you, in exile, made manifest! (*Ibid.* §5.)

And yet: *Why art thou sad, O my soul? and why dost thou trouble me? Hope in God, for I will still give praise to Him,*[21] when error has vanished from reason; pain [of wavering] from the will; and every fear from the memory; and in their place

[15] I Corinthians XV, 28.
[16] Romans VIII, 20.
[17] Psalm CII, 5.
[18] Psalm XXXVII, 11.
[19] *Ibid.*
[20] *Ibid.*
[21] Psalm XLI, 6.

there will be that wonderful tranquility for which we hope—perfect sweetness, eternal security. The first, God who is Truth will bring to pass; the second, God who is Charity; the third, God who is Supreme Power. Thus God will be all in all when the reason is flooded with inextinguishable light, when the will has attained inviolable peace and when the memory is for all eternity in intimate communication with an inexhaustible spring . . . (*Ibid.* § 6.)

In regard to the *way* [Redemption was accomplished], which if you remember, we defined as God's emptying-out of Self, there are also three points which I particularly commend to your consideration. For, that emptying-out was not a simple matter or limited. *But* (He) *emptied* HIMSELF[22] even to the extent of becoming flesh, of enduring death, even *the death of the cross.*[23] Who can adequately measure how great was the humility, the loving kindness, the condescension of the Lord of Majesty in being clothed in flesh, in being wounded unto death, in hanging, an unsightly thing, upon the cross? But someone asks: "Had not the Creator the power to repair the work of His creation without such difficulty as that?" He had the power, but He preferred to do it by inflicting upon Himself the punishment of sin in such a way that thenceforth man might have no grounds for that worst and most hateful of all vices, ingratitude. He took upon Himself much weariness that He might bind man as the debtor of much love and so that the difficulty of Redemption might constrain to the giving of thanks one whom the ease with which creation was accomplished had left rather lacking in devotedness. What, then, did man, created and ungrateful, have to say? "Through no

[22] Philippians II, 7. [23] *Ibid.* 8.

merit of my own I was fashioned, to be sure, but with no trouble or pain on the part of Him who fashioned me. He merely uttered a word and I was made, after the manner of everything in creation. What great boon is it that you have bestowed at a cost no greater than a word?" . . . But *the mouth is stopped of them that speak wicked things.*[24] It is clearer than the light of day how great a price He has paid for you, O man. He who was Lord did not disdain to become a servant; rich, to become a beggar; the Word of God, to become flesh; the Son of God, to become the Son of Man. Remember, then, that although you were made from nothing, you were not redeemed with nothing. In six days He fashioned all things, you among them. But for thirty whole years, *He wrought* (your) *salvation in the midst of the earth.*[25] Oh, how He suffered under the burden He bore! The needs of the flesh, the temptations of the enemy—did He not add the ignominy of the cross to the weight of these and crown them with the horror of death? . . . (*Ibid.* §7.)

Meditate upon these things, dwell long upon them.[26] With such perfumes as these restore the sweet fragance of your hearts which the rather noisome odor of your sins has too long made offensive. Thus will you abound in those ointments no less sweet than salutary. (*Ibid.* §8.)

[24] Psalm LXII, 12.
[25] Psalm LXXIII, 12.
[26] Cf. 1 Timothy IV, 15.

CHAPTER XI

THE OINTMENT OF PIETY, AND THE RESPECT THAT SHOULD BE SHOWN BY SUBJECTS TO THOSE WHO ARE PLACED OVER THEM

THERE IS AN ointment which far surpasses both penitence and devotion, and this I have called piety because it is made out of the needs of the poor, the anguish of those who are oppressed, the affliction of those who are sad, the faults of transgressors, and finally, out of all the troubles of the wretched whoever they may be even though they be enemies. Despicable those ingredients seem, but the ointment produced from them is beyond all other sweet-smelling spices. . . . Who, think you, is that happy man who *sheweth mercy and lendeth,*[1] who is easily moved to compassionate others and quick to help them, judging it *a more blessed thing to give rather than to receive,*[2] one who finds it easy to forgive, hard to become angry, and almost impossible to revenge a wrong, looking upon his neighbor's every necessity as his own? O whoever you are, a soul thus affected, thus imbued with the dew of mercy, thus abounding in the bowels of piety, thus making yourself *all things to all men,*[3] thus becoming *as a vessel that is destroyed,*[4] so that wherever you are, you may at once run to the assistance of others and bring them relief, thus, finally, dead to self that you may live to all men, you, happy soul that you are, you clearly possess that third and best ointment and

[1] Psalm CXI, 5.
[2] Acts, XX, 35.
[3] I Corinthians IX, 22.
[4] Psalm XXX, 13.

your hands have distilled the essence of all sweetness. It will not be dried up in an evil time nor will the fire of persecution exhaust it. But always God will be *mindful of all thy sacrifices:* and *thy whole burnt-offering* will be *made fat.*[5] (Sermon XII, §1.)

There are men of riches in the city of the Lord of virtues. I seek to know if among some of them this ointment may be found. And the first who occurs to me here as everywhere is Paul, the vessel of election, in truth a vessel of sweet-smelling spices, a vessel giving forth sweet odors and filled with every least particle of the ingredients of this ointment. For he was *the good odor of Christ unto God,*[6] in every place. Intense, indeed, was the sweetness of the fragrance which that heart diffused far and wide, oppressed as it was by *solicitude for all the churches.*[7] See what sweet spices he amassed for himself! *I die daily,* he said, *by your glory.*[8] And again: *Who is weak, and I am not weak? Who is scandalised, and I am not on fire?* [9] . . . It was fitting that the breast which nourished the members of Christ should be redolent of the best and purest ointments. For, Paul was certainly a mother to these, in labor again and again until Christ had been formed in them,[10] and as members, brought into conformity with their Head. (*Ibid.* §2.)

Hear how another, rich in this respect, kept at hand those spices from which he might produce the most precious ointments.[11] *The stranger,* he said, *did not stay without, my door was open to the traveller.*[12] Again: *I was an eye to the blind, and a foot to the lame. I was the father of the poor.*[13] . . . With how

[5] Psalm XIX, 4.
[6] 2 Corinthians II, 15.
[7] 2 Corinthians XI, 28.
[8] 1 Corinthians XV, 31.
[9] 2 Corinthians XI, 29.
[10] Cf. Galatians IV, 19.
[11] Cf. Isaias, XXXIX, 2.
[12] Job XXXI, 32.
[13] *Ibid.* XXIX, 15-16.

sweet an odor did such a man besprinkle the earth in those deeds. His several deeds were as so many perfumes. With these he replenished his own conscience, to lessen the noisomeness of rotting flesh with the exhalation of internal sweetness. (*Ibid.* §3.)

Joseph, after he had made all Egypt run after him in the odor of his ointments, exhaled the same fragrance even to those who sold him into slavery. He did, indeed, utter chiding words with an angry countenance. But tears burst forth from his fulness of heart, not as signs of wrath but as betrayers of forgiveness.[14] Samuel mourned for Saul who sought to kill him,[15] and when he was melted within, his heart glowing with the fire of charity, the fulness of his pity flowed out through the channels of his eyes. On account of the good odor which his reputation diffused on every side, Scripture says of him: *all Israel from Dan to Bersabee knew that Samuel was a faithful prophet of the Lord.*[16] What shall I say about Moses? With what fatness and richness did he replenish his soul! Not even that *provoking house*[17] in which he was for a time occupied, could ever in all its murmuring and wrath destroy the ointment of the spirit with which he had once been anointed. Hence, in the midst of incessant strifes and daily disputes he persevered to the end in his meekness. Deservedly did the Holy Spirit bear witness in his regard that he was *a man exceeding meek above all men that dwelt upon earth.*[18] Even *with them that hated peace* he *was peaceful*[19] to such a degree that not only did he fail to become angry with an ungrateful and rebellious people but he even appeased God when He was angry with them, by his intercession, as

[14] Cf. Genesis XLIII, 30: XLV, 2.
[15] Cf. 1 Kings XV, 35: XVI, 2.
[16] *Ibid.* III, 20.
[17] Ezechiel II, 5.
[18] Numbers XII, 3.
[19] Psalm CXIX, 7.

it is written: *And He said that He would destroy them, had not Moses, His Chosen, stood before Him in the breach, to turn away His wrath, lest He should destroy them.*[20] Finally, *either forgive them this trespass,* he said, *or if Thou do not, strike me out of the book that Thou hast written.*[21] O! truly a man anointed with the ointment of compassion. . . . Thus Moses was not content to be admitted alone *into the joy of* his *Lord*[22] while his people remained outside. Even though they were inconstant and ungrateful, he clung to them as one who held the place of a mother and her love. (*Ibid.* §4.)

What greater model of meekness is there than David who grieved over the death of him who ceaselessly thirsted for his death?[23] What is more kind than that he lamented the decease of him whom he succeeded to the throne? Even at the death of a son who was at heart a parricide, how difficult it was to console him![24] Great indeed was the store of this best of ointments which such an affection revealed. And so he prayed with confidence, saying, *O Lord, remember David and all his meekness.*[25] Hence all these possessed those best of ointments, and even to this day their fragrance is diffused throughout the universal Church. Not only these, but also as many as have shown themselves thus kind and charitable in this life, who have thus striven to live on friendly terms with all men, inasmuch as every grace which they were seen to possess they did not keep to themselves but shared it in common, considering themselves debtors to enemies as well as to friends, *to the wise and to the unwise.*[26] Since they were of service to all, humble in all, hence they were beyond all others

[20] Psalm CV, 23.
[21] Exodus XXXII, 31-32.
[22] St. Matthew XXV, 21.
[23] Cf. 2 Kings I, 11.
[24] Cf. *Ibid.* XIX, 4.
[25] Psalm CXXXI, 1.
[26] Romans I, 14.

dear to God and men, they whose fragrance is held in benediction. . . . As sweet balm in the mouth is a brother of this sort in a religious congregation. He is pointed out and all say of him: *This is a lover of his brethren and of the people of Israel: this is he that prayeth much for the people and for all the holy city.*[27] (*Ibid.* §5.)

Let us have recourse to the Gospel and see if there is anything that pertains to these ointments. *Mary Magdalen, and Mary the mother of James, and Salome bought sweet spices, that coming they might anoint Jesus.*[28] . . . They came not to anoint any particular part of the Body alone—for instance, the feet or the head—but as it is written, *that coming they might anoint* JESUS, which includes His whole Body and is not restricted to a part. (*Ibid.* §6.)

You also if you put on the bowels of mercy, will appear generous and kind not only to your parents or relatives, or to those whom you regard as benefactors or hope will one day become your benefactors, for even *the heathens* do this; [29] but in keeping with Paul's advice strive to *work good to all men,*[30] so that for the sake of God you will consider that not even in the case of an enemy should any human service of body or soul be denied or withdrawn. Then it will be evident that you also are rich in the best of ointments and that not only the head or feet of the Lord, but indiscriminately, as far as lies within your power, you have undertaken to anoint His whole Body, which is the Church. And perhaps it was for this reason that the Lord Jesus was unwilling that the preparation which had been made for Him should be expended upon His dead body, so that it might be saved for It

[27] 2 Machabees XV, 14.
[28] St. Mark XVI, 1.
[29] St. Matthew V, 47.
[30] Galatians VI, 10.

living. For the Church is living and eats of *the Living Bread which came down from heaven.*[31] It is the Church that is the more precious Body of Christ which He would not suffer to taste death, whereas He surrendered His other Body to death, as every Christian knows. The Church is the Body which He wishes us to anoint and cherish. The weak members of this Body He desires to be made strong by warm lotions prepared with great care. (*Ibid.* §7.)

Sometimes I—if I may make a slight digression—when I sat down at Jesus' feet bemoaning my lot, offering the *sacrifice* of *an afflicted spirit*[32] at the remembrance of my sins; or certainly, if ever or rarely I stood at His head and rejoiced in the remembrance of His benefits, I have heard those who said, *To what purpose is this waste?*[33] That is, they complained because I was living for myself alone, I, who, as they thought, could do good to many. And they said: *For this might have been sold for much and given to the poor.*[34] But it would not be a good exchange for me, even if I gained the whole world, to destroy myself and effect my own damnation.[35] Hence understanding that those remarks are the *dying flies* of which the Scripture speaks, which *spoil the sweetness of the ointment,*[36] I recalled that divine utterance: *O my people, they that call thee blessed, the same deceive thee.*[37] But let those who find fault with me for my leisure, as it were, let them hear the Lord making excuse and answering for me. *Why,* he asks, *do you trouble this woman?*[38] That is to say, "You look upon the external form and you draw your conclusions from appearances. That is not a man, as you think, one

[31] St. John VI, 41.
[32] Psalm L, 19.
[33] St. Matthew XXVI, 8.
[34] *Ibid.* 9.
[35] Cf. St. Mark VIII, 36-37.
[36] Ecclesiastes X, 1.
[37] Isaias III, 12.
[38] St. Matthew XXVI, 10.

who can put his hand to powerful deeds, but a woman. Why do you try to lay upon him a yoke for which I see he is unequal? He is doing *a good work upon Me.*[39] Let him continue in what is good so long as he has not grown strong enough for what is better. If some time he progresses from a woman to a man, and a perfect man, he may then even be employed in the work of perfection." (*Ibid.* §8.)

Brothers, let us look upon bishops with reverence, but upon their labors with fear. If we reflect upon the labors, we shall not be ambitious for the honors. . . . It would be uncivil to criticise the works of those whose burdens we shun. It would be an impertinence in a woman at home, spinning, to rebuke a man returning from battle. . . . You do well in keeping a watchful guard over yourself, but he who is of assistance to many does even better and acts more like a man. If in this matter he is incapable of meeting his obligations without some injustice, that is, without some irregularity in his life and dealings with others, remember, *charity covereth a multitude of sins.*[40] (*Ibid.* §9.)

But let us return to the ointments of the Spouse. Do you not see how preferable beyond others is that ointment of piety of which alone none is allowed to go to waste? So impossible is waste in its regard that not even a gift of cold water is permitted to go unrewarded.[41] The good ointment of contrition which is composed of the remembrance of sins is applied to the feet of the Lord, because *a contrite and humbled heart* God *will not despise.*[42] But far better do I consider that which is called devotion, made from the remembrance of God's benefits, because it is considered suitable for the head so that God speaks of it thus:

[39] *Ibid.*
[40] 1 St. Peter IV, 8.
[41] Cf. St. Matthew X, 42.
[42] Psalm L, 19.

The sacrifice of praise shall glorify Me.[43] But far surpassing both of these is the ointment of piety which is made of consideration for the wretched and is poured out upon the whole body of Christ. By the *body* I mean not that which was crucified, but that body of His which he acquired by the Passion (*i.e.* the Church, the Mystical Body of Christ). (*Ibid.* §10.)

. . . Who among us possesses even one of these qualities fully and perfectly, so that he is not at times unfruitful in word and lukewarm in deed? But there is one who may glory in this praise deservedly and with no hesitancy. I mean the Church. . . . She it is who confidently and securely calls herself the Spouse of Christ. . . . But although no one of us would dare presume to such a degree that he would make bold to call his soul the Spouse of the Lord, nevertheless, because we are members of the Church which rightly glories in this title and in this reality, not unjustly we appropriate to ourselves a share in this glory. For, what we all together possess fully and wholly, that, as individuals, we must share. Thanks to Thee, Lord Jesus, Who have deigned to add us to the flock of your beloved Church, not only that we might be among the Faithful, but that after the manner of a spouse we might be joined to you in embraces joyous, chaste and eternal, when, in the revelation of Your Countenance we are admitted into the contemplation of Your glory, which You have equally and in common with the Father and the Holy Ghost forever. *Amen.* (*Ibid.* §11.)

[43] Psalm XLIX, 23.

CHAPTER XII

THE NAME OF JESUS IS A SALUTARY MEDICINE FOR ALL FAITHFUL CHRISTIANS IN ALL ADVERSITIES

MANY, INDEED, ARE the names of the Spouse you read scattered over every page that is divinely inspired, but all these I shall include in two. You will discover none, I think, which does not signify the beauty of mercifulness or the power of majesty. It is thus the Holy Spirit speaks through one of his more familiar instruments: *These two things have I heard, that power belongeth to God, and mercy to Thee, O Lord, for Thou wilt render to every man according to his works.*[1] . . . Some names sound forth His majesty; the rest, His mercy. Which of these, then, *is as oil poured out?*[2] Clearly the name of majesty and power is in some way or other transfused into that of mercy and grace, and the result is abundantly poured out through Jesus Christ Our Savior. The name, for instance, which is *God,* does it not blend and become transfused into *God with us,* that is, *Emmanuel?*[3] . . . (Sermon XV, §1.)

Where now is that which among the ancients used to be spoken with a voice of thunder so awful and so frequent: *I am the Lord thy God?*[4] To me there is dictated a prayer the beginning of which, sweet with the name *Father,* gives confidence that the

[1] Psalm LXI, 12-13.
[2] Canticle I, 2.
[3] St. Matthew I, 23.
[4] Exodus XX, 2.

petitions that follow will be granted. *Servants* are called *friends*,[5] and the resurrection is announced not only to disciples but to *brethren*.[6] (*Ibid.* §2.) *It behooved Christ to suffer and to rise again from the dead . . . and that penance and the remission of sins should be preached in His name*,[7] not only throughout Judea but throughout *all nations*, inasmuch as from one name which is *Christ*, thousands upon thousands of believers shall be called *Christians* and shall say: *Thy name is as oil poured out.* (*Ibid.* §3.)

I recognize the name which I read in Isaias: (the Lord God) *shall call His servants by another name in which he that is blessed upon the earth shall be blessed in God, Amen.*[8] O blessed name! O oil everywhere poured out! To what extent? From Heaven it spreads into Judea, and thence into every land, and from the whole earth the Church sends up the cry: *Thy name is as oil poured out. Poured out* to the last drop, since not only has it flooded the heavens and the earth, but it has sprinkled even the dwellers beneath the earth to such an extent, *that in the name of Jesus every knee should bow, of those that are in heaven, on earth, and under the earth, and that every tongue should confess*,[9] and say, *Thy name is as oil poured out* . . . I share the name. I also have a part in the inheritance. I am a Christian. I am a brother of Christ. If I am what I am said to be I am an heir indeed of God, and a *joint-heir with Christ*.[10] And what wonder if the *name* of the Spouse was poured out, since *He Himself* was poured out? For He *emptied Himself, taking the form of a servant*.[11] Hence it is said: *I am poured out like water*.[12] The fulness of divinity was poured out, dwelling corporally upon the

[5] Cf. St. John XV, 15.
[6] Cf. St. Matthew XXVIII, 10.
[7] St. Luke XXIV, 46-47.
[8] Isaias LXV, 15-16.
[9] Philippians II, 10-11.
[10] Cf. Romans VIII, 17.
[11] Philippians II, 7.
[12] Psalm XXI, 15.

earth, so that all of us who bear about a body of death might partake of that fulness, and replenished with its life-giving odor, say; *Thy name is as oil poured out.* (*Ibid.* §4.)

There is beyond doubt an analogy between oil and the name of the Beloved. Not without reason does the Holy Spirit compare one with the other. I say that the reason lies in that threefold property of oil which gives forth light, nourishes and heals. It feeds the flame, it nourishes the flesh, it alleviates suffering; light, food, medicine. Notice now that the same is true of the name of the Spouse. Preached, it gives light to the mind; meditated upon, it feeds the soul; invoked in prayer, it soothes and heals the spirit. . . . (*Ibid.* §5.)

Whence do you think throughout the whole world was the light of faith so great and so sudden, unless from *Jesus,* preached? Is it not by the light of this name that God calls us into *His marvellous light?* [13] To us thus enlightened and seeing the Light by that light, Saint Paul justly says: *For you were heretofore darkness, but now light in the Lord.*[14] This, finally, is the name which the same Apostle was commanded *to carry . . . before the Gentiles and Kings, and the children of Israel.*[15] And this name he carried as a light, and he lighted up his native land and cried out, everywhere: *The night is passed and the day is at hand. Let us therefore cast off the works of darkness and put on the armour of light. Let us walk honestly, as in the day.*[16] And he pointed out to all *the lamp . . . upon the candlestick,*[17] everywhere preaching Jesus and Him *crucified.*[18] How that light shone into the eyes of all beholders and dazzled them, when, coming forth from the

[13] 1 St. Peter II, 9.
[14] Ephesians V, 8.
[15] Acts IX, 15.
[16] Romans XIII, 12-13.
[17] Ecclesiasticus XXVI, 22.
[18] Cf. 1 Corinthians I, 23.

mouth of Peter, like lightning, it gave strength to the bodily *feet and soles* of one who was lame,[19] and gave sight to many spiritually blind! Did it not flash fire when he said: *In the name of Jesus Christ of Nazareth, arise and walk?* [20]

But the name of Jesus is not only light, it is also food. Do you not feel strengthened as often as you recall it to mind? What so nourishes the mind of him who thinks upon it? What so repairs the spent powers of the senses, strengthens virtues, quickens good and honorable habits, fosters chaste affections? Dry is every food of the soul if this oil be not poured over it: it is tasteless if it be not seasoned with this salt. . . . If you write, it does not satisfy my taste unless I read there, *Jesus*. If you are having a discussion or if you are deliberating about some matter, it has no savor for me unless *Jesus* is there heard. *Jesus* is honey in the mouth, music in the ear, a shout of gladness in the heart.

It is also a remedy. Is any one of you sad? Let *Jesus* come into the heart and hence spring to the lips, and behold as the light of that name rises like the sun, it scatters every semblance of cloudy weather and restores a clear sky. Is anyone falling into sin? Is he, moreover, rushing into the snare of death? [21] If he calls upon the life-giving name will he not straightway breathe again the breath of life? In whom was the presence of that saving name ever withstood by hardness of heart, common as it is, by the sluggishness of sloth, rancor of mind, or the lassitude of weariness? To whom has it ever happened that when the fount of his tears was dried up and Jesus was invoked, that it did not gush forth more abundantly and flow more sweetly? To what soul, trembling and agitated in the presence of dangers, did not that

[19] Acts III, 7.
[20] *Ibid*. III, 6.
[21] 2 Kings XXII, 6.

name of power when invoked, immediately bring confidence and cast out fear? Who ever, I ask, laboring in doubt and uncertainty did not perceive the clear light of certitude shine forth at the invocation of that enlightening name? Who that has lost confidence in the midst of misfortunes and is at the very point of giving up, if he has pronounced that name full of help, has ever been wanting in courage? Truly these are the maladies and weaknesses of the soul, and this is the remedy. And, in fine, this can be proved. *Call upon Me,* it is written, *in the day of trouble: I will deliver thee, and thou shalt glorify Me.*[22] Nothing so restrains the violence of anger, allays the swellings of pride, heals the wounds of envy, checks the unrestraints of the flesh, extinguishes the flame of lust, tempers the thirst of avarice and banishes the unlawful desire of everything unseemly. For when I name the name *Jesus* I see before me a man *meek and humble of heart,*[23] kind, temperate, chaste, merciful and distinguished for everything that is upright and holy, the Same who is himself God the Almighty who restores me to health by His example and strengthens me by His help. All these things sound in my ear whenever I hear the name *Jesus.* I derive an example from Him as Man, and help from Him as the Mighty One. (*Ibid.* §6.)

[22] Psalm XLIX, 15. [23] St. Matthew XI, 29.

CHAPTER XIII

THE THREE DEGREES OF LOVE WITH WHICH WE LOVE GOD

SAINT PAUL SAYS: *If any man love not our Lord Jesus Christ, let him be anathema.*[1] Truly He should be loved by me above all else, through Whom I exist and live and have the power of understanding. If I am ungrateful, I am also unworthy. He is clearly deserving of death who refuses to live for You, Lord Jesus. In fact he is already dead. He who does not use the gift of understanding for You, is a fool. He who strives to live for anything except You, is worth nothing, and *is* nothing. Ultimately, *what is man* unless *Thou art made known to him?*[2] For Yourself, O God, you have made all things. He who wishes to exist for himself and not for You, is beginning to be a mere nothing among all the things that are. *Fear God and keep His commandments: for this,* it is written, *is the whole man.*[3] If this, therefore, is *the whole man,* without this, *the whole man* is nothing . . . (Sermon XX, §1.)

God, moreover, has loved us tenderly, wisely and bravely. Tenderly, I would say, because He clothed Himself in flesh; wisely, because in His prudence He avoided the least stain of sin; bravely, because He endured death . . . (*Ibid.* §3.) Learn, O Christian, from Christ how you should love Christ. Learn to love tenderly, to love with prudence, to love bravely. Tenderly,

[1] I Corinthians XVI, 22.
[2] Psalm CXLIII, 3.
[3] Ecclesiastes XII, 13.

lest we be seduced; prudently, lest we be deceived; bravely, lest being overcome we flee from the love of the Lord. That you may not be seduced by the glory of the world or the delights of the flesh, let Christ who is wisdom grow sweeter to you than these. That you may not be misled by the spirit of lies and deceit, let Christ who is Truth be your light. That you may not grow faint in adversity, let the courage of God, who is Christ, strengthen you . . . (*Ibid.* §4.)

Notice that the love [of Christ] that springs from the heart is in a way carnal because it especially moves the human heart to be attracted to the Humanity of Christ and to what He did and commanded in the flesh . . . I think that the chief reason why the Invisible God wished to become visible in the flesh, and to live as a Man among men, was manifestly this—that He might first win back the affections of fleshly creatures who could not love otherwise than in the flesh, to the salutary love of Himself in the Flesh, and thus step by step lead them finally to a love that is purely spiritual. Was it not, ultimately, in this degree [of love] that they were standing who said: *Behold we have left all things, and have followed Thee?* [4] Indeed, it was only because of the love of His bodily presence that they had left all things, so that they could not bear to hear a single word about His saving Passion and Death; and afterwards, they could not gaze upwards at His glory as He ascended to Heaven, except with hearts heavy with grief. This is what He meant when He said: *because I have spoken these things to you sorrow hath filled your heart.*[5] Thus it was, that in the meantime while they were being attracted by the grace of His bodily presence alone, He had checked their love of everything merely carnal. (*Ibid.* §6.)

[4] St. Matthew XIX, 27.

[5] St. John XVI, 6.

Therefore, to express it briefly, to love with the whole heart is to prefer the love of His incorruptible Body to the allurements of the flesh in ourselves or others. And among the allurements of the flesh I include also the glory of the world because the glory of the world is the glory of the flesh and they who find their delight in it are, beyond the shadow of a doubt, carnal-minded. (*Ibid.* §7.)

But although it is a gift and a great gift of the Holy Spirit—such devotion as this to Christ in the flesh—nevertheless I would say that this love is carnal, in comparison, at least, with that love which has as its object not so much the Word that is Flesh, as the Word that is Wisdom, the Word that is Justice, the Word that is Truth, the Word that is Holiness, Piety, Power and anything else that can be spoken of as possible. And Christ, to be sure, is all of these, He *who of God is made unto us wisdom and justice and sanctification and redemption.*[6] Does it seem to you that two persons are equally affected and in one and the same way—one of whom, for example, piously suffers with Christ suffering, is filled with remorse of conscience, and is easily moved at the remembrance of what He has endured, and, fed by the sweetness of this devotion, thus derives strength for whatever is salutary, upright and pious: while the other, always on fire with zeal for justice is everywhere zealous for truth; burns with a love for wisdom; one to whom sanctity of life and discipline of character are a delight; whose character is such that he blushes at ostentation, abhors detraction, knows no envy, abominates pride, not only shuns all human glory but loathes and disdains it; detests and strongly strives without ceasing against every impurity of

[6] I Corinthians I, 30.

the flesh and of the heart, and finally spurns, as it were naturally, every evil and embraces what is good? (*Ibid.* §8.)

But although it is good, that love is carnal by which the life of the flesh is shut out and the world is contemned and overcome. It makes progress in this, that it becomes rational. It becomes perfect when it is made spiritual, as well. Love is rational when in all the sentiments it should feel concerning Christ, the grounds of the credibility of faith (*ratio fidei*) are adhered to so tenaciously that this love cannot in any detail be turned aside from the purity of Catholic teaching by the mere semblance of truth, nor by heretical or diabolical deception. Likewise in our personal dealings with others precautions must be taken so that no boundary fixed by discretion will be violated by superstition or levity or by the eagerness of a spirit that is, as it were, too fervent. And I have already said above, that this is to love God with the whole soul. If there also be added a force of the sustaining Spirit so great that no power of pains or torments and not even the fear of death can prevail upon the soul to abandon the ways of justice, then God is loved with the whole strength, and the love is spiritual. And I think that this name is especially appropriate to such love as this because of the prerogative of the fulness of the Spirit in which it excels. (*Ibid.* §9.)

CHAPTER XIV

THE MANNER IN WHICH THE SPOUSE, THAT IS, THE CHURCH, DESIRES TO BE DRAWN TO HER BELOVED

Draw me: we will run after Thee to the odor of Thy ointments.[1] Was it the Church, perhaps, who said that, when she beheld her Beloved ascending to Heaven passionately longing to follow Him and to be assumed with Him in glory? But every soul of however great perfection, so long as it groans under *the body of this death* [2] and is kept confined in the prison of this wretched world, bound by necessities, tortured by sins, must of necessity rise rather slowly and gradually to the contemplation of heavenly things, nor is it altogether free to follow the Bridegroom *whithersoever He goeth.*[3] Hence that tearful cry of lamentation: *Unhappy man that I am, who shall deliver me from the body of this death?* [4] Hence that suppliant prayer: *Bring my soul out of prison.*[5] Therefore let her say, let even the Spouse say: *Draw me after Thee,* because *the corruptible body is a load upon the soul, and the earthly habitation presseth down the mind that museth upon many things.*[6] . . . (Sermon XXI, §1.)

Now, in truth, because she said: *Draw me after Thee* [and not, "*to* Thee"], she seems to me to ask rather that she might have strength to follow in His footsteps in His dealings with

[1] Canticle I, 3.
[2] Romans VII, 24.
[3] Apocalypse XIV, 4.
[4] Romans VII, 24.
[5] Psalm CXLI, 8.
[6] Wisdom IX, 15.

others, so that she may be able to strive after virtue and hold fast to a rule of life, and be able to attain discipline of character. In these things, to be sure, there is the greatest necessity of that help from which the soul derives strength to deny herself and to take up her cross and thus follow Christ. In this, above all, the spouse has need to be drawn, and to be drawn by no other than by Him who says: *Without Me you can do nothing.*[7] "I know," she says, "that I can never attain to You except by following after You, step by step. But neither can I do this unless helped by You. Hence it is that I pray that You may draw me. *Blessed,* indeed, *is the man whose help is from Thee: in his heart he hath disposed to ascend by steps,*[8] so that finally he may attain to Thee upon the mountains of joy. How few are they, O Lord Jesus, who are willing to follow Thee! Yet there is no one who is not willing to attain to Thy presence, for this is known to all, that, *at Thy right hand are delights even to the end.*[9] And for this reason all are willing to share Your delights, but not to follow Your example. They long to share the Kingdom, but not to share the sufferings. Of this number was he who said: *Let my soul die the death of the just, and my last end be like to them.*[10] He was desirous of the end to which the just attained, but not of the beginnings they made. The carnal-minded desire for themselves such a death as spiritual men die, but they shudder at the life they lead. Yet they know that the death of the saints is a precious thing, for, *When He shall give sleep to His beloved, behold the inheritance of the Lord;*[11] and because, *Blessed are the dead who die in the Lord;*[12] while, on the contrary, according to

[7] St. John XV, 5.
[8] Psalm LXXXIII, 6.
[9] Psalm XV, 11.
[10] Numbers XXIII, 10.
[11] Psalm CXXVI, 2-3.
[12] Apocalypse XIV, 13.

the thought expressed by the prophet: *The death of the wicked is very evil.*[13] . . . (*Ibid.* §2.)

Thus it is that Your beloved having left all things for Your sake longs to follow after You, to walk in Your footsteps, and to follow You whithersoever You go, knowing that Your *ways are beautiful ways and all* Your *paths are peaceable,*[14] and that he who follows You, *walketh not in darkness.*[15] But she asks to be drawn, since *Thy justice is as the mountains of God,*[16] and her own strength is not sufficient to attain it . . . (*Ibid.* §3.)

Therefore, in the day of strength feel not secure but cry out to God with the prophet: *when my strength shall fail, do not Thou forsake me.*[17] Likewise, in the time of temptation be comforted and say with the spouse: *Draw me: we will run after Thee to the odor of Thy ointments.* Thus hope will not desert you in the time of evil, nor will prudence be wanting to you in the time of prosperity. In the midst of the adversity and the prosperity of time with its changes, you will be one who retains, as it were, the image of eternity in that inviolable and unshaken equanimity of a constant soul, blessing the Lord *at all times,*[18] and hence amidst the uncertain events of changing time and its certain failures, laying claim for yourself to a state of perpetual unchangeableness, as it were, you will begin to renew and reform yourself according to that glorious and ancient likeness of the eternal God, *with Whom there is no change, nor shadow of alteration.*[19] Thus, as He is so also you will be in this world, neither faint-hearted in adversity nor reckless in prosperity . . . (*Ibid.* §6.)

And what wonder if the spouse needs to be drawn onward, she

[13] Psalm XXXIII, 22.
[14] Proverbs III, 17.
[15] St. John VIII, 12.
[16] Psalm XXXV, 7.
[17] Psalm LXX, 9.
[18] Cf. Psalm XXXIII, 1.
[19] St. James I, 17.

who is hastening after a Giant, she who strives to overtake Him who leaps *upon the mountains* and skips *over the hills?* [20] *His word,* it is said, *runneth swiftly.*[21] She has not the strength to keep pace with Him. She cannot rival the speed of Him who rejoices *as a giant to run the way.*[22] She cannot do this of her own strength and for this reason she asks to be drawn onward. "I am exhausted," she says, "I am falling behind; do not abandon me, but *draw me after Thee* lest I begin to wander about in search of other lovers, or *run as at an uncertainty.*[23] . . . The time will come when I shall not need to be drawn since we shall run willingly and with all swiftness. It is not I alone who shall run, although I alone pray to be drawn onward. *Young maidens* [24] will run with me. We shall run together: we shall run side by side: I, incited by the perfume of Your ointments: they, inspired by my example and exhortation; and thus we shall all run in the fragrance of Your ointments." The spouse has her imitators, just as she is an imitator of Christ. And for that reason she does not say in the singular, "*I* shall run," but "*we* shall run." (*Ibid.* §9.)

[20] Cf. Canticle II, 8.
[21] Psalm CXLVII, 15.
[22] Psalm XVIII, 6.
[23] 1 Corinthians IX, 26.
[24] Canticle I, 2.

CHAPTER XV

THE FOUR OINTMENTS OF THE BRIDEGROOM AND THE FOUR CARDINAL VIRTUES

LEAVING THEREFORE TO every individual soul whatever, perchance, more sublime or more subtle has been given it to feel and know from experience because of a special function of the spouse's ointment, I place before you for common use what I have received from a common Source. For He it is who is the very *fountain of life,*[1] the Same who is a *sealed fountain* flowing out from *a garden enclosed*[2] through the mouth of Saint Paul as a conduit. Truly He is that *wisdom* which, according to the conception of holy Job, *is drawn out of secret places.*[3] This Fountain has poured itself forth in four streams and has directed its waters into the by-ways, where, to be sure, it reveals to us Him *who of God is made unto us wisdom and justice and sanctification and redemption.*[4] From these four streams as from most precious ointments—for there is nothing to prevent understanding them both as water and ointment; water, because it cleanses; ointment because it exhales perfume—from these four, I repeat, as from very precious ointments made of balms of heaven upon the mountains of sweet spices, a fragrance so rich has filled the nostrils of the Church, that straightway from the four corners of the earth, attracted by

[1] Psalm XXXV, 10.
[2] Canticle IV, 12.
[3] Job XXVIII, 18.
[4] 1 Corinthians I, 30.

that sweetness she hastened to the heavenly Spouse. In this she was truly like that *queen of the south* who *came from the ends of the earth to hear the wisdom of Solomon,*[5] incited by the sweet odor of his fame.[6] (Sermon XXII, §4.)

Consider now the fourfold ointment. Consider the abundant and inestimable sweetness of Him whom the Father *hath anointed . . . with the oil of gladness above* His *fellows.*[7] You were sitting, O man, in darkness and in the shadow of death through ignorance of the truth. You were sitting bound by the chains of sin. He came down to you in prison not to torture you, but to rescue you from the power of darkness. And first the Teacher of truth dispelled the darkness of ignorance by the light of His wisdom. Then by *the justice of faith*[8] he loosed the bonds of sin, freely justifying the sinner.[9] By this twofold benefit He fulfilled that word of holy David: *the Lord looseth them that are fettered: the Lord enlighteneth the blind.*[10] To these benefits He added living holily among sinners, thus giving them a model of life, a way, as it were, along which you might return to your fatherland. Finally to crown His devotedness He surrendered His soul to death, and from His own side He drew forth the price of redemption with which to render satisfaction to the Father. In this way He applied to Himself the verse: *with the Lord there is mercy: and with Him plentiful redemption.*[11] Truly *plentiful* because not a drop, but a flood of blood poured forth abundantly through the five wounds of His Body. (*Ibid.* §7.)

. . . Four ointments, then, you have, pointed out to you: the first of wisdom, the second of justice, the third of sanctification,

[5] St. Matthew XII, 42.
[6] Cf. 3 Kings X, 1-7.
[7] Psalm XLIV, 8.
[8] Romans IV, 13.
[9] Cf. Romans III, 23-24.
[10] Psalm CXLV, 7-8.
[11] Psalm CXXIX, 7.

the fourth of redemption. Remember their names. Breathe in their fragrance. And do not seek to know how they are made or the number of ingredients out of which they are composed. For these things cannot easily be made manifest to us in regard to the ointments of the Bridegroom, as those of the bride were in previous considerations. In Christ, to be sure, the fulness of things is without number and without limit. For, *of His wisdom there is no number,*[12] and *Thy justice is as the mountains of God,*[13] as the mountains of eternity. His holiness is such as is found only in Him. And His redemption is beyond the power of man to fathom. (*Ibid.* §9.)

[12] Psalm CXLVI, 5.

[13] Psalm XXXV, 7.

CHAPTER XVI

THREE WAYS OF CONTEMPLATING GOD, FIGURATIVELY EXPRESSED

The King hath brought me into His storerooms.[1] Behold whence the fragrance! Behold the goal towards which we run! The bride had declared that we must run and in what strength we must run. But whither we must run she had not declared. Therefore [she tells us now] we must run towards the storerooms and run in the fragrance that is exhaled from them. For the bride with her accustomed keenness first detects this fragrance and eagerly desires to be admitted into its fulness. But what do we consider should be understood by these storerooms? For the present let us think of them as certain places redolent of sweet odors, belonging to the Bridegroom, rich in perfumes and filled with delights. For it is in a storehouse of this sort that the better produce from the garden or whatever is particularly worth saving from the field is stored away. Hither, therefore, all run together. Who? Souls on fire with the Holy Spirit. The bride runs. The *young maidens* run. But she who loves more intensely, runs more swiftly and reaches the goal sooner. . . . And she, however great the progress she makes, however far she advances [along the road of perfection], she will never be separated from the care, the protection and the love of those whom she has begotten in the Gospel. She never forgets her own flesh

[1] Canticle I, 3.

and blood. (Sermon XXIII, §1.) And so, let her say to them: "Rejoice! Be confident! *The King hath brought me into His storerooms.* Be persuaded that thereby you, no less than I, have been brought in. I alone seem to have been brought in. But this privilege is not conferred on one only. Every advantage of mine belongs to every one of you. It is for you I go forward. With you I shall share whatever, perchance, I shall merit more than you." (*Ibid.* §2.)

Now since the literal sense is clear from what I have already said, let us see what spiritual profit we ought to derive from a consideration of *the storerooms.* In subsequent verses mention is also made of a *garden* and a *bedchamber.* And let us seek, if you will, those three things in Holy Scripture—a garden, a storeroom and a bedchamber. . . . And so let the *garden* be the simple and plain historic sense. Let the *storeroom* be the moral sense. Let the *bedchamber* be the secret of interior contemplation. (*Ibid.* § 3.)

Let us come now to the bedchamber. What, then, is it? And shall I presume to know what it is? Far be it from me to lay claim to an experience of a thing so sublime. Nor do I boast of a prerogative which is reserved for the bride alone, being careful according to that saying of the Greeks, to know myself so that *I may* also *know* with the Prophet, *what is wanting to me.*[2] However if I knew nothing at all, I would say nothing. What I know I do not begrudge you, nor do I withhold it from you. What I do not know, may *He* teach you *that teacheth man knowledge.*[3] . . . Not to everyone is it given to enjoy the gratifying and secret presence of the Bridegroom, but only to whomsoever that enjoyment has been prepared by His Father. For it is not we who have

[2] Psalm XXXVIII, 5. [3] Psalm XCIII, 10.

chosen Him but He who has chosen us and has appointed us to our respective places.[4] And where anyone has been placed by Him, there He is. Thus one woman filled with repentance was assigned a place at the feet of the Lord Jesus,[5] while another—if indeed it was another—found the fruit of her devotion at His head.[6] Furthermore, Thomas attained the grace of this secret in His side; [7] John on His breast,[8] Peter in the bosom of the Father,[9] Paul in the third heaven.[10] (*Ibid.* § 9.)

Who of us is competent to draw a distinction between these differences in merits or rather in rewards? Lest we may seem to have passed over altogether what we ourselves have known, the first woman assumed her place in the security of humility, the second in the dominion of hope, Thomas in the solid ground of faith, John in the breadth of charity, Paul in the depth of wisdom, Peter in the light of truth. Thus therefore where the Bridegroom dwells *there are many mansions,*[11] and whether it be a queen or a wife or even one of the number of maidens, whoever it be she receives there a place and boundaries in keeping with her merits, until it is permitted her to advance further by contemplation and to enter into the joy of her Lord and to explore the sweet secrets of the Bridegroom. (*Ibid.* § 10.)

But there is a place where the Lord is perceived truly at peace and tranquil. It is in fact the place not of a judge, not of a teacher, but of a Bridegroom. And it is to me certainly (for I know nothing concerning others) a real bedchamber if from time to time it is my privilege to be admitted to it. But, alas! at what wide intervals and for how short a time! Clearly there it is recognized

[4] Cf. St. John XV, 16.
[5] Cf. St. Luke VII, 38.
[6] Cf. St. Matthew XXVI, 7.
[7] Cf. St. John XX, 27-28.
[8] Cf. *ibid.* XXI, 20.
[9] Cf. St. Matthew XVI, 17.
[10] Cf. 2 Corinthians XII, 2.
[11] Cf. St. John XIV, 2.

how *the mercy of the Lord is from eternity and unto eternity upon them that fear Him.*[12] O truly blessed is he *to whom the Lord hath not imputed sin!*[13] . . . It suffices me for attaining to all righteousness, to have Him alone propitious toward me against Whom alone I have sinned. . . . Not to sin is the righteousness of God: man's righteousness is God's forgiveness. I have seen these things and I have understood the truth of that saying: *Whosoever is born of God, committeth not sin; for His seed abideth in him.*[14] *His seed* is the eternal predestination by which God has loved his elect. . . . These I have regarded as those who have never sinned, as it were, because although they are seen to have sinned in some things in time, they do not appear to have done so in eternity, because the charity of their Father covers a multitude of sins. And He calls them blessed, *whose iniquities are forgiven and whose sins are covered.*[15] (*Ibid.* § 15.)

O place of true repose and which not unfittingly I choose to call by the name of bedchamber! . . . If it should happen to any one of you to be caught up and hidden for a time in this secret place and in this sanctuary of God, . . . such a one will in truth be able when he returns, to glory and say: *The King hath brought me into His storerooms.*[16] But I would not rashly affirm that this is the very bedchamber in which the bride rejoices. It is, nevertheless, a bedchamber and a bedchamber of the King. . . . In it He deigns to reveal Himself not as altogether terrible, nor so much wonderful as lovable, tranquil and serene and *sweet and mild, and plenteous in mercy*[17] unto all who look to Him. (*Ibid.* § 16.)

[12] Psalm CII, 17.
[13] Psalm XXXI, 2.
[14] 1 St. John III, 9.
[15] Psalm XXXI, 1.
[16] Canticle I, 3.
[17] Psalm LXXXV, 5.

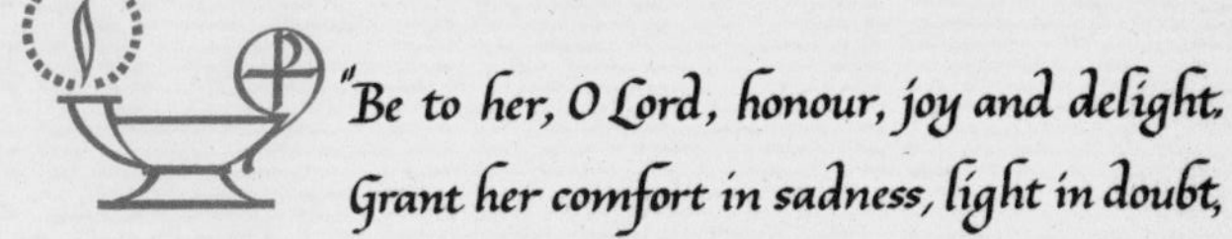

"Be to her, O Lord, honour, joy and delight.
Grant her comfort in sadness, light in doubt,
protection in injustice; Give her patience in tribulation,
abundance in poverty; in fasting be her food and beverage,
in illness her remedy and cure. May she find all things in
Thee who desires to love Thee above all."

From the Pontifical for the consecration of virgins.

CHAPTER XVII

THE BRIDE—THE CHURCH OR THE SOUL—IS BLACK BUT BEAUTIFUL

If we consider the outward appearance of the saints which strikes our senses, how lowly it is and even abject and despised by a lack of care! Nevertheless, within, they are at the same time continually *beholding the glory* of God *with open face*, they *are transformed into the same image from glory to glory, as by the Spirit of the Lord.*[1] Will not such souls justly seem to us able to reply to those reproaching them for their black color: *I am black but beautiful?*[2] Do you wish, then, that I should show you a soul that was at the same time black and beautiful? *For his epistles indeed, say they, are weighty and strong; but his bodily presence is weak and his speech contemptible.*[3] This was Paul. So you, *O daughters of Jerusalem*, judge Paul by his *bodily presence* and you despise him as one colored and deformed, because you observe a man of small stature suffering distress *in hunger and thirst . . . in cold and nakedness . . . in many more labors, in prisons more frequently, in stripes above measure, in deaths often.*[4] These are the things which make Paul black. Because of such things the Doctor of the Gentiles is reputed as one without glory, without renown, black, obscure, in a word, as the offscouring of this world. Yet is it not he who was caught up into Para-

[1] 2 Corinthians III, 18.
[2] Canticle I, 4.
[3] 2 Corinthians X, 10.
[4] 2 Corinthians XI, 27, 23.

dise, who passing through the first and second heaven, attained, because of his purity, even to the third? [5] . . . This soul do you call black? She is *black but beautiful.* She is black in your estimation, but beautiful in the judgment of God and of His angels. (Sermon XXV, § 5.)

With good reason, then, every concern of the saints, after contemning the unnecessary adornment and care of the *outward man* who certainly *is corrupted,*[6] directs itself with all diligence and continuously to cultivating and adorning *the inward man* who is made to the image of God and *is renewed day by day.*[7] For they are certain that there can be nothing more acceptable to God than His image, if it has been restored to its original beauty. Therefore all their glory is within. . . . Clearly that is no ordinary glory that is within, in which the Lord of glory deigns to be glorified when David says: *All the glory of the King's daughter is within.*[8] . . . But the saints glory in tribulations as well as in hope. *Gladly* says the Apostle, *will I glory in my infirmities, that the power of Christ may dwell in me.*[9] That infirmity should be the object of our desires, which is compensated for by the power of Christ. Who will give me not only to be burdened with infirmities, but even to be made destitute and wanting in all things within, on my own account, that I may be made strong by the power of *the Lord of hosts?* [10] *For power is made perfect in infirmity.*[11] And finally it is said: *For when I am weak, then am I powerful.*[12] (*Ibid.* §7.)

The very ignominy of the cross is welcome to him who is not ungrateful to the Crucified. It is blackness, but it is the image

[5] Cf. 2 Corinthians XII, 2
[6] 2 Corinthians IV, 16.
[7] *Ibid.*
[8] Psalm XLIV, 14.
[9] 2 Corinthians XII, 9.
[10] Psalm XXIII, 10.
[11] 2 Corinthians XII, 9.
[12] *Ibid.* 10.

and likeness of the Lord. Go to holy Isaias and he will describe Him to you as he beheld Him in spirit. For whom else does he call *a man of sorrows and acquainted with infirmity;* and that *there is no beauty in Him nor comeliness?* [13] . . . Behold what made Him black! Add to this that statement of holy David, *Thou art beautiful above the sons of men,*[14] and you have everything in the Bridegroom that the bride here bears witness to concerning herself. [*i.e. I am black but beautiful.*] (*Ibid.* §8.)

Blessed is he, Lord Jesus, who diligently observing You in these matters, a Man dealing with men, strives to imitate You, according to his strength. Already Your *beautiful one* [the Church] has received this share of blessedness as the first-fruits of her dowry, being neither slow to imitate what is beautiful in You, nor ashamed to share what is black. Hence she said: *I am black but beautiful, O ye daughters of Jerusalem,* and added the comparison, *as the tents of Cedar, as the curtains of Solomon.*[15] (*Ibid.* § 9.)

Cedar, which is interpreted darkness seems to agree well enough with the idea of blackness, but *the curtains of Solomon* does not seem equally to agree with *beauty*. Then, who does not see that *tents* falls in, no less, with the same interpretation. For what are *tents* unless they are our bodies in which we are sojourning? *For we have not here a lasting city but we seek one that is to come.*[16] And also we carry on warfare in our bodies as in tents, for *the kingdom of heaven* is for *the violent.*[17] In fine, *the life of man upon earth is a warfare,*[18] and as long as we carry on a warfare in this body, we are in exile from the Lord,

[13] Isaias LIII, 2-3.
[14] Psalm XLIV, 3.
[15] Canticle I, 4.
[16] Hebrews XIII, 14.
[17] Cf. Matthew XI, 12.
[18] Job VII, 1.

that is, from the light. For the Lord is the Light and to the degree that anyone is not with Him, he is in darkness, that is, in *Cedar*. Let him, then, acknowledge that tearful cry as his own: *Woe is me that my sojourning is prolonged! I have dwelt with the inhabitants of Cedar: my soul hath been long a sojourner.*[19] This abode of our body, therefore, is not the dwelling of a citizen or the home of a native, but either the tent of a soldier or the lodging of a traveller. This body is, I repeat, a tent, the tent of Cedar which projecting itself, as it were, before the soul deprives it now, for a while, of the Light that is infinite, nor does it suffer the soul to see the Light except *through a glass*, as it were, and *in a dark manner*, but not *face to face.*[20] (Sermon XXVI, § 1.)

I have examined and explained how the bride is *black . . . as the tents of Cedar*. How, then, is she *beautiful . . . as the curtains of Solomon?* (Sermon XXVII, § 1.). . . . Notice, especially, what is said about curtains in the Psalm: *Who stretchest out the heaven like a curtain.*[21] . . . A most beautiful curtain which, like a great canopy covering the whole face of the earth, delights men's gaze with the variety and beauty of the stars, the sun and the moon! What is more beautifully adorned than the heavens? Yet not even these can in any wise be compared to the glory and adornment of the bride, because of the very fact that they are passing, that the very *fashion* of these things *passeth away,*[22] since they are physical and the objects of bodily sense. *For the things which are seen are temporal; but the things which are not seen are eternal.*[23] *(Ibid.* § 2.)

[19] Psalm CXIX, 5-6.
[20] 1 Corinthians XIII, 12.
[21] Psalm CIII, 2.
[22] Cf. 1 Corinthians VII, 31.
[23] 2 Corinthians IV, 18.

But the beauty of the bride is of a kind that pertains to the mind. It is a spiritual likeness and is itself eternal because it is an image of eternity. Her comeliness, for instance, is charity. And *charity,* as you read, *never falleth away.*[24] It is also, beyond doubt, justice. And her *justice remaineth for ever and ever.*[25] It is patience, as well. And you read, none the less, that *the patience of the poor shall not perish forever.*[26] What of voluntary poverty? What of humility? Does not the one merit an eternal kingdom[27] and the other, likewise, eternal exaltation?[28] In her, also, one sees *the fear of the Lord, . . . holy, enduring for ever and ever.*[29] Thus prudence, temperance, fortitude and whatever other virtues there may be, what are they but pearls, as it were, for the adornment of the bride, gleaming with undying lustre. (*Ibid.* § 3.)

[24] 1 Corinthians XIII, 8.
[25] Psalm CXI, 3.
[26] Psalm IX, 19.
[27] Cf. St. Matthew V, 3.
[28] Cf. St. Luke XIV, 11.
[29] Psalm XVIII, 10.

CHAPTER XVIII

THE BLACKNESS AND BEAUTY OF THE BRIDEGROOM. HEARING RATHER THAN SIGHT AVAILS IN MATTERS OF FAITH AND IN THE ATTAINMENT OF TRUTH

WHAT I HAVE said of the saints is true also of our Lord. Within is the splendor of Divinity, the comeliness of virtues, the light of glory, the purity of innocence. But the ignoble complexion of infirmity conceals these, *and His look* is *as it were hidden and despised.*[1] (Sermon XXVIII, § 1.). . . . In fact, the Prophet says: *the chastisement of our peace was upon Him . . . and the Lord hath laid on Him the iniquity of us all.*[2] *Wherefore it behooved Him in all things to be made like unto His brethren,* as the Apostle says, *that He might become merciful.*[3] Hence, *the voice indeed is the voice of Jacob; but the hands are the hands of Esau.*[4] What is heard from Him is His: what is seen in Him is ours. What He speaks is spirit and life: what He appears is corporal and death. One is seen and the other is believed. Bodily sense declares that He is black. Faith proves that He is fair and beautiful. He is black only to the eyes of the foolish. For to the minds of the faithful He is altogether beautiful. He is *black but beautiful*—black in the opinion of Herod, beautiful in the con-

[1] Isaias LIII, 3.
[2] *Ibid.* 5-6.
[3] Hebrews II, 17.
[4] Genesis XXVII, 22.

fession of the thief and in the faith of the centurion. (*Ibid.* § 3.)

How beautiful He was, he had noticed who cried out: *Indeed this man was the Son of God.*[5] . . . If he had been intent upon what was visible to the bodily eye, how could he have called Him beautiful and the Son of God? . . . Whence, therefore, did he perceive the beauty of the Crucified and that He was the Son of God, He who *was reputed with the wicked?*[6] It is not fitting that we should answer that nor is it necessary, for the care of the Evangelist has not overlooked it. Hence you have: *And the centurion who stood over against Him, seeing that crying out in this manner He had given up the ghost, said: Indeed this man was the Son of God.*[7] Therefore it was at the sound of the voice that he believed. He recognized the Son of God by His voice, not by His appearance . . . (*Ibid.* § 4.)

Hearing discovered what sight did not. External appearance deceived the eye. Truth communicated itself through the ear. The eye pronounced Him weak, to the eye He was defiled, to the eye He was an object of pity, to the eye He was one condemned to a most ignominious death. But to the ear He was the Son of God; it was to the ear that He became known as beautiful. . . . The ear, the first gate of death!—let it be the first opened to life. Let hearing, which destroyed sight, restore it, because unless we believe we shall not understand.[8] Therefore hearing pertains to merit; sight to the reward. Hence the Prophet says: *To my hearing Thou shalt give joy and gladness,*[9] because the Beatific Vision is the reward of faithful hearing, and the merit [which is

[5] St. Mark XV, 39.
[6] Isaias LIII, 12.
[7] St. Mark XV, 39.
[8] Cf. Isaias VII, 9.
[9] Psalm L, 10.

the title] of the Beatific Vision is faithful hearing. *Blessed are the clean of heart for they shall see God.*[10] Furthermore, it is by faith that the eye that is to see God must be purified as you read: *purifying their hearts by faith.*[11] (*Ibid.* § 5.)

[10] St. Matthew V, 8. [11] Acts XV, 9.

CHAPTER XIX

THE EXCELLENCE OF THE VISION OF GOD. IN THE PRESENT LIFE THE DELIGHT OF THE DIVINE PRESENCE FELT BY HOLY MEN DIFFERS ACCORDING TO THE DIFFERENT DESIRES OF THE SOUL

THE WORD WHO is the Bridegroom often appears to zealous minds, and not under one form. Why is this true? Doubtless because He is not yet seen *as He is.* (Sermon XXXI, § 1.). . . . Such a vision is not for the present life, but it is reserved for our final state—for those, at least, who can say: *We know that when He shall appear we shall be like to Him, because we shall see Him as He is.*[1] And now, even, He appears to whom He will; but as He wills, not as He is. No man of wisdom, no saint, no prophet can see Him as He is, or ever could see Him in this mortal body. But he who will be considered worthy will be able to see Him, in a body that is immortal. (*Ibid.* § 2.) But that will be hereafter, as I have said. Meanwhile so great a variety of forms and so great a number of *species* in created things—what are they but rays of the Sun of Divinity, as it were, showing indeed that He truly *is* from whom they derive their being, but not defining *what* He is! . . . This manner of seeing is common to all men. For it is easy, according to the Apostle, for everyone with the use of reason to see clearly the invisible things of God, *being understood by the things that are made.*[2] (*Ibid.* § 3.)

It was, beyond doubt, in another way, formerly, that the fre-

[1] 1 St. John III, 2.

[2] Romans I, 20.

quent and familiar intercourse of the divine presence was graciously bestowed upon the Patriarchs, although even to them God was not visible as He is, but as He was pleased to manifest Himself. Nor was this done in one way for all, but, as the Apostle says, *at sundry times and in divers manners.*[3] . . . And this manifestation was, to be sure, common to all men, but nevertheless it was made from without, that is to say, by appearances that the eye could see and by words that the ear could hear. But there is a divine contemplation different from these inasmuch as it is interior, when God of His own accord deigns to visit the soul who is seeking Him. But it must be a soul that devotes herself to that seeking with entire love and longing. And this is the sign of His coming in this way, as we are taught by him who has experienced it: *A fire shall go before Him and shall burn His enemies round about.*[4] For it is necessary that the ardor of holy longing should go before His face in every soul to which He is to come, a longing which will consume the rust of sin and thus prepare a place for the Lord. Then the soul knows that *the Lord is nigh*[5] when she feels herself aflame with that fire, and she will say with the Prophet: *From above He hath sent fire into my bones and hath chastised me:*[6] and again, *My heart grew hot within me, and in my meditation a fire shall flame out.*[7] (*Ibid.* § 4.)

But beware lest you think that in this mingling of the Word and the soul, we are sensibly aware of anything corporal or imaginary. We are saying only what the Apostle says, that *he who is joined to the Lord is one spirit.*[8] The raising up of the

[3] Hebrews I, 1.
[4] Psalm XCVI, 3.
[5] Psalm XXXIII, 19.
[6] Lamentation I, 13.
[7] Psalm XXXVIII, 4.
[8] 1 Corinthians VI, 17.

pure soul to God, or the hallowed descent of God to the soul, we express in our own words as we are able, comparing spiritual things with spiritual. And so it is in the spirit that this union is brought about because *God is a Spirit,*[9] and longs for the beauty of that soul which, perchance, He may have observed walking in the spirit and having no desire to *fulfil the lusts of the flesh,*[10] especially if He perceives it burning with love of Him. A soul therefore thus affected and thus beloved will in no wise be content with that manifestation of the Bridegroom which is granted to many through the things which are made, or that which is granted to a few through visions and dreams. Such a soul will not be satisfied unless by special prerogative she receives Him in the most intimate of affections, and that in the innermost recesses of the heart; and unless she possesses Him whom she desires, present not in some outward form, but intimately united to her, within: not appearing to her without, but affecting her internally. Nor can there be any doubt but that He will be a source of delight greater according to the degree that He is within, not without. For He is the Word making no sound, but penetrating the soul; not full of words, but powerful in effects; not sounding in the ears, but speaking the language of love to the affections. His countenance is not confined to a particular form, but it moulds the countenances of others. It is not such as strikes the eyes of the body, but it rejoices the sight of the heart . . . (*Ibid.* § 6.)

I would not say, however, that when He appears in this wise, He manifests Himself as He is, although He does not manifest Himself as altogether different than He is. Nor will He be constantly manifest in this manner even to the most devout minds.

[9] St. John IV, 24.

[10] Cf. Galatians V, 16.

And neither will He manifest Himself in one and the same way to all. For according to the various desires of the soul, the savor of the divine presence must vary, and the infused taste of heavenly sweetness must delight the palate of the hungry soul now in one way, now in another. Also, you have noticed in this Song of Love how often He has changed His countenance and with *how great a multitude of sweetness*[11] he is pleased to be transformed in the presence of His beloved; and how at one time like a modest Bridegroom he seeks the secret embraces of the holy soul and finds His delight in kisses. But at another time He appears as a Physician with oil and ointments, because of those delicate and weak souls who still have need of lenitives and medicines and hence are designated by the tender name of *young maidens.* If anyone murmurs at this, let him hear, that *they that are in health need not a physician, but they that are ill.*[12] Now, again, a Traveller, as it were, He joins the company of the spouse and the young maidens who accompany her and He lightens the fatigues of the journey for the whole company by His conversation delightful beyond measure, so that they say as He departs: *Was not our heart burning within us whilst He spoke in the way* about Jesus?[13] . . . Again, at times He comes as the very wealthy head of a family, so to speak, whose house is rich in bread; or rather as a King great and powerful who comes to dispel the diffidence of His poor bride, to stimulate her desire by showing her all the desirable things of His glory, the riches of His wine-presses and storehouses, the abundance of His gardens and fields and finally, even admitting her into the very secrets of His inner chamber. Truly *the heart of her Husband trusteth*

[11] Psalm XXX, 20.
[12] St. Matthew IX, 12.
[13] St. Luke XXIV, 32.

in her[14] and there is nothing of all His possessions which He thinks should be hidden from her whom He has rescued from destitution, whom He has proved faithful, whom He embraces as worthy of His love. And thus He does not cease in one internal way or another to manifest Himself without ceasing to the gaze of those who seek Him, so that the word may be fulfilled which said: *behold I am with you all days, even to the consummation of the world.*[15] (*Ibid.* § 7.)

In all these manifestations He is *sweet and mild and plenteous in mercy.*[16] . . . Thus throughout the whole text of this Canticle you will find the Word appearing as a shadow, under such likenesses as we have seen. Hence I think that is the significance of what is found in the Prophet where he says: *The breath of our mouth, Christ the Lord . . . under* His *shadow we shall live among the Gentiles,*[17] because, it is clear, *We see now through a glass in a dark manner, but then face to face.*[18] But that is only while we are living *among the Gentiles,* for among the Angels it will be otherwise when, enjoying the same happiness as theirs, with them we too shall see Him as He is, that is, *in the form of God*[19] and not as a shadow. (*Ibid.* § 8.)

But the shadow of faith is a good thing. . . . It tempers the Light to the weakness of the eye and prepares the eye for the Light Itself. For it is written: *purifying their hearts by faith.*[20] And so faith does not extinguish the light, but preserves it. Whatever vision an angel sees, that the shadow of faith preserves for me hidden away in its faithful bosom, to be revealed in due time. (*Ibid.* § 9.)

[14] Proverbs XXXI, 11.
[15] St. Matthew XXVIII, 20.
[16] Psalm LXXXV, 5.
[17] Lamentation IV, 20.
[18] 1 Corinthians XIII, 12.
[19] Philippians II, 6.
[20] Acts XV, 9.

CHAPTER XX

CHRIST COMES AS A BRIDEGROOM TO A SAINTLY SOUL, AND AS A PHYSICIAN TO THE WEAK AND IMPERFECT. THE ORIGIN OF GOOD AND EVIL THOUGHTS

ALTHOUGH THOSE WORDS in which the visions and likenesses [of God] are described seem to signify corporal things and things pertaining to the body, they are, nevertheless, spiritual things which are communicated to us in this way, and for this reason it is in the spirit, likewise, that we must inquire into the causes and reasons for them. And who is competent to search into and to comprehend so many of the soul's affections and ways of progress in which this grace of the Bridegroom's presence is communicated in so many ways? Nevertheless, if we enter into ourselves and if the Holy Spirit is pleased to show us by His light what by His constant workings He does not disdain to effect again and again in us, I think we shall not remain altogether without understanding of these matters. For I am confident, that *we have received not the spirit of this world, but the spirit that is of God, that we may know the things that are given us from God.*[1] (Sermon XXXII, § 1.)

If, therefore, any one of us finds with the Prophet that *it is good . . . to adhere to . . . God*[2] and, that I may speak more

[1] 1 Corinthians II, 12. [2] Psalm LXXII, 28.

clearly, if any one among us is so much *a man of desires* [3] that he has *a desire to be dissolved and to be with Christ,*[4] and moreover desires it ardently, feels a burning thirst for it, and meditates upon it without ceasing, he certainly will receive the Word at the time of His visitation in no other wise than as a Bridegroom. I am speaking of the hour when he will feel himself inwardly clasped in the arms of Wisdom and then will be aware that the sweetness of divine love has been infused into his soul. For the desire of his heart will be granted him although he is still in the body of his exile—but in part only, and that for a time, and a very short time. For when [the Lord] has been sought in watchings and prayers and with great effort and a flood of tears, He suddenly slips away at the very moment when we think we are holding Him fast. And once again coming to the soul that, weeping, pursues Him, He suffers Himself to be grasped but not to be retained, for suddenly, He again slips from our hands, as it were. But if the devout soul continues to pursue Him with prayers and tears, He will return again and He will not withhold *from him the will of his lips.*[5] But presently He will disappear again and will not be seen unless He be sought again with the whole desire of the heart. Thus, therefore, even in this body of ours the joy of the Bridegroom's presence is frequently felt, but not the fulness of it, for although His visitation gladdens the heart, the alternation of His absence makes it sad. And this the beloved must of necessity endure until she has once laid down the burden of the body of flesh, when she too will fly aloft borne up on the wings of her desires, freely making her way through the realms of contemplation and with unimpeded mind following her Beloved *whithersoever He goeth.*[6] (*Ibid.* § 2.)

[3] Daniel IX, 23.
[4] Philippians I, 23.
[5] Psalm XX, 3.
[6] Apocalypse XIV, 4.

Nevertheless, He will not be thus present to every soul, even in passing, but only to that soul whose great devotion and intense desire and sweetest affection prove her a bride, and a worthy one, for whom the Word puts on His beauty[7] to visit her, assuming the form of a Bridegroom. For whoever is found, not yet affected in this way, but rather filled with sorrow at the remembrance of his sins, speaking in the bitterness of his soul, he says to God: *Do not condemn me.*[8] Or perhaps, drawn away and seduced by his own concupiscence he is still being dangerously tempted. Such a soul as this does not need a Bridegroom but a Physician, and for this reason receives not kisses or caresses, surely, but only remedies for wounds, in oil and ointments. Have we not felt thus, time beyond number, and while at prayer have we not had this experience, we who are still daily tempted by our present excesses or filled with remorse for those of the past? Ah! from how great bitterness of soul have you often delivered me, O Good Jesus, coming to me! . . . How often has prayer taken me on the brink of despair, and restored me to the state of soul of one exulting in joy and confident of forgiveness. Those who are afflicted in this way, behold they know that the Lord Jesus is truly a Physician *Who healeth the broken of heart and bindeth up their bruises.*[9] . . . (*Ibid.* § 3.)

There are those who, tired of their spiritual exercises and fallen into tepidity and so being in a kind of faintness of spirit, walk the ways of the Lord in sadness. With a heart that is dry and weary they come to whatever is enjoined them and often they murmur. They complain of long days and long nights, saying with holy Job: *If I lie down to sleep I shall say: When shall*

[7] Cf. Psalm XX, 6.
[8] Job X, 2.
[9] Psalm CXLVI, 3.

I arise? and again I shall look for the evening and shall be filled with sorrows even till darkness.[10] Therefore whenever it befalls us that we suffer something of this sort, if the Lord moved to compassion hastens to us in the way in which we walk and begins to talk of Heaven—He who is from Heaven—and also to sing something pleasing from the songs of Sion, and to tell us about the city of God, about the peace of that city, about the eternity of peace, about the state of eternity, I tell you this joyous narrative will be as a means of transport for the sleeping and indolent soul so that it will drive out every aversion from the mind of him who hears it, and all weariness from the body. Does it not seem to you that this is what he suffers and this is what he prays for who says: *My soul hath slumbered through heaviness: strengthen Thou me in Thy words?*[11] And will he not cry out when his prayer has been answered: *O how I have loved Thy law, O Lord! it is my meditation all the day.*[12] (*Ibid.* § 4.)

You, therefore, when you are conscious of such things as these revolving in your mind, do not think it is your reflection, but recognize Him speaking who says through the Prophet: *I that speak justice.*[13] . . . And in the Gospel He says: *from the heart come forth evil thoughts.*[14] . . . And the Apostle says: *Not that we are sufficient to think anything of ourselves, as of ourselves: but our sufficiency is from God.*[15] . . . *I will hear,* says the Psalmist, *what the Lord God will speak in me: for He will speak peace unto His people.*[16] (*Ibid.* § 5.) . . . But see to it that the word which comes forth from the mouth of God does not return

[10] Job VII, 4.
[11] Psalm CXVIII, 28.
[12] *Ibid.* 97.
[13] Isaias LXIII, 1.
[14] St. Matthew XV, 19.
[15] 2 Corinthians III, 5.
[16] Psalm LXXXIV, 9.

to Him void, but that it shall prosper and do all things for which He sent it,[17] so that you also may be able to say: *His grace in me hath not been void.*[18] (*Ibid.* § 7.)

Now, to be sure, I think the Word appears at times in the guise of a great father of a family or of royal majesty, to those who, coming *to a deep heart,*[19] have become more magnanimous because of a greater liberty of spirit and purity of conscience. They were wont to essay higher things—restless, to be sure, and curious to penetrate into the greater secrets and to grasp the more sublime, to attempt the more perfect, not only in the physical order, but in the spiritual order, as well. And these on account of the greatness of their faith are found worthy to be admitted into the complete fulness of grace. And there is not among all the repositories of wisdom any from which *the Lord God of all knowledge*[20] judges that they should be excluded who are eager for truth and know no vanity. Such was Moses who made bold to say to God: *If therefore I have found favor in Thy sight, shew me Thy face.*[21] Such was Philip who prayed that the Father be shown to him and to his fellow-disciples. . . . Such, too, was David who himself said to God: *My face hath sought Thee: Thy face, O Lord, will I still seek.*[22] Such souls dare great things because they themselves are great. And what they dare they obtain, according to the word of promise to them, namely: *Every place that your foot shall tread upon shall be yours.*[23] For great faith merits great rewards. And wherever you set down the foot of hope among the goods of the Lord, they will be yours. (*Ibid.* § 8.)

[17] Cf. Isaias LV, 11.
[18] 1 Corinthians XV, 10.
[19] Psalm LXIII, 7.
[20] 1 Kings II, 3.
[21] Exodus XXXIII, 13.
[22] Psalm XXVI, 8.
[23] Deuteronomy XI, 24.

Thus the Great Bridegroom will appear to great souls and He will glory to treat with them, communicating to them His light and His truth, leading them on and bringing them to His holy mountain and into His tabernacles so that whoever is a soul of this sort may say: *He that is mighty hath done great things to me.*[24] (*Ibid.* § 9.)

[24] St. Luke I, 49.

CHAPTER XXI

THE THINGS WHICH A DEVOUT SOUL OUGHT TO SEEK WITHOUT CEASING. THE MEANING OF *Midday*. FOUR KINDS OF TEMPTATIONS AGAINST WHICH WE MUST ALWAYS BE ON OUR GUARD

Shew me, O Thou whom my soul loveth where Thou feedest, where Thou liest in the midday.[1] . . . Who will grant me to see the happy sheep and myself, likewise, feeding upon the mountains together with those ninety-nine which we read were left there when their Shepherd went down to seek the one which had gone astray.[2] . . . With good reason does the bride sigh for and look with longing towards that place of pasturage and of peace, that place of rest and safety, of rejoicing and wonder and ecstasy. For I, alas! wretched that I am, so far removed from it, saluting it from afar!—the very thought of it moves me to tears and fills my soul with the feeling and cry of those who say: *Upon the rivers of Babylon, there we sat and wept when we remembered Sion.*[3] I too will cry out with bride and Prophet alike: *Praise thy God, O Sion. . . . Who hath placed peace in thy borders, and filleth thee with the fat of corn.*[4] Who would not fervently desire to be fed from thence for peace, for nourishment and for complete satisfaction? There is nothing to be feared, there, nothing that is distasteful, nothing that is wanting. Paradise is a

[1] Canticle I, 6.
[2] Cf. St. Matthew XVIII, 12.
[3] Psalm CXXXVI, 1.
[4] Psalm CXLVII, 12, 14.

safe abode. The Word is sweet nourishment. Eternity is abundance without limit. (Sermon XXXIII, § 2.). . . . Let us hasten, then, my children, let us hasten towards a place more secure, towards a pasture more sweet, towards a field richer and more fruitful. . . . You, O Lord, are the Lord of armies and the Shepherd of sheep. Therefore You feed Your sheep and You take Your rest—but not here! . . . (*Ibid.* § 4.)

. . . For here you feed Your sheep, but not to their complete satisfaction. Nor may You take Your rest here. You must stand and keep watch because of the *terror of the night.*[5] Alas! here the light is not clear, nor the nourishment complete, nor the dwelling-place secure. Hence, *Shew me . . . where Thou feedest, where Thou liest in the midday.* You call me blessed when I *hunger and thirst after justice.*[6] But what is this compared with the blessedness of those who are *filled with the good things of Thy house,*[7] who *feast and rejoice before God and* are *delighted with gladness?*[8] But if I *suffer anything for justice' sake,* you pronounce me *blessed.*[9] And certainly to be fed where one must be in dread of suffering, is agreeable but brings no sense of security. In fact, to be fed and to suffer at the same time—is it not a grievous joy? Everything of mine here below falls short of perfection, many are contrary to my deliberate desire, and nothing is secure. . . . *Shew me . . . where Thou feedest, where Thou liest in the midday.* I know well enough where *Thou feedest* but *liest* not down to rest. Show me where *Thou feedest* AND *liest down* to rest. (*Ibid.* § 7.)

There are, indeed, other shepherds who say that they are Your

[5] Cf. Psalm XC, 5.
[6] St. Matthew V, 6.
[7] Psalm LXIV, 5.
[8] Psalm LXVII, 4.
[9] 1 St. Peter III, 14.

companions and are not. They have their flocks and their fields filled with deadly weeds upon which they feed their flocks neither with You nor through You. Their pastures I have not entered, nor have I even approached near to them. They are the very ones who say: *Lo, here is Christ: lo, He is here,*[10] promising richer pastures of wisdom and of knowledge. And many believe them and flock to them and they make them the children of hell twofold more than themselves.[11] Why is this unless it be that with them there is no clear light of midday so that truth may be clearly recognized, and falsity is easily mistaken for it on account of its likeness to truth, and in dim light it is not easily distinguished from the real truth, especially since *stolen waters are sweeter, and hidden bread is more pleasant.*[12] And on this account I pray that you show me *where Thou feedest, where Thou liest in the midday.* (*Ibid.* § 8.)

To me, however, it seems that not only for the reasons given but also because of the wiles of invisible powers such as the seductive spirits lying in ambush, preparing *their arrows in the quiver, to shoot in the dark the upright of heart*[13]—because of them, I repeat, and especially because of them, it seems to me that the midday should also be desired by us, so that by its clear light we may be able to detect the devices of the devil and easily distinguish our own angel from that angel of Satan who *transformeth himself into an angel of light.*[14] For we are powerless to protect ourselves from *invasion* and *the noonday devil,*[15] except by the light of midday. (*Ibid.* § 9.)

The noonday devil is especially wont to lie in wait for the

[10] St. Mark XIII, 21.
[11] Cf. St. Matthew XXIII, 15.
[12] Proverbs IX, 17.
[13] Psalm X, 3.
[14] 2 Corinthians XI, 14.
[15] Psalm XC, 6.

perfect, those namely who as men of virtue have overcome all—pleasures, applause and honors. For what is left him who tempts, with which he may openly assail a man of this sort? He comes, therefore, in disguise—he who dares not come as he is. And he endeavors to overthrow with an apparent good the man whom he knows well enough from experience as one who looks with horror upon every manifest evil. Such souls can say with the Apostle: *For we are not ignorant of his devices.*[16] The more perfect they become, the more careful they are to be on their guard against any such snare. Hence it is that Mary was troubled at the angelic salutation,[17] suspecting some evil intent (unless I am mistaken). And Josue did not receive the angel as a friend until he knew for certain that he was a friend.[18] . . . The Apostles, also, on a certain occasion when they were laboring at the oars, with the wind against them tossing their little boat about, seeing the Lord walking upon the water and thinking it was an apparition, so that they cried out for fear—did they not betray a suspicion of the noonday devil? . . . Presently He who is the true Noonday manifested Himself to the Apostles in what they heard: *It is I, fear ye not,*[19] and the suspicion of deception was at once dispelled. Would that, whenever hidden untruth attempts to steal upon us, the true Noonday, *The Orient from on high,*[20] would send forth His light and His truth to expose it, and again divide *the light from the darkness*[21] so that we may not be spoken of by the Prophet as putting *darkness for light, and light for darkness.*[22] (*Ibid.* § 13.)

[16] 2 Corinthians II, 11.
[17] Cf. St. Luke I, 29.
[18] Cf. Josue V, 13-15.
[19] St. Matthew XIV, 24-27.
[20] St. Luke I, 78.
[21] Cf. Genesis I, 4.
[22] Isaias V, 20.

CHAPTER XXII

HUMILITY

If thou know not thyself, O fairest among women, go forth, and follow after the steps of the flocks and feed thy kids beside the tents of the shepherds.[1] Once Moses, a man of great holiness, because he presumed much on the grace and favor he had found in God's sight, aspired to attain to a certain great vision, so that he said to God: *If therefore I have found favor in Thy sight, shew me Thy face.*[2] But instead of this, he received a much lesser vision by means of which, however, he might one day attain to the one which he desired.[3] The sons of Zebedee, too, walking in the simplicity of their hearts, also made bold to ask something great. But nevertheless they were reduced to a state from which they were to ascend to a higher. Thus, and in the same way, the bride, since she seems to request a thing sublime, is reproved, to be sure, with a reply that is rather austere but very helpful and true. For one who aspires to higher things must have a humble opinion of himself. . . . And as without humility the greatest favors can in no way be obtained, he who is to make progress is humbled by reproof and merits by humility. You, therefore, when you see yourself being humbled, take it as a good sign, even as certain proof of approaching grace. For as the heart *is lifted up before a fall,*[4] so, before it is lifted up it is

[1] Canticle I, 7.
[2] Exodus XXXIII, 13.
[3] Cf. *ibid.* 18-23.
[4] Proverbs XVI, 18.

humbled. Both of these truths are found in the law, namely, that *God resisteth the proud and giveth grace to the humble.*[5] . . . (Sermon XXXIV, § 1.)

Do you see that it is humility that is our justification? Humility, I say, and not humiliation. How many are humiliated who are not humble! Some receive humiliations with bitterness, some with patience, and some with joy. The first are guilty of sin, the second are without blame, the last are those who are justified. Blamelessness, to be sure, is a part of justice. But the perfection of justice is found in the humble. And he who can say: *It is good for me that Thou hast humbled me,*[6] is truly humble. (*Ibid.* § 3.)

[5] St. James IV, 6.

[6] Psalm CXVIII, 71.

CHAPTER XXIII

KNOWLEDGE AND IGNORANCE OF GOD AND OF SELF

You remember that you agreed with me that no one can be saved without self-knowledge which is the source of humility—the mother of salvation—and of fear of the Lord which is the beginning of Wisdom, as it is the beginning of salvation. . . . But what if you know nothing about God? Can there be any hope of salvation where there is ignorance of God? By no means. For you can neither love him whom you do not know, nor possess him whom you do not love. Hence you must know yourself that you may fear God. You must know Him that you may, also, love Him. In the one you are merely introduced to wisdom; in the other you arrive at the perfect knowledge of it, because *the fear of the Lord is the beginning of Wisdom,*[1] and *love . . . is the fulfilling of the law.*[2] Both kinds of ignorance must be equally avoided by you, for without the fear and the love of God no one can be saved. All other kinds of knowledge are indifferent. If they are acquired they do not bring salvation, nor, if they are not known, do they compass our damnation. (Sermon XXXVII, § 1.)

If every one of us were clearly to know their state of soul in God's sight, we would be constrained to assume a place neither higher nor lower than this, conforming to the truth in all things.

[1] Psalm CX, 10.

[2] Romans XIII, 10.

But now, since this judgment [of God] has *made darkness* its *covert,*[3] and the expression of it is concealed from us so that no one knows *whether he be worthy of love or hatred,*[4] it is better and more secure, certainly, according to the counsel of Him who is Truth itself, that we choose for ourselves the lowest place from which we may afterwards, in honor, be conducted to a higher, rather than usurp the higher which, presently, we shall have to yield, with shame.[5] (*Ibid.* § 6.)

There is no danger, therefore, however much you humble yourself, however much you account yourself less than you are, that is, less than Truth considers you. But it is a great evil and a fearful danger if you exalt yourself even in the least degree above what you are in truth, or if in your own judgment you place yourself before a single person, even, whom Truth, it may be, judges to be your equal or even your superior. When you are passing through a door where the lintel is too low, there is nothing to fear, however low you stoop. But there is much to fear, if you raise your head higher than the doorway, even by so much as the breadth of a finger, so that you strike it and dash your bruised head against it. (*Ibid.* § 7.)

[3] Psalm XVII, 12.
[4] Ecclesiastes IX, 1.
[5] Cf. St. Luke XIV, 9-10.

CHAPTER XXIV

IGNORANCE OF GOD LEADS TO DESPAIR. THE BEAUTY OF THE BRIDE AND OF THE BRIDEGROOM

What, therefore, does ignorance of God beget in us? . . . We have said, despair. But how this is brought about we must now consider. Imagine a man *returning to himself*,[1] perchance, and becoming anxious about himself for all the evil he has done, pondering how to recover a view of life in keeping with reason, and how to turn from all his evil ways, and the way of the flesh in his dealings with others. If he is ignorant of how good God is, how *sweet and mild*,[2] and how willing to pardon, will not his carnal reason accuse him and say: "What are you doing? Do you wish to lose this life and the life to come? Your sins are very great and beyond number. Never will you be able to make satisfaction for them, so many and so great are they, not even if you strip the very skin from your body. Your constitution is delicate, your life has been a life of luxury, you will not easily overcome your habitual way of living." Because of these and similar difficulties the wretched man starts back in despair, not knowing how easily Omnipotent Goodness Who wills not that anyone should perish, would cause all his difficulties to melt into thin air. And so the result is final impenitence which is the

[1] St. Luke XV, 17. [2] Psalm LXXXV, 5.

greatest of sins and the blasphemy which is beyond forgiveness.[3] . . . Thus it is, then, that from ignorance of God comes the consummation of all evil, which is despair. (Sermon XXXVIII, § 1.)

The Apostle says, *some have not the knowledge of God.*[4] But I say that all who are unwilling to be converted to God, have not the knowledge of God. For, without doubt, it is for nothing else that they hold back, unless it be that they imagine that He who is kind, is harsh and severe; that He who is merciful, is hard and inexorable; that He who is loveable, is one who inspires fear and dread. . . . Thus iniquity lies to itself,[5] fashioning an idol for itself to take the place of Him—an idol that in nothing resembles Him as He is. *Why are you fearful, O ye of little faith?*[6] Because He is unwilling to forgive sins? He nailed them to the cross together with His own hands.[7] Because you are delicate and accustomed to a life of ease? But *He knoweth our frame.* [*He remembereth that we are dust.*][8] Because you have grown accustomed to evil and are bound by the fetters of habitual sin? But *the Lord looseth them that are fettered.*[9] Are you, perhaps, fearful lest, angered by the greatness and number of your sins He will be slow to extend a helping hand? But *where sin abounded, grace did more abound.*[10] (*Ibid.* § 2.)

God forbid, however, that we should think that the bride has been warned against such a danger, that is, ignorance of God. She has been blest, I do not say with the mere knowledge of Him who is at once her God and her Bridegroom, but with friendship and familiarity to such a degree that she merits His

[3] Cf. St. Matthew XII, 31.
[4] 1 Corinthians XV, 34.
[5] Cf. Psalm XXVI, 12.
[6] St. Matthew VIII, 26.
[7] Cf. Colossians II, 14.
[8] Psalm CII, 14.
[9] Psalm CXLV, 7.
[10] Romans V, 20.

frequent conversation and embraces, and says with the daring of an intimate: *Shew me . . . where Thou feedest, where Thou liest in the midday.*[11] Here, clearly, she asks not that He Himself, but *the place where* His *glory dwelleth*[12] be shown her, although His place and His glory are not distinct from Himself. But He thinks it well to reprove her for presumption, and to warn her about her knowledge of self in which matter she who has considered herself worthy of so great a vision, has seemed at times to grope about in the dark. This is either because, through an excess of love, she has paid too little attention to the fact that she is still in the body, or because vainly hoping that even while remaining in the body, she may be able to attain to that brightness inaccessible. Therefore she is straightway recalled to herself, convicted of ignorance and rebuked for presumption. *If thou know not thyself,* it is written, *go forth.*[13] Fearfully does the Bridegroom thunder forth against the bride, not as a Bridegroom but as a Master, and not as One who would vent His anger upon her, but as One who would strike her with terror that she might be purged of every stain, and thus purified be made worthy of the vision for which she longs. For that Vision is reserved for the clean of heart. (*Ibid.* § 3.)

Let the soul cease, then, so long as it is on earth, to inquire too curiously into the things which are in heaven, lest, perchance, the *searcher of majesty shall be overwhelmed by glory.*[14] . . . "That Vision which you ask to be shown is far beyond your powers, O my spouse," says the Bridegroom, "nor are you now strong enough to look upon the marvellous light of midday

[11] Canticle I, 6.
[12] Psalm XXV, 8.
[13] Canticle I, 7.
[14] Proverbs XXV, 27.

wherein I dwell. . . . That is reserved for you until the Last Day when I shall reveal myself to you and you are filled with glory, *not having spot or wrinkle or any such thing.*[15] . . . How can you who are not yet all beautiful, consider yourself worthy to behold Him who is the Sum of all beauty?" (*Ibid.* § 5.)

[15] Ephesians V, 27.

CHAPTER XXV

THE FACE OF THE SOUL—ITS BEAUTY AND ITS UGLINESS. MODESTY AND SOLITUDE OF SOUL

DELICATE IS THE bride's modesty, and at the Bridegroom's reproof, I believe, her face blushing red makes her more lovely and straightway He makes bold to say: *Thy cheeks are beautiful as the turtle-dove's.*[1] . . . In order to complete the figure of this proposed comparison, understand the face of the soul as the intention of the mind, for it is from this that the rectitude of a deed is judged just as physical beauty is determined by the face. (Sermon XL, § 1.)

There are two things in the intention which we call the face of the soul, which are essential—the act and the reason for the act, that is, what you intend to do and why you do it. And from these two, to be sure, the beauty or deformity of the soul is judged. Thus, for instance, to a soul wherein both of these are upright and pure it is justly and rightly said: *Thy cheeks are beautiful as the turtle-dove's.* (*Ibid.* § 2.). . . . Therefore to seek God alone for His sake only, this is clearly to have both cheeks of the soul's countenance beautiful by reason of the two elements of the intention. And this is the special prerogative of the bride whose singular distinction justly entitles her to hear: *Thy cheeks are beautiful as the turtle-dove's.* (*Ibid.* § 3.)

[1] Canticle I, 9.

But why, *as the turtle-dove's?* That bird is chaste and does not consort with many but is said to be content to spend her life with only one mate, so that if she lose him she will not seek another, but live thenceforth alone. You, then, who hear these words, . . . if you feel moved by promptings of the Holy Spirit such as these, and if you burn with a desire so to act that you may make your soul the bride of Christ, see to it that both cheeks of your intention are beautiful. . . . *Forget thy people and thy father's house. And the King shall greatly desire thy beauty.*[2] O soul that is sanctified, remain in solitude so that you may preserve yourself for Him only, Whom you have chosen for yourself from among all others. Shun the public. Shun even those of your own household. Withdraw from friends and intimates and even from him who serves you. Do you not know that you have a very modest Bridegroom and One who does not at all wish to honor you with His presence in the presence of others? Withdraw, therefore, but let your withdrawal be in mind, not in body—in intention, in devotion, in spirit. A Spirit before your face is Christ the Lord, and He requires solitude of soul, not of body. Yet, to retire sometimes from the company of others, as the opportunity presents itself, is not unprofitable especially in the time of prayer. (*Ibid.* § 4.)

The only solitude that is enjoined you, then, is solitude of mind and spirit. You are alone if you do not think of common things, if you are not affected by things present, if you despise what many admire, if you loathe what all desire, if you avoid strife, if you do not feel temporal losses, if you do not dwell upon past injuries. Otherwise you are not really alone, even if there is no one with you. Do you not see that you can be alone in the midst

[2] Psalm XLIV, 11-12.

of a multitude, and that you can be in the midst of a multitude when you are alone? You are alone however great be the crowd in which you move, if only you are on your guard not to inquire curiously into the conduct of others, and if you do not judge them rashly. Even if you discover some evil deed or other, do not judge your neighbor, but rather excuse him. Excuse the intention if you cannot excuse what is done. Attribute it to ignorance. Attribute it to a lack of deliberation. Attribute it to a mistake. But if the case is so clear that it cannot in any way be excused, persuade yourself, at least, to say: "The temptation was a very violent one. What would it have done to me if it had taken possession of me with power so great?" (*Ibid.* §5.)

CHAPTER XXVI

THE NATURE OF CONSOLATION WHICH THE BRIDE DERIVES FROM THE CONTEMPLATION OF DIVINE GLORY IN THIS LIFE, BEFORE SHE ATTAINS TO THE CLEAR VISION OF IT

Thy neck is as jewels.[1] . . . We must now invoke the Holy Spirit so that, as He was pleased to enable us to discover the spiritual cheeks of the bride, He will deign to show us, likewise, what is to be understood in a spiritual sense by her *neck*. To my mind (since I am under an obligation to tell you what I feel is true) nothing appears to come nearer the truth and to be more probable than that the *intelligence* of the soul is designated by the word *neck*. . . . Does it not seem to you that, in a way, the neck performs the same function for the body as the intellect does for the soul? For it is through the intellect that the soul takes in the lifegiving food of the spirit and directs it through the digestive organs of the affections and deliberate acts of the will. This, the bride's neck, therefore,—the intellect pure and simple—since it shines forth enough in the plain unadorned brilliance of truth, has no need of ornamentation, but rather itself, like a precious jewel fittingly adorns the soul, and hence is described as being *as jewels*. . . . But the intellect of merely natural philosophers and heretics has not in itself any of the lustre of purity and truth and hence they take great care to give it ar-

[1] Canticle I, 9.

tificial coloring and to hide it under the glistening adornments of words and in sophistries couched in syllogisms, lest their intellect appear as it really is and at the same time reveal the ugliness of untruth. (Sermon XLI, §1.)

There follows, *We will make thee chains of gold inlaid with silver.*[2] . . . These words we may attribute to the Bridegroom's companions who are, as it were, consoling the bride with a promise such as this, namely, that until she attains to that vision of Him for which her soul is consumed with longing, they will fashion beautiful and precious chains for her such as are used to adorn the ears. . . . Inasmuch as *faith cometh by hearing*[3] and since by faith the sight is purified, it is fitting that they should strive to adorn the bride's ears, since the hearing, as reason teaches, is a preparation for sight. (*Ibid.* §2.)

We must now consider what kind of chains they offer. *Gold,* it is said, *and inlaid with silver. Gold* is the splendor of Divinity and *the wisdom that is from above.*[4] . . . This, in my opinion, is nothing else than to fashion certain spiritual similitudes in which to impart the purest meanings of Divine Wisdom to the soul who ponders them, so that she may see *through a glass,* at least, and *in a dark manner*[5] what she is not yet in any wise equal to beholding face to face. These things of which we speak are divine and altogether unknown except to those who have had experience of them. They alone know how while still in this mortal body, while yet in the state of faith and while the very substance of Light is not yet made manifest to our view—even now, at times, the contemplation of pure truth undertakes to perform its functions within us to a degree, at least. As a result, any one of us

[2] Canticle I, 10.
[3] Romans X, 17.
[4] St. James III, 17.
[5] 1 Corinthians XIII, 12.

to whom this has been given may apply to himself those words of the Apostle: *Now I know in part,*[6] and, *We know in part and we prophesy in part.*[7] But when suddenly, and as it were with the speed of a flash of lightning something more divine becomes clearly manifest to the mind when the soul is raised in ecstasy, straightway—though I know not whence they come—there are present to the mind certain imaginative pictures of lower [earthly] things, either to temper a splendor that is too intense or to be used in teaching [others the nature of what has been seen]. They are appropriately adapted to the thoughts divinely infused, and by them that most pure and dazzling ray of truth is, as it were, toned down so that it becomes more bearable to the mind and more capable of being imparted to whomsoever we will. I believe that these images are formed in us by the suggestions of holy Angels, just as, on the other hand, there can be no doubt that the contrary evil imaginings are presented to the mind through the agency of evil spirits. (*Ibid.* §3.)

But see how the bride desires one thing and receives another: how upon one striving after the quiet of contemplation, the work of preaching is imposed, and upon one athirst for the presence of the Bridegroom there is enjoined the care of the Bridegroom's children who must be brought into the world and nourished. . . . . Do we not find that the same thing was prefigured of old in the holy patriarch Jacob, when he was deprived of the embraces of Rachael which he so desired and awaited so long, and instead of a wife who was sterile but beautiful he unwillingly and unknowingly received one who was fruitful but *blear-eyed?*[8] Thus, therefore, now, the bride desiring and striving to know

[6] *Ibid.*
[7] *Ibid.* 9.
[8] Cf. Genesis XXIX.

where her Beloved pastures and reposes at midday, carries away, instead of this knowledge, *chains of gold inlaid with silver,* that is, wisdom together with eloquence, to be used, there can be no doubt, in the work of preaching. (*Ibid.* §5.)

From this we are taught, surely, that the sweet kisses [of divine contemplation] must often be interrupted to give suck to the little ones. And life must not be lived for one's self alone, but for all. Those who have received the grace to know God well and to speak eloquently of Him, woe to them if they look upon devotion as a matter of personal advantage only, if they turn into vain glory what they have received to be expended in gaining souls for God! (*Ibid.* §6.)

CHAPTER XXVII

TWO KINDS OF HUMILITY: THE ONE BORN OF TRUTH, THE OTHER OF LOVE

While the King was at His repose my spikenard sent forth the odor thereof.[1] These are the words of the bride. . . . This is the reply made by her, not, however, to the Bridegroom but to His companions. (Sermon XLII, §1.) . . .

The good odor of humility which goes up from this vale of tears, having diffused itself all around, penetrates the very bed-chamber of the King with grateful sweetness. Spikenard is a lowlying plant. And those who are at pains to examine into the properties of plants declare that it is of a warm nature. And hence not inappropriately, it seems to me, I take it to mean in this context, the virtue of humility, but the humility which glows with the warmth of holy love. I say this, really, because there is a humility which truth engenders in us and it has no warmth. And there is a humility which charity produces in us and sets on fire. One consists in affection; the other in knowledge. As a matter of fact if you examine yourself within, in the light of truth and without dissimulation, and draw your conclusion fearlessly, I have no doubt that you will be humbled in your own eyes, although, it may be, you cannot yet bear to appear thus in the eyes of others. You will as a consequence be humble, but as yet

[1] Canticle I, 11.

only through the working of truth and not in the least through the infusion of love. For if you had been affected by love, as you have been enlightened by the splendor of truth which has truthfully and profitably proved to you what you are, you would without doubt have wished, as far as lies within your power, that everyone would hold the same opinion about you as you know Truth itself holds in your regard. . . . (*Ibid.* §6.)

You see, therefore, that it is one thing for a man constrained by the light of truth, to have a lowly opinion of himself. It is quite another for him, assisted by the grace of charity, freely to *consent to the humble.*[2] The one is a matter of necessity. The other is a free act of the will. . . . And Our Lord says: *Learn of Me, because I am meek and humble of heart.*[3] (*Ibid.* §7.)

If in your own sight you are humble with that necessary humility which Truth *that searcheth the reins and hearts*[4] produces in the senses of a watchful soul, exert your will and make a virtue of necessity, since there is no virtue without the concurrence of the will. . . . *Diverse weights and diverse measures, both are abominable before God.*[5] . . . Do you, in private, under-value yourself in your own eyes after having weighed yourself in the scales of truth, and, outwardly pretending to be worth something else, do you offer yourself to us for sale at a greater price than you received from truth itself? Fear God and do not commit this worst of evils, the result of which is that the will exalts one whom Truth humbles. For this is to resist the truth. This is to fight against God. . . . And, *Shall not my soul,* it is written, *be subject to God?*[6] (*Ibid.* §8.)

[2] Romans XII, 16.
[3] St. Matthew XI, 29.
[4] Apocalypse II, 23.
[5] Proverbs XX, 10.
[6] Psalm LXI, 2.

But it is not enough to be subject to God, unless you *be subject to every human creature for God's sake.*[7] . . . Be subject to your equals. Be subject to those who are less than you are. *For so it becometh us to fulfil all justice.*[8] Do you, then, go to him who is less than you, if you wish to be perfect in justice—defer to your inferior; bow down before him who is younger than you. For, doing this, you appropriate to yourself the words of the bride who said: *My spikenard sent forth the odor thereof.* The odor is devotedness. The odor is a good reputation which has come to the knowledge of all so that you may everywhere be *the good odor of Christ,*[9] known to all and worthy of the love of all. This is impossible for the humble man upon whom the truth forces humility, since he keeps it to himself and does not suffer it to escape so that it may spread its perfume abroad. . . . But the humility of the bride, like spikenard, gives forth a sweet odor, is warm with love, alive with devotedness, redolent of good fame. The humility of the bride is voluntary. It is constant. It is fruitful. It cannot be deprived of its perfume by blame or praise. . . . The greater she hears herself made, the more she humbles herself in all things. . . . It is as if with the voice of the Virgin Mary she said: "God *hath regarded the humility of His handmaid.*"[10] For what else is, *My spikenard sent forth the odor thereof,* but, "my humility has been pleasing to God?" (*Ibid.* §9.)

[7] 1 St. Peter II, 13.
[8] St. Matthew III, 15.
[9] 2 Corinthians II, 15.
[10] St. Luke I, 48.

CHAPTER XXVIII

MEDITATION UPON THE PASSION AND SUFFERINGS OF CHRIST ENABLES THE BRIDE, THAT IS, THE SOUL, TO PASS UNSCATHED THROUGH THE PROSPERITY AND ADVERSITY OF THIS WORLD

A little bundle of myrrh is my Beloved to me, He shall abide between my breasts.[1] Before, He was *King*: now He is *Beloved*. . . . Great is the virtue of humility to which even the majesty of the Godhead so easily bends down. Quickly has the name of reverence been changed into the name of friendship, and He who was afar off has straightway been brought near. *A little bundle of myrrh is my Beloved to me.* Myrrh, a bitter thing, means the hard and austere things of tribulation. The bride foreseeing what awaits her because of her Beloved, utters this sentiment with joy, confident that she will bravely endure all. *And they indeed went from the presence of the council, rejoicing that they were accounted worthy to suffer reproach for the name of Jesus.*[2] For this reason, then, she does not call her Beloved, "a bundle," but *a little bundle,* because on account of her love of Him she reckons as *little* whatever of pain or suffering lies before her. Well said —*a* LITTLE *bundle,* because *a* CHILD *is born to us.*[3] Well said —*a* LITTLE *bundle,* because *the sufferings of this time are not worthy to be compared with the glory to come, that shall be revealed in us.*[4] *For that which is at present momentary and light*

[1] Canticle I, 12.
[2] Acts V, 41.
[3] Isaias IX, 6.
[4] Romans VIII, 18.

of our tribulation, worketh for us above measure exceedingly an eternal weight of glory.[5] He, therefore, will be for us an immensity of glory, Who is now *a little bundle of myrrh.* Is He not *a little bundle,* whose *yoke is sweet and burden light?*[6] Not that it is light in itself (for neither the severity of suffering nor the bitterness of death is light) but it is light, nevertheless to him who loves. And hence the bride does not say merely: *a little bundle of myrrh is my Beloved,* but she adds, *to me*—to me who loves—He is *a little bundle of myrrh.* (Sermon XLIII, §1.)

I remember that in one of my former talks[7] I interpreted the breasts of the bride as being *Congratulation* [the faculty of sharing the joy of those who rejoice] and *Consolation* [the faculty of sharing the grief of those who sorrow]. This is according to the teaching of Saint Paul when he says: *Rejoice with them that rejoice; weep with them that weep.*[8] But because the bride dwells in the midst of prosperity and adversity she knows that dangers are not wanting on either side. For this reason she desires to have her Beloved between her breasts, so that strengthened by His unfailing protection, joy will not unduly lift her up nor sorrow cast her down. You, too, if you are wise, will imitate the bride's prudence and never permit this cherished little bundle of myrrh to be snatched from the centre of your heart, even for an hour. . . . (*Ibid.*, §2.)

How *many* are the *prophets and kings* who *have desired to see . . . and have not seen!*[9] They have labored and I *have entered into their labors.*[10] I have gathered the myrrh which they planted. It is for me that this grace-giving bundle of myrrh has been pre-

[5] 2 Corinthians IV, 17.
[6] St. Matthew XI, 30.
[7] Cf. Sermon X, §1.
[8] Romans XII, 15.
[9] St. Luke X, 24.
[10] St. John IV, 38.

served. No one shall take it from me. Between my breasts it shall remain. To meditate upon these things, I have said, is wisdom. In them I have placed the perfection of justice for myself; in them the fulness of knowledge; in them the riches of salvation; in them the abundance of merit. From them there is given me, at times, a draught of saving bitterness; from them, again, the sweet unction of consolation. They raise me up in adversity. In prosperity they restrain me. And amid the joys and sorrows of this present life they give me guidance along the royal road safe from whatever I encounter on either side, routing the evils that lie in wait for me at every turn. . . . Hence these truths are often on my lips, as you know. They are in my heart always, as is known to God. They are the cherished and frequent themes of my pen, as is evident. While I am in this life this more sublime philosophy will be mine—*to know . . . Jesus Christ, and Him crucified.*[11] I do not inquire, as the bride does, where He lieth *in the midday*[12] whom I embrace with joy, as He abides between my breasts. I do not inquire where He feedeth, for I gaze upon Him, my Savior, upon the cross. What the bride asks is more sublime. What I ask is sweeter. . . . (*Ibid.* §4.)

Let it be this *little bundle* so precious, that you, also, my dearly beloved ones, gather for yourselves. Keep it in the depths of your heart. With it guard the approach to your affections, so that He will abide between *your* breasts, as well. Have Him always, not behind you on your shoulders, but before your eyes. Otherwise, carrying Him as a burden and not inhaling the fragrance of His sweetness, the burden will weigh you down and the sweet odor will not revive you. (*Ibid.* §5.)

[11] I Corinthians II, 2. [12] Canticle I, 6.

CHAPTER XXIX

THE TWOFOLD BEAUTY OF THE SOUL, INNOCENCE AND HUMILITY

Behold thou art fair, my Beloved, and comely.[1] . . . Let us inquire into this twofold beauty of the soul. . . . Now the comeliness of the soul is humility. I do not say this of myself, since a prophet has said it before: *Thou shalt sprinkle me with hyssop and I shall be cleansed.*[2] By that herb [*hyssop*], humble and purgative of the heart, was meant humility. By it he who was king and prophet was confident, after falling into serious sin, that he would be cleansed and thus regain the snowy whiteness of his former innocence. But in him who has seriously sinned, humility, although attractive, is not surprising. But if a man has preserved his innocence and joins to it humility, does he not seem to you to possess a twofold beauty of soul? The Blessed Virgin lost no sanctity of soul and she was not lacking in humility. Hence *the King* greatly desired her *beauty*[3] because she joined humility to innocence. And it was she who said: *He hath regarded the humility of His handmaid.*[4] Therefore blessed are they who *have not defiled their garments,*[5] that is, their robes of simplicity and innocence, if they also take care to put on the beauty of humility. He, certainly, who is found to be such a soul will hear:

[1] Canticle I, 15.
[2] Psalm L, 9.
[3] Cf. Psalm XLIV, 12.
[4] St. Luke I, 48.
[5] Apocalypse III, 4.

Behold thou art fair, my Beloved, and comely. Would that even once you might say to my soul, Lord Jesus: *Behold thou art fair!* Preserve my humility for me, I pray, for I have ill kept my first robe [of baptismal innocence]. (Sermon XLV, §2.)

CHAPTER XXX

THE MANNER IN WHICH, BY AN ACTIVE LIFE SPENT UNDER OBEDIENCE, THE LIFE OF CONTEMPLATION MAY BE OBTAINED

Our bed is strewn with flowers. The beams of our houses are of cedar, our rafters of cypress trees.[1] . . . You who hear or read these words spoken by the Holy Spirit, do you not think that you could apply to yourself some of the things that are said? Can you not recognize in yourself any of the bride's felicity which is sung by the Holy Spirit in this song of love? Let it not be said of you: *thou hearest His voice, but thou knowest not whence He cometh and whither He goeth.*[2] Perhaps you, also, desire the quiet of contemplation. And you do well. But do not forget the flowers with which you read the bride's bed is strewn. Take care, therefore, that your bed [your conscience] is covered with the flowers of good works, with the practice of virtues—a flower, as it were, that must precede the fruit of sacred rest [attained in contemplation]. You would wish to sleep the sleep of the self-indulgent, if, without having practiced virtue, you were to desire to rest. . . . Moreover, it is altogether contrary to the right order of things, to look for a reward before you have earned it and to accept a meal before you have done any work, since the Apostle says: *If any man will not work, neither let him eat.*[3] And it is written: *By Thy commandments I have had understanding,*[4] so that you may know

[1] Canticle I, 15-16.
[2] St. John III, 8.
[3] 2 Thessalonians III, 10.
[4] Psalm CXVIII, 104.

that the taste of contemplation is due only to obedience to the commandments. . . . The Bridegroom will never grace that bed which you have strewn with the poison-oak and nettles of disobedience instead of the flowers of obedience. As a consequence He will not hear your prayers. When called, He will not come, for He will not give His riches to one who is disobedient—He who is so great a Lover of obedience that He preferred to die rather than to disobey.[5] I fear the more, lest there fall upon you that terrifying sentence that so thundered against the treachery of the Jews: *My soul hateth your new moons and your solemnities: they are become troublesome to me, I am weary of bearing them.*[6] (Sermon XLVI, §5.)

I am greatly astonished at the impudence of some who are among us. When they have caused us all great trouble because of their singular ways, have provoked us by their impatience, have shown their contempt for authority by contentiousness and insubordination, they have the boldness, nevertheless, to invite, with all the importunance of their prayers, the Lord of all purity to the defiled bed of their conscience. But, *when you stretch forth your hands,* He says, *I will turn away my eyes from you: and when you multiply prayer I will not hear.*[7] . . . The Centurion would not suffer Him to enter under his roof because of his own unworthiness. And yet his faith gave forth a sweet odor that spread throughout all *Israel.*[8] . . . The Prince of the Apostles cried out: *Depart from me for I am a sinful man, O Lord.*[9] And do you say: "Come to me, O Lord, for I am sinless?" (*Ibid.* §6.)

Everyone who walks not according to the flesh but according

[5] Cf. St. Matthew XXVI, 39.
[6] Isaias I, 14.
[7] Isaias I, 15.
[8] Cf. St. Matthew VIII, 8-10.
[9] St. Luke V, 8.

to the spirit, should know that he is a spiritual house of God. *For the temple of God is holy, which you are.*[10] Take care, therefore, brethren, of this spiritual edifice which you are, lest, perhaps, when it begins to rise higher, it should totter and crash to the ground, if it be not built and supported by strong beams. Take care, I say, to supply it with rafters that are firm and will not decay—*the fear of the Lord is holy, enduring for ever and ever;*[11] patience, of which it is written: *the patience of the poor shall not perish for ever;*[12] perseverance, too, which, lasting till the end unchangeable under the weight of any superstructure, endures throughout the endless ages of the life of blessedness. For, according to Our Savior, speaking in the Gospel: *He that shall persevere unto the end, he shall be saved.*[13] But above all, make use of charity which *never falleth away,*[14] because, it is said: *love is strong as death.*[15] (*Ibid.* §8.)

[10] 1 Corinthians III, 17.
[11] Psalm XVIII, 10.
[12] Psalm IX, 19.
[13] St. Matthew X, 22.
[14] 1 Corinthians XIII, 8.
[15] Canticle VIII, 6.

CHAPTER XXXI

CHARITY IS REGULATED BY DISCRETION

The King brought me into the cellar of wine, He set charity in order in me.[1] . . . When, in answer to her prayers, the bride enjoyed for a while, sweet and familiar converse with the Beloved, He left her and the bride returned again to the young maidens. She appeared so refreshed and stimulated by the appearance and conversation of the Beloved that she seemed like one inebriated. The maidens astonished, as it were, by the change in her and asking the cause of it, she replied that it was no wonder she appeared to be stimulated by wine, she who had been brought *into the cellar of wine.* This is the meaning according to the literal sense. According to the mystical meaning, the bride does not here deny that she was inebriated—but with love, not with wine, unless it be that love is wine. (Sermon XLIX, §1.)

When the disciples, filled with the Holy Spirit, were thought by the people to be drunk with wine, Peter, as a friend of the Bridegroom speaking for the bride, standing in the midst of them said: *These are not drunk, as you suppose.*[2] Notice that he did not altogether deny that they were drunk, but that they were drunk in the way in which the people supposed. For they were drunk with the Holy Spirit, not with wine. . . . And as if they would bear witness to the people that they had, in truth, been

[1] Canticle II, 4.

[2] Acts II, 15.

brought *into the cellar of wine,* Saint Peter again speaking in their name, said: *But this is that which was spoken of, by the prophet Joel: "And it shall come to pass, in the last days (saith the Lord) I will pour out of my Spirit upon all flesh: and your sons and your daughters shall prophesy and your young men shall see visions and your old men shall dream dreams."* [3] Does it not seem to you that *the cellar of wine* was the house in which the disciples were gathered together when, *suddenly there came a sound from heaven, as of a mighty wind coming, and it filled the whole house where they were sitting,*[4] and fulfilled the prophecy of Joel? And every one of them coming forth *inebriated with the plenty of* that *house,*[5] and having drunk *of the torrent of pleasure* so great,[6] could he not say, with good reason: *The King brought me into the cellar of wine?* (*Ibid.* §2.)

Let us suppose that someone, in prayer, is raised in ecstasy and admitted into the hidden secrets of the Divinity, whence he returns all aflame with divine love and burning with zeal for justice, glowing with excessive fervor in the performance of all his spiritual duties and in all spiritual pursuits. As a result, he can say: *My heart grew hot within me: and in my meditation a fire shall flame out.*[7] He, surely, . . . will not without reason claim that he has entered into *the cellar of wine.*

Now, there are two kinds of ecstasy in divine contemplation, one in the intellect and the other in the will. One consists in the enlightenment of the understanding, the other in an increase of love. One is knowledge, the other is devotion. . . . And by everyone to whom it is given to come forth from prayer with an

[3] Acts II, 16-17.
[4] *Ibid.* II, 2.
[5] Psalm XXXV, 9.
[6] *Ibid.*
[7] Psalm XXXVIII, 4.

abundance of these gifts, it can in truth be said: *The King brought me into the cellar of wine.* (*Ibid.* §4.)

The Bride goes on to say: *He set in order charity in me.*[8] This follows as an absolute necessity. For zeal without knowledge is an insupportable thing. Therefore where zeal manifests itself most intensely, the greatest discretion is necessary. And this is the setting in order of charity. . . . Discretion puts order into every virtue. And order makes for moderation and attractiveness and stability, as well. Finally, *By Thy ordinance the day goeth on.*[9] This is said, calling virtue, *the day.* Discretion, then, is not so much a virtue as the mistress and guide of virtues, as well as the one who regulates the affections and teaches right conduct. Take discretion away and virtue will become vice, and even natural affection will be turned into an unbridled passion that will destroy nature itself. (*Ibid.* §5.)

[8] Canticle II, 4.

[9] Psalm CXVIII, 91.

CHAPTER XXXII

TWO KINDS OF CHARITY—OF THE AFFECTIONS AND OF ACTION

THERE IS CHARITY in action and there is charity in affection. And it was concerning that which looks to the deed, that I think the law was given to men and the [first] commandment was drawn up. For who can possess the charity of affection to the degree set down in the commandment? Therefore one kind of charity is commanded as a necessary condition of merit. The other is given by way of reward. We do not deny that, in the latter, a beginning may be made and a degree of progress attained even in this life by means of divine grace. But, clearly, we hold that its consummation is in the happiness that is to come. How, then, could that charity be imposed upon us as an obligation, which could in no wise be attained? Or if you prefer to think that the commandment was given concerning charity of affection, I have nothing to say so long as you agree with me that never in this life has any man been able perfectly to fulfil it or will be able to do so in the future. For who would dare arrogate to himself what Saint Paul confesses that he had not attained? [1] And it was not hidden from the Divine Legislator that the weight of the commandment is greater than man's strength. But He judged it helpful that men should thus be reminded of their own insufficiency, and that they might also know toward what goal of justice they had an obligation to strive according to their powers.

[1] Cf. Philippians III, 13.

Therefore by commanding the impossible He made men not transgressors but humble; *that every mouth may be stopped, and all the world may be made subject to God. Because by the works of the law no flesh shall be justified before Him.*[2] (Sermon L, §2.)

That the commandment applies rather to charity of action appears perfectly clear from the fact that when the Lord had said, *Love your enemies,* He immediately added concerning actions, *do good to them that hate you.*[3] In similar strain the Old Testament says: *if thy enemy be hungry, give him to eat: if he thirst give him water to drink.*[4] And here you see there is reference to action, not affection. But listen to the Lord imposing the commandment concerning the love of Himself: *If you love Me,* He says, *keep my commandments.*[5] (*Ibid.* §3.)

Now I do not say that we should be without affection, and that with dry heart we should employ our hands only in the performance of external deeds. Among other things which the Apostle sets down as the great and grave evils of men, I have read this one also mentioned, namely, to be *without affection.*[6] There is an affection begotten of the flesh, and there is one which reason governs, and there is one rich with the savor of wisdom. The first is that which the Apostle says neither is nor can be *subject to the law of God.*[7] The second, on the contrary, he describes as giving *consent to the law, that it is good.*[8] And there is no doubt that these two are different from each other, since one is obstinately opposed to the law and the other is willingly subject to it. But the third is far removed from both of these. It tastes and under-

[2] Romans III, 19, 20.
[3] St. Luke VI, 27.
[4] Proverbs XXV, 21.
[5] St. John XIV, 15.
[6] Romans I, 31.
[7] Cf. Romans VIII, 7.
[8] *Ibid.* VII, 16.

stands that *the Lord is sweet.*[9] It excludes the first. It is the reward of the second. For the first is sweet, surely, but vile. The second is dry but strong. The last is full of unction and is sweet. It is, then, through the second that deeds are performed and in it charity consists—not that of the affections, . . . but rather, as it were, of act. Although it does not as yet refresh the soul with that sweet love just mentioned, yet it inflames our hearts with an intense love of that love itself. *Let us not love in word,* it says, *nor in tongue, but in deed and in truth.*[10] (*Ibid.* §4.)

He set in order charity in me,[11] says the bride. Which of these two kinds of charity is meant? Both. But the order in one is just the reverse of the order in the other. For charity of act looks to the lower order; charity of affection, to the higher. In a soul rightly disposed in the matter of charity of affection, there is no doubt, for instance, but that love of God is placed before the love of man, and among men themselves the more perfect are preferred to the less perfect, heaven is preferred to earth, eternity to time, the soul to the body. But in well-ordered charity of action often, if not always, the reverse order is found. For we are more concerned about the care of our neighbor and more often occupied with it. It is the weaker of our brethren that we assist with more painstaking zeal. We give our attention to the peace of earth rather than to the glory of heaven, and this we do by the law of our human nature and by the very necessity of our condition. Because of the demands of temporal cares we scarcely find time to think at all about matters eternal. Almost continuously we are engaged in administering to the needs of the body, after having neglected the care of the soul. And finally, we surround

[9] Psalm XXXIII, 9.
[10] 1 St. John III, 18.
[11] Canticle II, 4.

our weaker members with *more abundant honor,*[12] according to the saying of the Apostle. In this way we fulfil, after a fashion, the word of the Lord which you have heard: *The last shall be first, and the first last.*[13] . . . That sort of charity is clearly kind and just, for it is no respecter of persons, and does not consider the price of things, but the needs of men. (*Ibid.* §5.)

But it is not thus in the case of the charity of affection. Its order begins with that which is first. For it is wisdom through which, to be sure, all things are valued according to their real worth. For instance, things which by their nature are of greater worth, wisdom makes the object of greater affection; things of less worth, of less affection; and those of least worth, of least affection. (*Ibid.* §6.)

Now, as for your neighbor—whom, truly, you must love as yourself—so that in your eyes and in his own he may be esteemed according to his real worth, you must have the same esteem for him as you have for yourself. For he is what you are. He is a man. And so, you who do not love yourself for any other reason than because you love God, as a consequence, you love as yourself, all who love Him as you do. But in the case of an enemy [one who deliberately hates you], since he is nothing, for the reason that he does not love God,[14] you cannot, surely, love him as yourself—you who love God. But you will love him so that he may in the future be brought to love God. . . . Hence, in order that in your eyes and in his own he may be esteemed according to his real worth, you must esteem him not for what he is, for he is nothing, but for what he may one day become. (*Ibid.* §7.)

[12] 1 Corinthians XII, 23.
[13] St. Matthew XX, 16.
[14] Cf. 1 Corinthians XIII, 2.

CHAPTER XXXIII

THE MYSTICAL MEANING OF FLOWERS AND FRUITS AND THE BRIDEGROOM'S HANDS

Stay me up with flowers, compass me about with apples: because I languish with love.[1] The bride's love has grown stronger because the incentives of love have become greater. For you see what a wealth of favors were granted her in this last meeting—not only of seeing the Bridegroom, but of conversing with Him. . . . It is not to be supposed that the bride came forth thirsty from the *cellar of wine* into which she was brought. But on the contrary, she must indeed be thirsty because; *they that drink Me,* it is said, *shall yet thirst.*[2] After all those favors, when the Bridegroom according to His wont retires, the bride declares that she languishes with love, that is, because of an excess of love. For the more delight she has experienced in His presence, the more grievously she feels His subsequent absence. The taking away of the thing you love, is the increase of longing for it. And what you long for more ardently, you miss with the greater pain of separation. Hence the bride asks to be lovingly consoled, meanwhile, with the sweet odors of flowers and fruits, until such time as He returns Whose absence she can scarcely endure. (Sermon LI, §1.)

If, according to the moral sense, you wish to attribute to one

[1] Canticle II, 5. [2] Ecclesiasticus XXIV, 29.

soul both of these, namely, both flowers and fruits, understand faith as a flower, and good works as fruit. And this will not seem incongruous, I think, if you notice that just as a flower necessarily goes before fruit, a good work must be preceded by faith. Moreover *without faith it is impossible to please God,* Saint Paul assures us.[3] Rather, we learn on his authority: *all that is not of faith is sin.*[4] And so there is no fruit without a flower, nor good work without faith. But even *faith without works is dead,*[5] just as it is futile for a flower to appear where no fruit follows. . . . Therefore the mind accustomed to quiet draws consolation from good works rooted in unfeigned faith whenever, as often happens, the light of contemplation is withdrawn. For who is there who can enjoy the light of contemplation—I do not say continuously, but even occasionally—while he still remains in the body? But as often as he falls from the contemplative way, he devotes himself to the active, whence, as from a neighboring retreat he will be able to return better acquainted, to his former state. For these two ways of life are companions one to the other and they live under the same roof on terms of equality. Martha, surely, is Mary's sister. And although she falls from the light of contemplation, she does not stumble into the darkness of sin or into the sloth of inactivity, but keeps herself in the light of doing good. And that you may know, also, that good works are a light, *let your light shine,* says Our Lord, *before men.*[6] And there is no doubt that this was said concerning good works, which men could see. (*Ibid.* §2.)

Stay me up with flowers, compass me about with apples: because I languish with love. When what is loved is present, love

[3] Hebrews XI, 6.
[4] Romans XIV, 23.
[5] St. James II, 20.
[6] St. Matthew V, 16.

grows strong. When it is absent, love languishes. This is nothing else than a kind of exhaustion brought on by the impatient longing with which the mind of one who loves intensely must of necessity be affected when he whom she loves is absent. And while he is the only object for which she waits, she considers speed howsoever great, as slow. And hence the bride entreats that she may heap up for herself the fruits of good works with the sweet odor of faith, wherein she may find refreshment while the Bridegroom tarries. I speak to you of an experience which I myself have had. If at times I have learned that some of you have made progress because of my counsels, then I felt no regrets, I confess, that I had preferred the trouble of speaking, to my own leisure and quiet. . . . There is not, I tell you, any reason for my feeling sad for having interrupted the pursuit of pleasant contemplation, when I have been surrounded with such flowers and fruits of piety. . . . For charity which *seeketh not her own,*[7] easily persuaded me of this long ago—that I should prefer nothing that is the object of my own desires, to those which are for your advantage. To pray, to read, to write, to meditate, and if there are any other things pertaining to spiritual studies *that were gain to me, the same I have counted loss* for your sakes.[8] (*Ibid.* §3.)

Stay me up with flowers, compass me about with apples: because I languish with love.[9] . . . I know that I have explained this passage more fully and in a different sense in the book "On the Love of God." (Cf. Chap. III, §1.) Whether that explanation is better or worse than this, let the reader judge if it please him to look at both. Surely I shall not be condemned by any person of

[7] 1 Corinthians XIII, 5.
[8] Philippians III, 7.
[9] Canticle II, 5.

prudence for these different interpretations, so long as truth sustains both. And charity, the rule for interpreting Scripture, will edify more readers, according as, in its work of edification, it discovers more meanings that are in conformity with truth. For why should anyone find this practice distasteful in regard to the meanings of Scripture, when we are constantly adopting it in the use of things? For instance, to how many uses is water alone put for the good of our bodies? In the same way any divinely inspired statement will not fail of its purpose if it bears different meanings adapted to the various needs and habits of souls. (*Ibid.* §4.)

There follows: *His left hand is under my head, and His right hand shall embrace me.*[10] . . . It appears that the Bridegroom is present again, I believe, to console with His presence His languishing bride. For how could it be that in His presence she would not be revived who was reduced to a state of exhaustion by His absence? He, then, cannot endure the bride's anxiety. He is at hand. For, called back by desires so ardent He can make no delay. And because he has found her, during His absence, faithful to good works and clearly striving for [spiritual] gain in this, that she had directed flowers and fruit to be gathered for her, He has returned now with a more abundant recompense of grace. . . . Happy the soul which reclines upon the breast of Christ and takes its rest within the arms of the Word. *His left hand is under my head, and His right hand shall embrace me.* She does not say, *embraces,* but SHALL *embrace me,* so that you may know that she is not ungrateful for the first grace, and that she anticipates the second by an expression of thanks. (*Ibid.* §5.)

Learn not to be slow or dilatory in returning thanks. Learn to give thanks for every individual gift. *Consider diligently,* it is

[10] Canticle II, 6.

said, *what is set before thy face,*[11] so that none of the gifts of God may be allowed to pass without the expression of thanks due them, whether they be great, indifferent or very small. Indeed we are bidden to *gather up the fragments, lest they be lost,*[12] that is, not to forget the very least of the benefits conferred upon us. For is not that *lost* which is given to one who is ungrateful? Ingratitude is an enemy of the soul—the emptying out of merit, the routing of virtue, the ruin of God's benefits. Ingratitude is a burning wind, drying up the fount of piety, the dew of mercy, the flowing waters of grace. On this account the bride as soon as she felt the grace received from the left hand of the Bridegroom, gave thanks, not waiting for the plentitude of grace in His right hand. (*Ibid.* §6.)

[11] Proverbs XXIII, 1.

[12] St. John VI, 12.

CHAPTER XXXIV

THE MYSTICAL SLEEP OF THE BRIDE. THE ECSTASY CALLED CONTEMPLATION IN WHICH THE BRIDEGROOM CAUSES A HOLY SOUL TO ATTAIN PEACE AND REST

I adjure you, O ye daughters of Jerusalem, . . . that you make not *the beloved to awake till she please.*[1] It is to the young maidens that this prohibition is addressed. The Bridegroom calls them *daughters of Jerusalem* because although they are charming and gentle, and still weak, as it were, with girlish affections and ways, nevertheless they cling to the bride in the hope of going forward and reaching Jerusalem. These, therefore, are restrained from disturbing the sleeping bride, lest, contrary to her desire they should presume in any way whatever to awaken her. . . . And now, as Holy Scripture goes on to say, the Bridegroom Himself becomes the bride's guard and most graciously and tenderly watches over her lest, disturbed by the frequent little needs of the young maidens she should be awakened. . . . (Sermon LII, §1.)

Now there are not lacking among our kind, those who are happy in having merited to be gladdened by this service of the Bridegroom, and who have thus enjoyed the personal experience of the sweetest hidden delight. Otherwise we are altogether lacking in faith in the passage of Holy Scripture which we have be-

[1] Canticle II, 7.

fore us, where the Heavenly Bridegroom is clearly represented as most zealous for the repose of a certain bride of His, anxious to hold her in His own arms while she is sleeping, so that she might not, perchance, be aroused from so sweet a sleep by any trouble or annoyance. (*Ibid.* §2.) . . . For there is, in truth, a sleep which does not, however, steep the senses in forgetfulness but transports them. It is also a death. This I may say without hesitation, since the Apostle by way of commendation speaks thus to some still living in the flesh: *You are dead: and your life is hid with Christ in God.*[2] (*Ibid.* §3.)

I may, then, without absurdity, call the bride's ecstasy, death. But it is a death that takes away not life, but life's snares, so that she can say: *Our soul hath been delivered as a sparrow out of the snare of the fowlers.*[3] For the soul is cast into the midst of snares in this life. But they hold no terrors for us so long as the soul is transported out of itself by some holy and intense reflection. . . . Would that I might often suffer a death such as this so that I might escape the snares of death, so that I might not feel the fatal allurements of a life of pleasure, so that I might be insensible to the inordinate desires of the flesh, to the passion of avarice, to the goads of anger and impatience, to the torments of anxiety and the disquiets of care. *Let my soul die the death of the just,*[4] so that no deceit may ensnare it, no sin seduce it. Happy death which does not take away life, but transforms it into a better! Happy, because it does not strike down the body, but raises up the soul. (*Ibid.* §4.)

Truly this is the death of men. But let my soul die the death

[2] Colossians III, 3.
[3] Psalm CXXIII, 7.
[4] Numbers XXIII, 10.

of Angels, if I may so speak. . . . Such, I believe, is that ecstasy which alone, or in a special manner, is called contemplation. For to live unfettered by a desire of earthly things is the part of human virtue. But to meditate upon truth and not to have it clothed in material images pertains to angelic purity. Yet both are God's gifts. Both go beyond your natural powers and both carry you out of yourself. But one carries you far; the other, only a little way. Blessed is he who can say: *Lo, I have gone far off flying away; and I abode in the wilderness.*[5] He was not content to go away unless he could go far away so that he could find rest. You have made rapid progress against the delights of the flesh so that you no longer yield to its concupiscence, nor are you mastered by its allurements. You have gone forward. You have cut yourself off from the world. But as yet you have not attained complete solitude of soul unless by virtue of your purity of mind you have the power to rise above the phantasms of material images forcing themselves upon you on every side. Until you have attained to this, do not promise yourself rest. You are mistaken if you think that this side of it you can find the place of rest, the retirement of solitude, the clarity of light, the abode of peace. . . . Truly it is a place in a solitude and a dwelling-place in light. According to the Prophet it is indeed, *a tabernacle for a shade in the daytime from the heat, and for a security and covert from the whirlwind and from rain.*[6] And of it holy David also says: *He hath hidden me in His tabernacle; in the day of evils He hath protected me in the secret place of His tabernacle.*[7] (*Ibid.* §5.)

Understand, therefore, that it was into this solitude that the bride retired and there, overcome by its delightfulness, sweetly

[5] Psalm LIV, 8.
[6] Isaias IV, 6.
[7] Psalm XXVI, 5.

fell asleep in the arms of the Bridegroom. By this we are to understand that she was rapt in ecstasy from which the young maidens were forbidden to arouse her until she herself should please. . . . It is left to her choice both to employ her leisure for her own advantage and to devote herself to the care of the young maidens, according to her own choice. For it is forbidden them to awaken her unless she herself please. (*Ibid.* §6.)

CHAPTER XXXV

THE BRIDE'S QUIET OF CONTEMPLATION IS SECURED BY THE BRIDEGROOM'S VOICE

The voice of my Beloved.[1] The bride seeing the unaccustomed timidity of the young maidens and their timorous fear inasmuch as they no longer dared to intrude upon her holy repose, nor presume *as yesterday and the day before*[2] to trouble the quiet of her contemplation, realized that this had been brought about by the care and effort of the Bridegroom. . . . And rejoicing in spirit . . . she declares that it was the voice of the Beloved that effected this change in them. For he who has the care of others, seldom if ever feels that he may take time for his own needs. He is always afraid that he is niggardly towards his subjects and that he is not pleasing to God because he prefers the quiet and sweetness of his own contemplation, to the common good. No little joy and reassurance is given him as he sweetly rests from his labors, when from a certain fear and reverence for him divinely infused into the hearts of his subjects, he understands that his quiet is pleasing to God. For it is He who brings it about that subjects would rather bear their own needs with patience, than presume to disturb the grateful rest of their spiritual father. (Sermon LIII, §1.)

[1] Canticle II, 8.

[2] 1 Machabees IX, 44.

CHAPTER XXXVI

THE *Wall,* THE *Windows* AND THE *Lattices* OF THE INCARNATION

Behold He standeth behind our wall, looking through the windows, looking through the lattices.[1] . . . The Bridegroom drew near to the wall when He assumed flesh. The flesh is the wall. The taking of it unto Himself by the Bridegroom is the Incarnation of the Word. Moreover, the windows and the lattices through which He is said to look are, as I understand it, the bodily senses and the human affections through which He began to have experimental knowledge of all human needs. In fine, *He hath borne our infirmities and carried our sorrows.*[2] He made use, therefore, of human affections and bodily senses as openings and windows, so that, being made man He might know by personal experience the miseries of men, and so that *He might become merciful.*[3] (Sermon LVI, §1.)

[1] Canticle II, 9.
[2] Isaias LIII, 4.
[3] Hebrews II, 17.

CHAPTER XXXVII

THE SOUL'S ALERTNESS FOR THE VISITATIONS OF THE LORD. THE SIGNS BY WHICH THESE VISITATIONS MAY BE KNOWN

Behold my Beloved speaketh to me.[1] . . . See the progress of grace. Mark the advances of divine condescension. Notice the devotedness and the fine sense of perception of the bride—how with watchful eye she awaits the Bridegroom's coming, and then diligently watches everything about Him. He comes. He makes haste. He draws near. He is present. He looks. He speaks. And nothing in all these movements eludes her diligence or escapes her notice. He comes in the Angels. He makes haste in the Patriarchs. He draws near in the Prophets. He is present in the Flesh. He looks upon us in miracles. He speaks to us in the Apostles. Or we may understand it thus: He comes in love and in the desire to compassionate us; He makes haste in the zeal to redeem us; He draws near in humbling Himself; He is present to those who are of His generation; He looks forward to those who are to come; He speaks *of the kingdom of God,*[2] teaching and convincing. Such, therefore, is the coming of the Bridegroom. . . . (Sermon LVII, §1.)

Who is wise and understands these things so that he can distinguish one from another, and so that he is able to describe them, every one, and explain them so that others can understand them?

[1] Canticle II, 10. [2] Acts I, 3.

If that is expected of me, I would prefer to hear these things from one who knows them from experience and who is accustomed to such things and well versed in their application. But such a man as this, modestly prefers to hide in silence what in silence he has gained, and thinks it safer to keep his secret to himself. But I as Superior have an obligation to speak and it is not right for me to remain silent. . . . If, then, I have been warned either by man from without or by the Holy Spirit within to guard justice and preserve equity, such salutary advice will be for me, certainly, an indication that the coming of the Holy Spirit is at hand, and a kind of preparation for worthily receiving the heavenly Visitor. The Prophet points this out to me when he says: *Justice shall walk before him.*[3] And again he speaks thus to God: *Justice and judgment are the preparation of Thy throne.*[4] . . . And Scripture says: *Holiness becometh Thy house, O Lord,*[5] and, *His place is in peace,*[6] and, *The clean of heart . . . shall see God.*[7] (*Ibid.* §5.)

Also, if *the just man shall correct me in mercy and shall reprove me,*[8] I shall feel the same way, knowing that the zeal of a just man and his goodwill, *make a way for Him who ascendeth upon the west.*[9] . . . Therefore the reproof of the just man is not to be scorned. It is the destruction of sin. It is health to the heart. And it is even the path of God to the soul. . . . If you hear a discourse that is pleasing and agreeable inasmuch as having suppressed any natural aversion you listen with eagerness, then you must believe not only that the Bridegroom is coming, but that He is making haste, that is, He is coming with eager desire. For His desire be-

[3] Psalm LXXXIV, 14.
[4] Psalm LXXXVIII, 15.
[5] Psalm XCII, 5.
[6] Psalm LXXV, 3.
[7] St. Matthew V, 8.
[8] Psalm CXL, 5.
[9] Psalm LXVII, 5.

gets yours. The fact that you are making haste to receive the word of God is a sign that He is making haste to enter into your soul. . . . For it is not we who have first loved Him, but, *He hath first loved us.*[10] If now you feel the word of God as a flame and that your conscience has caught fire from it in the remembrance of sin, then recall of Whom it is that Scripture says: *A fire shall go before Him,*[11] and doubt not that He is near. For, *the Lord is nigh unto them that are of a contrite heart.*[12] (*Ibid.* §6.)

But if you are not only filled with remorse at the word, but are entirely converted to the Lord, swearing and determining *to keep the judgments of* His *justice,*[13] you may know that He is present to you, especially if you feel your heart beginning to glow with the fire of love. . . . Indeed Moses says of Him: *The Lord Thy God is a consuming fire.*[14] . . . In truth, the fire which is God consumes, to be sure, but it does not destroy. It burns sweetly. It leaves one desolate unto bliss. It is truly a desolating burning, but one which directs the flame of fire against sin in such a way that it has the effect of unction upon the soul. (*Ibid.* §7.)

When every stain of sin and the blight of faults have been consumed by this fire, if when the conscience is already purified and at peace there follows a certain sudden and extraordinary expansion of mind, and the infusion of light that illuminates the intellect for the understanding of the Scriptures or the knowledge of mysteries—one of which I believe is given for our own comfort, the other for the help of our neighbor—this is without doubt the eye of the Bridegroom looking [through the window], bringing

[10] 1 St. John IV, 10.
[11] Psalm XCVI, 3.
[12] Psalm XXXIII, 19.
[13] Psalm CXVIII, 106.
[14] Deuteronomy IV, 24.

forth *thy justice as the light and thy judgment as the noonday.*[15] This is according to the word of Isaias: *Thy light shall rise up in darkness and thy darkness shall be as the noonday.*[16] But surely it is not through wide-open doors, but through narrow openings that this ray of such splendor pours itself in upon us, at least while this dilapidated wall of the body is still standing. You are mistaken if you have other aspirations, however great the purity of heart to which you have attained, for he who was a distinguished contemplative says: *We see now through a glass in a dark manner; but then face to face.*[17] (*Ibid.* §8.)

After this look of so great condescension and compassion, there comes a voice gently and softly making known the divine will. This voice is nothing else than love itself which cannot remain idle, inciting and urging you on to the things which are of God. Finally the bride hears that she must arise and make haste, there can be no doubt, for the winning of souls. This is a characteristic of true and pure contemplation, that the mind which is all aflame with the fire that is divine, contemplation fills, from time to time, with so great a zeal and desire of winning to God those who will love Him as she does, that she freely interrupts the time of contemplation for the work of preaching. Again, when she has accomplished what she desired to do, at least to some extent, she returns to contemplation with greater fervor in proportion as she feels that her interruption has been productive of fruit. Likewise when she has tasted again of contemplation, she returns with her usual eagerness to the quest for souls. But during these alternations her mind is very often troubled, being apprehensive and altogether beside herself lest, perchance, while she is being

[15] Psalm XXXVI, 6.
[16] Isaias LVIII, 10.
[17] I Corinthians XIII, 12.

drawn hither and thither by her affections she might become attached to one of these more than to the other, and thus in either deviate from the divine will even in a slight degree. And perhaps it was something like this, that Holy Job was experiencing when he said: *If I lie down to sleep, I shall say: When shall I arise? and again I shall look for the evening.*[18] That is: "When I am enjoying prayerful quiet I accuse myself of neglecting my work. And when I am exteriorly occupied I accuse myself of disturbing my prayerful quiet." (*Ibid.* §9.)

Every soul among us who is watchful as the bride, like her will be greeted as *love,* consoled as *dove,* and embraced as *beautiful.*[19] Every man will be reputed as perfect, in whose soul these three things are found to be present, existing in harmony and with all propriety, so that he knows how to weep for himself and rejoice in God, and at the same time is able to do good to his neighbor—a man pleasing to God, circumspect in his own regard, helpful to others. (*Ibid.* §11.)

[18] Job VII, 4.

[19] Canticle II, 10.

CHAPTER XXXVIII

THE BRIDE INSPIRED TO LEAVE CONTEMPLATION FOR EXTERNAL ACTS OF CHARITY IS ACCOMPANIED BY THE BRIDEGROOM. THE NECESSITY OF SELF-EXAMINATION AND SELF-IMPROVEMENT

ALMOST AT THE same moment the Bridegroom forbids that the bride be awakened, and then awakens her Himself. *Arise,* He says, *and come.*[1] . . . As is His wont, the Bridegroom when He perceives that His beloved has rested for a little while upon His bosom, does not hesitate to lead her forth anew to those things which seem more practicable—not, however, as if she were unwilling. For He Himself would not do what He has forbidden to be done.[2] But for the bride to be drawn away by the Bridegroom, is for her to receive a desire from Him by Whom she is drawn—a desire of good works, a desire to bring forth fruit unto the Bridegroom. . . . (Sermon LVIII, §1.)

Arise . . . and come! . . . From this the bride understands that she is not so much sent as led, and that the Bridegroom will come with her wherever she goes. What can she consider difficult for herself, with such a companion? *Set me beside Thee,* it is written, *and let any man's hand fight against me.*[3] And again: *Though I should walk in the midst of the shadow of death, I will fear no evils, for Thou art with me.*[4] (*Ibid.* §2.)

[1] Canticle II, 10.
[2] Cf. Canticle II, 7.
[3] Job XVII, 3.
[4] Psalm XXII, 4.

Arise . . . and come. For winter is now past, the rain is over and gone.[5] . . . I trust that for us, too, the *winter is now past.* Do you know of what winter I speak? That fear which has no part in charity. Although it is for all *the beginning of wisdom,*[6] it brings no one to the consummation thereof, because charity as it grows in perfection drives out *fear*[7] as summer drives out winter. For the summer of the soul is charity. If it has already come —rather, because it has already come (as it is right for me to feel in your regard)—it must have dried up every drop of winter rain, that is, every anxious tear which the bitter remembrance of sin, and fear of judgment were wont to wring from you. . . . But summer also has its showers, sweet and fruitful. . . . What is sweeter than the tears of charity? For charity weeps from love, not from sorrow. It weeps from desire. It weeps *with them that weep.*[8] . . . (*Ibid.* §11.)

Therefore if the *winter is now past,* and *the rain is over and gone,* if at last, *the flowers have appeared in our land,* and presently the vernal mildness of spiritual grace, as it were, proclaims *the time of pruning,*[9] what is left us to do, except hereafter to devote ourselves whole-heartedly to this work so holy, so necessary? *Let us,* as the Prophet says, *search our ways,*[10] and our attachments. And in doing so let each one judge that he has made progress, not when he finds nothing to correct but when he corrects what he finds. Then only you have not examined yourself in vain, if you have noticed that another examination is necessary. And as often as your investigation has not withheld anything from you, you will be of the opinion that it should be re-

[5] Canticle II, 10-11.
[6] Psalm CX, 10.
[7] Cf. 1 St. John IV, 18.
[8] Romans XII, 15.
[9] Canticle II, 11-12.
[10] Lamentations III, 40.

peated. But if you do this whenever it is necessary, you will always be doing it. Always, therefore, remember the need you have of help from on high, and of the mercy of the Bridegroom of the Church, Jesus Christ Our Lord Who is, above all, God forever blessed. (*Ibid.* §12.)

CHAPTER XXXIX

THE BRIDEGROOM OF OUR SOUL SHARES OUR NATURE AND OUR NATIVE LAND

The voice of the turtle is heard in our land.[1] . . . It is the Bridegroom who speaks. . . . He says, *in* OUR *land*. . . . Think how sweet it is that the God of Heaven says, *in* OUR *land. You that are earth-born and you sons of men,*[2] listen! *The Lord hath done great things for us.*[3] Great are His dealings with the earth, great His dealings with the bride whom He was pleased to take from the earth. *In* OUR *land,* He says. That is not the language of sovereignty, but of equality and friendship. He speaks here as Bridegroom, not as Lord. What? He is the Creator and He makes Himself as one of us! Love speaks and love knows nothing of a lord and master. . . . (Sermon LIX, §1.)

God Himself is made as one of us! I have fallen short of the truth. He is not made *as* one of us, but literally, *one* of us. It is not enough for Him to be on terms of equality with men. He is a Man! He lays claim to our earth as His own, but as His native land, not as a possession. Why should He not make such a claim? From hence He took His bride; from hence the substance of His Body; it is from hence that He Himself became the Bridegroom; from hence [He and His bride] are *two in one flesh.*[4] If one flesh, why not one country? (*Ibid.* §2.)

[1] Canticle II, 12.
[2] Psalm XLVIII, 3.
[3] Psalm CXXV, 3.
[4] St. Matthew XIX, 5.

CHAPTER XL

THE TEMPTATIONS OF BEGINNERS AND OF THOSE ADVANCED IN THE SPIRITUAL LIFE

Catch us the little foxes that destroy the vines.[1] . . . These vines are nothing else than spiritual men whose every interior faculty has been cultivated, putting forth leaves and blossoms, bearing fruit and bringing forth the spirit of salvation . . . (Sermon LXIII, §5.)

The foxes are temptations. It is necessary that temptations come. For who will be crowned, *except he strive lawfully?*[2] Or how will they strive if there be no one with whom to fight? Therefore, *when thou comest to the service of God, stand in justice and in fear and prepare thy soul for temptation,*[3] certain that, *all that will live godly in Christ Jesus, shall suffer persecution.*[4] Now temptations are different according to the difference of the time when they occur. In the beginning, like the tender blossoms of young plants that have just been set out, intense cold attacks us in the open. . . . But contrary forces never dare openly to oppose themselves to those who are making progress in sacred pursuits. But they are accustomed to lie in wait for them in hiding like crafty little foxes, as it were,—in outward appearance virtues, but in reality vices. How many, for example, having en-

[1] Canticle II, 15.
[2] 2 Timothy II, 5.
[3] Ecclesiasticus II, 1.
[4] 2 Timothy III, 12.

tered upon *the ways of life,*[5] and having advanced towards the better things, going on well and securely, making progress along *the paths of justice,*[6] how many such have I known in my personal experience—oh, the pity of it!—shamefully worsted by the deceit of these little foxes and too late lamenting aloud the fruits of virtue blighted in them. (Sermon LXIV, §1.)

[5] Acts II, 28.

[6] Psalm XXII, 3.

CHAPTER XLI

THE MYSTICAL EXHALATIONS OF GRACE. THE SPECIAL ATTENTION WHICH THE BRIDEGROOM GIVES THE BRIDE, AND SHE TO HIM

My Beloved to me and I to Him.[1] . . . These words of the bride are as sweet unto grace as they are rich in meanings and deep in mysteries. (Sermon LXVII, §1.) . . . It is her affection that has spoken, not her intelligence . . . (*Ibid.* §3.) It is an exhalation of love. . . . The bride is a good vase of my Lord and sweet is the perfume that arises from her. (*Ibid.* §4.)

What can be more fragrant than the exhalations of Saint John who smells sweet unto me of the eternity, the generation and the divinity of the Word? What shall I say of the exhalations of Saint Paul that have filled the earth with such intense sweetness? In truth he was *the good odor of Christ, . . . in every place.*[2] Surely the words he heard were unspeakable. Although he does not utter them so that I can hear them, he does, however, present them to me as the object of my desires, and so that I am allowed to enjoy the fragrance of what I am not permitted to hear. I do not know why it is that the more secret things are, the more pleasing they are, and we sigh the more eagerly after things denied us . . . (*Ibid.* §7.)

My Beloved to me and I to Him. One thing is certain—in this passage there burns the flame of mutual love. But in the love of

[1] Canticle II, 16. [2] 2 Corinthians II, 14, 15.

one there is supreme felicity; in the other's, marvellous condescension. For this common accord and union is not between equals. But what it is that the bride glories in having been bestowed upon her in virtue of this prerogative of love, and which she, in turn, has reciprocated, who will presume that he has clearly understood, unless he be one who because of singular purity of mind and holiness of body has merited to experience something of this sort in himself? It is a matter of the affections. It is not attained by reasoning, but by conformity of will. How few there are who can say: *But we all beholding the glory of the Lord with open face, are transformed into the same image from glory to glory, as by the spirit of the Lord.*[3] (*Ibid.* §8.)

But in order that what is read in our text may be reduced to a form that the human intelligence can more easily grasp, I shall leave to the bride her unique secret the knowledge of which, for the time being, is not given us to attain, especially while we are so imperfect. As a consequence we must apply to ourselves a meaning better adapted to ordinary powers because it is more familiar—a meaning which will at the same time give an interpretation to the words of our text, and *understanding to little ones.*[4] (*Ibid.* §9.)

She who is truly the bride, confesses that she has received a two-fold grace—that which is first and by which she is prevented, and that which comes afterwards and completes. And so she says now: *My Beloved to me and I to Him,* attributing the beginning of the work of grace to the Beloved. Subsequently she adds: *I to my Beloved, and my Beloved to me,*[5] equally attributing to Him the completion of the work. (*Ibid.* §12.)

[3] 2 Corinthians III, 18.
[4] Psalm CXVIII, 130.
[5] Canticle VI, 2.

It seems to me, then, that it is sufficient for us if in saying, *My Beloved to me,* we understand the bride to say: "He has given His special attention to me." Then the meaning will be: "My Beloved gives His special attention to me, and I to Him." (*Ibid.* §9.)

Is it then true that He who is Majesty itself, with Whom rests the government and administration of the universe, and the care of all the things of time, turns His attention alone to the occupations of the bride, and even to the repose and desires of her love? Yes, clearly. For she is the Church of the elect of whom the Apostle says: *all things for the sake of the elect.*[6] (Sermon LXVIII, §2.) Does not the end of all things depend upon the state and consummation of the Church? Take this away, and in vain does *a creature* of the lower order wait for *the revelation of the sons of God.*[7] Take this away and neither the Patriarchs nor any of the Prophets will be made perfect. For Saint Paul says that God has so provided for us, *that they should not be perfected without us.*[8] Take this away and the very glory of the holy Angels will be incomplete for lack of numbers and the very City of God will not glory in the integrity of all its parts. (*Ibid.* §4.)

Do you think that Our God will have the complete praise due His glory, before they come who, *in the sight of the Angels,*[9] will sing to Him: *We have rejoiced for the days in which Thou hast humbled us: for the years in which we have seen evils?*[10] This kind of rejoicing the heavens have not known except through the children of the Church. No one who is never without joy, can ever rejoice with such joy as this. Grateful is joy that comes after

[6] 2 Timothy II, 10.
[7] Romans VIII, 19.
[8] Hebrews XI, 40.
[9] Psalm CXXXVII, 1.
[10] Psalm LXXXIX, 15.

sadness; rest, after labor; the harbor, after shipwreck. A sense of security is gratifying to all, but especially to him who has known fear. . . . To have passed from death to life, doubles the joy of life. This is my portion at the celestial banquet, a portion unshared by the very Angels themselves. I make bold to say that the very happiness of the Angels has no share in my peculiar beatitude, unless they be pleased to confess that through their charity they share my beatitude in me and through me. . . . In fine, the Angels rejoice at the repentance of a sinner.[11] But if my tears of repentance are the delight of Angels, what will my delight be to them? Every action of theirs is to praise God. But there is something lacking to that praise if there is no one who can say: *We have passed through fire and water, and Thou hast brought us out into refreshment.*[12] (*Ibid.* §5.)

There is no reason why you should now ask on what merits we place our hope for good things, especially when you hear through the Prophet: *It is not for your sake that I will do this, . . . but for My Holy Name's sake.*[13] In order to merit, it is enough to know that our merits do not suffice for us. But as for merit, it is enough not to presume upon our merits. So, to be lacking in merits is enough for our condemnation. . . . The want of merits is poverty that is ruinous. But false riches in them, is presumption of spirit. And hence the Wise Man says: *Give me neither beggary, nor riches.*[14] (*Ibid.* §6.)

[11] Cf. St. Luke XV, 10.
[12] Psalm LXV, 12.
[13] Ezechiel XXXVI, 22.
[14] Proverbs XXX, 8.

CHAPTER XLII

EVERYTHING OPPOSED TO THE KNOWLEDGE AND SERVICE OF GOD MUST BE REJECTED. THE ZEAL THAT SPRINGS FROM JUSTICE. THE ZEAL THAT SPRINGS FROM CHARITY. THE CLOSE RELATIONSHIP OF LOVE THAT EXISTS BETWEEN GOD AND A FAITHFUL SOUL

My Beloved to me and I to Him.[1] The preceding discourse attributed this utterance to the universal Church on account of the promises made her by God, promises of that life of hers which now is and will endure hereafter. But the question is raised of applying to the individual soul these words addressed to the universal Church. . . . Now, it is important to know to what sort of a soul they may be applied. For they may not be applied indiscriminately to everyone. The Church of God has her spiritual children, to be sure, who not only live faithfully in her fold, but who *deal confidently in* her *regard,*[2] speaking with God as with a friend, as it were, their conscience bearing witness, assuring them that they are seeking His glory. Who these are, is known only to God. But listen to what you must be if you wish to be such a one. What I say, however, I say not as one who knows from experience, but as one desiring to have this experience. Give me a soul who loves nothing but God and what should be loved on account of God, a soul to whom *to live* not only IS *Christ,*[3] but

[1] Canticle II, 16.
[2] Psalm XI, 6.
[3] Philippians I, 21.

has long been so, the object of whose activity and rest is to *set the Lord always in* his *sight,*[4] whose chief will, rather whose one will is to walk with the Lord his God and who does not lack the grace to do so. Give me, I say, such a soul as this and I, for one, do not deny that he is worthy the Bridegroom's care and special attention. . . . And if such a soul should *have a mind to glory,* he *will not be foolish,*[5] so long as he is mindful that *he that glorieth,* must *glory in the Lord.*[6] (Sermon LXIX, §1.)

The reasons enumerated above give confidence to the great multitude of the faithful. But there are two considerations that make a holy soul confident. First, that the divinity of the Bridegroom because of the absolute simplicity of His Nature has it in His power to regard, as it were, one as many, and many as one. Nor will He become many in proportion to the multitude He regards, nor few in proportion to the small number. He is neither divided to meet the demands of diversity, nor restricted by singularity. He is not troubled by cares, nor disturbed or agitated by anxiety. Thus, to be sure, He is especially attentive to one in such a way that he is not wholly occupied with him. And He gives His attention to many in such a way that He is not overburdened.

The second motive of confidence for a holy soul is the sweetest of all to prove by experience, as it is the rarest to have known in this wise. So great is the condescension of the Word, so great is the benevolence of the Father toward a soul that is well affected and well ordered—which is indeed the gift of the Father and the work of the Son—that after preventing and preparing the soul

[4] Psalm XV, 8.
[5] 2 Corinthians XII, 6.
[6] *Ibid.* X, 17.

with Their special blessing, They deign to honor her with Their presence and in such a way that not only do They *come* to her but They *make* Their *abode* with her.[7] For it is not enough that They be made manifest, unless They give the soul of Their abundance. What is it for the Word to come to the soul? To instruct her in wisdom. What is it for the Father to come? To affect her unto a love of wisdom so that she can say: *I became a lover of her beauty.*[8] (*Ibid.* §2.)

If ever I have felt that the Lord has *opened* my *understanding that* I *might understand the scriptures,*[9] or if I feel words of wisdom flowing forth, as it were, from the bottom of my heart, or if I am conscious of having received an infusion of heavenly light so that mysteries are made manifest, or at least if the ample bosom of heaven, as it were, seems to open to me and to pour down upon my soul more fruitful showers of meditation, I have no doubt that the Bridegroom is present. For these, surely, are the riches of the Word, and of His fulness we receive them. But if a certain humble but plentiful diffusion of deep devotion is likewise infused into my soul, so that the love of revealed truth begets in me an irresistible hatred and loathing of vanity, lest perchance either knowledge should puff me up or the frequency of [Divine] visitations exalt me—then I feel straightway that I am being treated with fatherly affection, and doubt not that the Father is with me. But if I shall have persevered always, as far as I am able, to respond to this [Divine] condescension with affections and deeds worthy of it, then the grace of God within me shall not have been *void,*[10] and the Father who nourishes, as well

[7] Cf. John XIV, 23.
[8] Wisdom VIII, 2.
[9] St. Luke XXIV, 45.
[10] Cf. 1 Corinthians XV, 10.

as the Son who teaches will make His abode with me. (*Ibid.* §6.)

It cannot be, in my opinion, that such a soul will fear to say, *My Beloved to me.* Inasmuch as she is conscious that she loves and loves ardently, she has no doubt that she is loved no less ardently in return. And from the singular attention, anxiety, care, labor, diligence and zeal with which she is ever eagerly on the alert to know *how* she *may please God,*[11] she recognizes all these characteristics without question in God Himself, recalling His promise: *With what measure you mete, it shall be measured to you again.*[12] But the bride in her prudence is rather cautious to claim as her own part, what is nothing else than the giving back of what was bestowed upon her by grace, knowing rather, that she has been prevented by the Bridegroom. Hence it is that she puts His work first, saying: *My Beloved to me and I to Him.* Hence, from the nature of her own characteristics she comes to a knowledge of God, and she who loves has no doubt that she is loved in return. . . . For I know not by what affinity of nature, when once the soul is enabled to behold *the glory of the Lord with open face,*[13] presently she is of necessity conformed to Him and *transformed into the same image.*[14] Hence, as you present yourself to God, such will God manifest Himself to you. *With the holy* He will be *holy: and with the innocent man* He will be *innocent.*[15] Why will He not, in the same way, be loving with him who loves, at rest with him who rests, attentive with him who is alert, and watchful with him who watches? (*Ibid.* §7.)

I love them that love Me, He says, *and they that in the morning early watch for Me, shall find Me.*[16] . . . Are you keeping

[11] 1 Corinthians VII, 32.
[12] St. Matthew VII, 2.
[13] 2 Corinthians III, 18.
[14] *Ibid.*
[15] Psalm XVII, 26.
[16] Proverbs VIII, 17.

watch? Arise at night at the very beginning of your vigils, hasten as you will to *prevent the watches,*[17] you will find Him there, you will not arrive before Him. It is rash of you in such a matter to attribute to yourself precedence in time or superiority in degree. He loves you more than you love Him, and He loved you before you loved Him. . . . I shall speak one last word to the more spiritual-minded among you, a word of wonder, but true—the soul that sees God sees Him in no other wise than as if she alone were seen by Him. . . . You are good, O Lord, to the soul that is seeking You! You run to meet her. You embrace her. You show yourself a Bridegroom—You Who are her Lord, yes, Who are over all things God blessed forever. (*Ibid.* §8.)

[17] Psalm LXXVI, 5.

CHAPTER XLIII

TRUTH, MEEKNESS AND JUSTICE ARE THE LILIES AMONG WHICH THE BELOVED FEEDS

My Beloved to me, and I to Him who feedeth among the lilies.[1] . . . He Who is Shepherd emptied Himself even to the extent of feeding like one of His sheep. He was found among the lilies and seen by the Church. Poor, He was loved by one destitute of all things [His spouse, the Church], and He became her Beloved because He was like her in poverty. Not for this reason only, but *because of truth and meekness and justice*[2]—because through Him promises were fulfilled, because sins were forgiven, because the demons of pride together with their chief were judged and condemned. Such, then, did He appear Who is so worthy of love—true in Himself, meek to men, just for men's sake. O truly to be loved, and Bridegroom to be embraced with every fibre of the heart! (Sermon LXX, § 4.)

Truth is an exquisite lily, resplendent in brightness, distinguished by its odor. For its brightness is *the brightness of eternal light,* the splendor and *image* of the Substance of God.[3] (*Ibid.* §5.) Truth, then, is a lily. And so is meekness. It has the brightness of innocence and the sweet odor of hope. . . . That justice is a lily, you recall from Scripture, because the just *shall spring forth as the lily and flourish forever before the Lord.*[4] . . . The

[1] Canticle II, 16.
[2] Psalm XLIV, 5.
[3] Cf. Wisdom VII, 26.
[4] Osee XIV, 6.

brightness of this lily, then, is found among the just. But its fragrance is diffused even among the wicked, but not for their good. For we have heard the just ones saying: *We are the good odor of Christ unto God in them that are saved, and in them that perish. To the one indeed the odor of death unto death: but to the others the odor of life unto life.*[5] (*Ibid.* §6.)

But I have erred in speaking of one lily. . . . One is not enough. Two at least are necessary. I refer to continence and innocence, one of which without the other will not avail for our salvation. . . . Absolutely speaking, these two can suffice. But because they may be found lacking in the midst of temptations —and, indeed: *The life of man upon earth is a warfare*[6]—there is great need of patience which is, as it were, protector and guardian of the other two. I think that if He who is the Lover of lilies comes and finds us thus, He will not disdain to feed among us and to eat the Pasch with us. (*Ibid.* §9.)

[5] 2 Corinthians II, 15-16. [6] Job VII, 1.

CHAPTER XLIV

THE NATURE AND MANNER OF THE BRIDEGROOM'S VISITATION OF A HOLY SOUL. SAINT BERNARD'S PERSONAL EXPERIENCE IN THIS MATTER, MODESTLY STATED FOR THE EDIFICATION OF HIS HEARERS

Return, . . . my Beloved![1] It is evident that He Who is called back, is not present, but that He was present and that, not so long before. For He seems to be called back, while He is still going away. . . . *Return,* entreats the bride. Very well! He was going away. He is called back. Who will reveal to me the secret meaning of this changeableness? Who will give me a fitting explanation of the going away and the coming back of the Word? (Sermon LXXIV, §1.)

When the soul is sensibly aware of grace, she recognises the presence of the Word. When she is not thus sensibly aware of it, she complains of His absence and begs Him to return again, saying with the Prophet: *My face hath sought Thee: Thy face, O Lord, will I still seek.*[2] . . . Thus, then, is the Word called back and He is called back by the soul's longing for Him when He is absent—but it is the soul of one upon whom He has once bestowed the favor of His sweetness. (*Ibid.* §2.)

And now give me a soul whom the Bridegroom-Word is accustomed to visit often, one whom intimate friendship has made

[1] Canticle II, 17. [2] Psalm XXVI, 8.

bold, one whom a taste has made hungry, and to whom a contempt of all things has brought peace—and I unhesitatingly attribute to this soul the voice as well as the name of bride, nor would I consider the passage we are now considering, inapplicable to her. Such indeed is the soul that is here introduced as speaking. For she proves beyond a doubt that she has already merited the company of Him whom she calls back, although not to the complete satisfaction of her desire. Otherwise she would not have called Him back, but would simply have called Him. . . . He comes and goes according to His good pleasure, as if visiting the soul *early in the morning* and *proving* her *suddenly*.[3] His going away is in some way or other entirely under His control. His return is a matter of His free will. And both are entirely a matter of His judgment. The reason for them is known only to Himself. (*Ibid.* §3.)

Now it is quite evident that in the soul such changes as this are the result of the going away and of the coming back of the Word, according as it is said: *I go away and I come unto you.*[4] Again: *A little while and you shall not see me; and again a little while and you shall see me.*[5] O little while and little while! O how long that little while is! Dear Lord, you call it *a little while* that we shall not see You! . . . It is a little while measured by our deserts; and a long while, measured by our desires. . . . Now the soul that loves is borne along by her desires, drawn on by her longing for Him who is absent. She makes little of her merits, closes her eyes to Majesty, opens them to the delights of love, setting Him *in safety,* and *dealing confidently in His regard.*[6] Fearless and unashamed she calls the Word back, and

[3] Job VII, 18.
[4] St. John XIV, 28.
[5] *Ibid.* XVI, 17.
[6] Psalm XI, 6.

with confidence begs the return of her former delights, calling Him, with her accustomed freedom, not *Lord,* but *Beloved. Return,* she entreats, *my Beloved.* (*Ibid.* §4.)

You ask how I can know that the Bridegroom is present since *His ways are unsearchable.*[7] *The Word of God is living and effectual.*[8] As soon as He has entered in, He has awakened my slumbering soul. He has stimulated and softened and wounded my heart which before was sick and hard as a rock. He has begun to *root up* and *pull down,* to *build* and to *plant,*[9] to water the dry places and to illuminate the dark ones, to open what was closed and to fill with warmth what was cold, to make the crooked straight and the *rough ways plain,*[10] so that *my soul* might *bless the Lord* and *all that is within me* might *bless His Holy Name.*[11] (*Ibid.* §6.)

The Bridegroom comes to the soul, *full of grace and truth.*[12] (*Ibid.* §7.) Both of these are necessary for me. . . . The visitation will not be complete if there is one without the other, since the severity of truth without grace may seem a sheer burden, and the joyousness of grace without truth may appear uncontrolled. Bitter is truth without the seasoning of grace, just as, without the bridle of truth even devotion itself may be unbalanced and know no restraint, and often may even grow insolent. For how many has it been no advantage to have received grace, because they have not at the same time received a proper measure of truth? As a consequence they have given themselves over to the enjoyment of grace more than they should, while they have felt no fear in contemplating [the warnings of] truth. . . . Hence it has hap-

[7] Romans XI, 33.
[8] Hebrews IV, 12.
[9] Jeremias I, 10.
[10] St. Luke III, 5.
[11] Psalm CII, 1.
[12] St. John I, 14.

pened that they were deprived of the grace which they had wished to enjoy by themselves. To such as these it could be said, even though too late: "Go, now, and learn what this means, *Serve ye the Lord with fear: and rejoice unto Him in trembling.*" [13] (*Ibid.* §8.)

Since this is so, neither gift suffices without the other. What I have said falls short of the truth. Neither is of any advantage without the other. How do we know this? *To him who knoweth to do good, and doth it not, to him it is sin.*[14] Again: *And that servant who knew the will of his Lord . . . and did not according to His will, shall be beaten with many stripes.*[15] But that pertains to the influence of truth without grace. What about the influence of grace without truth? It is written: *And after the morsel, Satan entered into him.*[16] It refers to Judas who after having received the gift of grace, because he did not walk in truth with the Master of truth, gave the devil a place in his soul. Listen again: *He fed them with the fat of wheat, and filled them with honey out of the rock.*[17] Whom did He feed? They were: *The enemies of the Lord* who *have lied to Him.*[18] Those whom He fed with honey and the fat of wheat, lied to Him and became His enemies, because they did not join truth to grace. Concerning them you have in another place: *The children that are strangers have lied to Me, strange children have faded away and have halted from their paths.*[19] Why would they not halt, content as they were with the one foot of grace and not putting down the other foot of truth? They are like their chief who himself *stood not in*

[13] Psalm II, 11.
[14] St. James IV, 17.
[15] St. Luke XII, 47.
[16] St. John XIII, 27.
[17] Psalm LXXX, 17.
[18] *Ibid.* 16.
[19] Psalm XVII, 46.

the truth, but was *a liar* from the beginning,[20] and hence heard: *Thou hast lost thy wisdom in thy beauty.*[21] (*Ibid.* §9.)

Do you ask what is that beauty so harmful and so dangerous? Yours. Still, perhaps, you do not understand? Listen to a more explicit answer. Your personal beauty—that which is your very own. We do not blame the gift, but the use made of it. Then, if you have noticed, it was not in beauty, but in *his own* beauty that the devil was said to have lost wisdom. And, unless I am mistaken, the one beauty of an angel and of a soul is wisdom. For without wisdom what is one or the other but a substance unformed and shapeless? . . . But Satan lost it when he made it his own. . . . Because he was wise in his own eyes, because he did not give glory to God, because he did not render grace for grace, because he walked not in wisdom according to truth, but twisted it according to his own will, that is why he lost it. Rather, that is in itself the loss of it. For to possess it thus, is to lose it. (*Ibid.* §10.)

But surely the foolish virgins, whom I consider foolish in no other wise than because, calling themselves wise they became foolish, these, I say, are doomed to hear from God: *I know you not.*[22] And likewise they who have used the grace of miracles for their own glory, will, despite this grace, be destined to hear: *I never knew you.*[23]

Grace and truth came by Jesus Christ, says Saint John Baptist.[24] If, therefore, the Lord Jesus Christ (for He is the Word of God, Bridegroom of the soul) ever knocks at my door bringing either one of these without the other, He will enter not as a

[20] Cf. St. John VIII, 44.
[21] Ezechiel XXVIII, 17.
[22] St. Matthew XXV, 12.
[23] *Ibid.* VII, 23.
[24] St. John I, 17.

Bridegroom, but as a Judge. God grant that this may never come to pass. May He *enter not into judgment with* His *servant.*[25] May He enter with peace. May He enter with delight and cheer. Still, may He enter with dignity and gravity, He who turns towards me the rather stern countenance of truth, as it were, while He curbs my boldness and chastens my joy. (*Ibid.* §11.)

[25] Psalm CXLII, 2.

CHAPTER XLV

THE TIME, THE PLACE, AND THE MANNER IN WHICH THE BRIDEGROOM SHOULD BE SOUGHT

In my bed by night I sought Him Whom my soul loveth.[1] The Bridegroom has not returned at the voice and desire of her who called Him back. Why? That her longing may increase, that her affection may be proved, that she may be initiated into the ways of love. The delay, then, is clearly a dissembling, not displeasure. But the result is that He must be sought, if indeed one seeking Him may find Him—He who when called has not come. For the Lord Himself says: *He that seeketh, findeth.*[2] . . . First she seeks Him *in bed,* but she fails to find Him. Then she *rises,* she goes *about the city,* she seeks Him up and down *the streets and the broad ways,*[3] and she does not meet Him, nor does she see Him. (Sermon LXXV, §1.)

But what does it mean, the fact that He who is the Bridegroom is not found when He has been sought, when a search is made for Him with such eagerness and diligence, now *in bed,* and now *about the city* and even *in the streets and the broad ways.* For He Himself says: *Seek and you shall find,* and *He that seeketh, findeth.*[4] (*Ibid.* §3.)

In vain throughout the nights of untruth [*v.g.* in heresy and

[1] Canticle III, 1.
[2] St. Matthew VII, 8.
[3] Canticle III, 2.
[4] St. Matthew VII, 7, 8.

schism] do you seek the Sun of Justice and the Light of Truth, that is, the Bridegroom, because there is no *fellowship* of *light with darkness.*[5] But someone says that the bride is not so foolish and so blind that she seeks light in darkness, that she seeks the Bridegroom among those who are ignorant and who do not love Him. As if, in truth, the bride were saying that she is now seeking Him by night, and not rather that she has been seeking Him. She does not say, "I am seeking," but, *I sought Him Whom my soul loveth.* And the sense is that when she *was a child,* she *understood as a child,* she *thought as a child,*[6] and she sought truth where it was not—wandering about and not finding it, according to what is written in the Psalm: *I have gone astray like a sheep that is lost.*[7] (*Ibid.* §10.)

[5] 2 Corinthians VI, 14.
[6] 1 Corinthians XIII, 11.
[7] Psalm CXVIII, 176.

CHAPTER XLVI

THE STRONG AND INDISSOLUBLE LOVE WITH WHICH THE SOUL CLINGS TO THE LORD, AND THE LORD, IN TURN, CLINGS TO THE SOUL

Have you seen Him Whom my soul loveth?[1] O love precipitate, passionate, impetuous, who suffer yourself to think of nothing but yourself, who loathe all else, who despise everything except yourself, content with yourself alone! You throw order into confusion, you disregard custom, you know no restraint. Everything that seems a matter of fitness, a matter of reason, a matter of propriety, a matter of prudence or judgment, you triumph over in your own name and bring into subjection. Thus everything that the bride thinks and everything that she says resounds of you, is redolent of you and of nothing else, so completely have you claimed as yours, both her heart and tongue. She says: *Have you seen Him Whom my soul loveth?* As if, in truth, they knew what she was thinking of. Do you seek information concerning Him Whom your soul loves? And He has no name? Who, then, are you, and who is He? I would speak in this wise on account of the singular nature of the discourse and the distinctive carelessness in the use of words, by which the passage of Scripture we are now considering, clearly appears unlike all others. Hence in this nuptial song it is not the words that must be pondered, but the affections. . . . Love speaks throughout it. And if any one of

[1] Canticle III, 3.

those who read it desires to attain to a knowledge of it, let him love. . . . For to him who does not love, the language of love will be a barbarous tongue. (Sermon LXXIX, §1.)

I found Him Whom my soul loveth: I held Him and I will not let Him go.[2] Nor, perhaps, does He desire any the less to be held. For He has declared: *My delights* are *to be with the children of men.*[3] And He promises to be with us, when he says: *Behold I am with you all days, even to the consummation of the world.*[4] What can be more powerful than this bond, strengthened by one and the same determined will in the two parties to it. *I held Him,* she says. But nevertheless she herself is, in turn, held by Him whom she holds. Elsewhere she says to Him: *Thou hast held me by my right hand.*[5] . . . She holds Him by the firmness of faith. She holds Him by the affection of devotion. But she could by no means hold Him long, if she were not held by Him. And she is held by the power and mercy of the Lord. (*Ibid.* §5.)

[2] Canticle III, 4.
[3] Proverbs VIII, 31.
[4] St. Matthew XXVIII, 20.
[5] Psalm LXXII, 24.

CHAPTER XLVII

THE SOUL, HOWEVER CORRUPT, CAN STILL, THROUGH CHASTE AND HOLY LOVE RECOVER ITS LIKENESS TO THE BRIDEGROOM, WHO IS CHRIST. A DESCRIPTION OF THAT LIKENESS AND OF THE SPIRITUAL MARRIAGE OF THE SOUL AND CHRIST

In my bed by night I sought Him Whom my soul loveth: I sought Him and found Him not.

I will rise, and will go about the city: in the streets and the broad ways I will seek Him Whom my soul loveth: I sought Him and I found Him not.

The watchmen who keep the city, found me: Have you seen Him Whom my soul loveth?

When I had a little passed by them, I found Him Whom my soul loveth: I held Him: and I will not let Him go, till I bring Him into my mother's house, and into the chamber of her that bore me.[1]

We have learned that every soul, although weighed down with sins, caught in the meshes of imperfections, held captive in exile, imprisoned in the flesh, sunk in mire, held fast in mud, fastened to the body, rendered helpless by anxieties, distressed by business considerations, grown suspicious because of fear, broken by sorrow, wandering about in the midst of errors, worried by cares, grown restless because of suspicions, and finally a stranger in the

[1] Canticle III, 1-4.

land of enemies, and according to the word of the Prophet, *defiled with the dead, . . . counted with them that go down into hell*[2]—although, I say, thus condemned and thus despairing, we have learned that nevertheless this soul can discover within herself not only the source whence she can breathe again in the hope of forgiveness, in the hope of mercy, but the source, as well, whence she may dare to aspire to the nuptials of the Word, not fearing to enter into an alliance of friendship with God Himself, nor afraid to draw the sweet yoke of love with Him Who is King of Angels. For what is there that she may not safely dare in the presence of Him Whose image, she discerns, gives her her distinction, and a likeness to Whom, she knows, makes her noble. What terror, I say, has Majesty for her to whom confidence is given by virtue of her very origin? It is necessary only that she take care to preserve by an upright life the purity of the nature given her at birth. Rather, let her strive to increase that heavenly beauty which is her birthright, and to adorn it with such shades of character and affection as it deserves. (Sermon LXXXIII, §1.)

What, then, is the reason why she is so sluggish in action? Activity is assuredly a great gift of nature in us. And if it fails to perform its functions, will not the rest of our nature be completely thrown into disorder, and be entirely covered over with rust of long standing? This certainly would be an injustice to the Creator. And indeed the Creator, God Himself, wished to preserve perpetually in the soul the distinction of divine generosity, so that she might always have within herself those attributes received from the Word by which she would ever be reminded either to remain with the Word, or to return to Him if ever she should be removed from Him. She is not removed from Him in

[2] Baruch III, 11.

passing from one place to another, or in walking on her feet. But she is removed (as a spiritual substance can be removed) by her affections. Rather, by her defects she falls from her high estate, as it were, when she renders herself unlike her natural self by the depravity of her life and character, and becomes degenerate. This unlikeness, however, is not the destruction of nature, but it is a vice exalting the good of nature by contrast with itself. To the same degree it defiles that good by conjunction with it. Again, the return of the soul is her conversion to the Word, to be reformed through Him and to be made conformed to Him. In what respect? In charity. For it is said: *Be ye therefore followers of God, as most dear children. And walk in love, as Christ also hath loved us.*[3] (*Ibid.* §2.)

Such conformity joins the soul in marriage to the Word, when, being already like unto Him in nature, she shows herself no less like unto Him in will, loving as she is loved. If, then, she loves perfectly, she has become His bride. What is more delightful than this conformity? What is more to be desired than charity? From it, it follows that not content with human guidance, O soul, in your own person you confidently draw near to the Word, you cleave to the Word consistently, on terms of familiarity you ask questions of the Word and consult Him about every thing, your capacity of mind being measured only by the fearlessness of your desires. Truly spiritual and a contract of holy marriage is such a relationship as this. It is an under-statement to call it a contract. It is an embrace—an embrace, surely, where to will and not to will the same thing, makes one spirit out of two. Nor should there be any fear that the inequality of the parties should make an agreement of wills defective in any way, because love

[3] Ephesians V, 1-2.

knows no reverential fear. It is from loving, not from showing respect, that love takes its name. By all means, let him show honor who trembles and stands aghast with fear, who is filled with apprehension, who is struck with awe. But all these have no place in the case of one who loves. Love more than suffices for itself. Love, when it comes to a soul, converts everything else into itself and takes the affections captive. The soul, therefore, who loves, loves, and knows nothing else. He Himself Who is worthy of honor, Who is rightly the object of fear and of awe, nevertheless, loves still more, to be loved. They are Bridegroom and bride. What other relationship do you seek between a bride and bridegroom, except to be loved and to love. This union dissolves even what nature has fashioned rather firmly, the bond between parents and children. *For this cause,* it is said, *shall a man leave father and mother, and shall cleave to his wife.*[4] (*Ibid.* §3.)

Add to this, that this Bridegroom is not only loving, but He is Love. Is He not Honor? Let who will, maintain that He is. I, for one, have never read it. But I have read, *God is Charity.*[5] And I have not read that He is Honor or Dignity. Not that God does not desire honor—He who says: *If then I be a Father, where is My honor?*[6] That He says as a Father. But if He presents Himself as a Bridegroom, I think that He will change what He has said, and say: "If I am a Bridegroom where is my love?" For previously He has spoken thus: *If I be a Master, where is my fear?*[7] It is fitting, therefore, that God be feared as Lord, be honored as Father, and that as Bridegroom He be loved. What one of these is best? What one stands out? Love, surely. With-

[4] St. Matthew XIX, 5.
[5] 1 St. John IV, 16.
[6] Malachias I, 6.
[7] *Ibid.*

out this, both *fear hath pain,*[8] and honor has no charm. Fear is servile so long as it is not emancipated by love. And honor which does not spring from love, is not honor but flattery. And indeed it is to God alone that honor and glory are due, but neither of these will God accept, unless they have been sweetened with the honey of love. Love is sufficient of itself. Of itself it pleases and for its own sake. It is itself its own merit and its own reward. It seeks no motive, no fruit beyond itself. It is its own fruit, its own enjoyment. I love because I love. I love in order that I may love. Love is a great thing if only it returns to its First Principle, if it has been restored to its Source, if having flowed back to its Fountain-head, it draws from thence the power to flow on forever. Out of all the motions of the soul those of the senses as well as those of the affections, it is love alone in which the creature can make a return to the Creator, although not on equal terms. For example, if God were angry with me, could I, in like manner, grow angry with Him in return? Certainly not. But I shall tremble and shake with fear, and pray forgiveness. Likewise if He rebukes me I shall not rebuke Him in return, but I shall justify Him. And if He condemns me I shall not condemn Him, but I shall adore Him. . . . If He exercises His power as my Lord and Master, I must act as His servant. If He commands, I must obey. . . . And now you must see how different it is in the case of love. For when God loves, He desires nothing else than to be loved. In fact, He loves for no other reason except that He may be loved, knowing that those who love Him have attained happiness by that very love itself. (*Ibid.* §4.)

Love is a great thing, but there are degrees in it. A bridegroom abides in the highest. For children also love, but they keep their

[8] 1 St. John IV, 18.

inheritance in mind. And while they are afraid that they may, in some way or other, lose it, they show him from whom they expect the inheritance, more respect than love. . . . The one inheritance and hope of a bride is love. In this the bride abounds. With this the bridegroom is content. He seeks nothing else. And she possesses nothing else. It is for this reason that he is a bridegroom and she is a bride. It is the prerogative of those who are wed, to which no one else can attain, not even a son. . . . But the love of the Bridegroom, rather, the Bridegroom who is Love, asks only a return of love, and fidelity. Let the bride, therefore, return love for love. (*Ibid.* §5.)

With good reason renouncing all other affections the bride gives herself wholly to love alone—she who in reciprocating love is constrained to make a return of love to Him who is love itself. For when she has poured out her whole being in love, what is this in comparison with the unceasing flow of the Fountain of Love? The waters of love do not flow with equal copiousness from the lover and from Him who is Love, from the bride and the Bridegroom, from the Creator and the creature. You might as well compare one who is thirsty and the fountain from which he drinks. What then? Will the hope of future nuptials cease on this account and become entirely void, together with the aspirations of one who sighs with longing, the ardor of one who loves, the trust of one who abounds in confidence, simply because she is unable to compete with a giant in a race, to rival honey in sweetness, a lamb in gentleness, a lily in radiant whiteness, the sun in brightness, and, in charity, Him Who is Charity itself? Assuredly not. For although a creature loves less because he is less, yet if he loves with his whole being, there can be nothing wanting. Hence, as I have said, to love thus is to have been joined in marriage with God, for it is impossible for the soul to love thus and to be imperfectly loved in return. And in the mutual consent of the two parties consists the integrity and perfection of marriage. But perhaps someone may doubt that the soul is first loved by the Word, and is more loved by Him. In very truth she is anticipated by Him in loving, and surpassed. Happy the soul who has deserved to be anticipated in the matter of a blessing so sweet. Happy the soul to whom it is given to experience an embrace of such intense delight. This is nothing else than love holy and chaste, love full of delight and sweet, love as untroubled as it is sincere, love that is mutual, intimate and strong, love which joins two together not in one flesh, but in one spirit, and makes these two no longer two, but one. As Saint Paul says: *He who is joined to the Lord, is one spirit.*[9] (*Ibid.* §6.)

[9] I Corinthians VI. 17.

NOTES ON THE BOOK ON THE LOVE OF GOD.

P. 4, l. 3. *The way (to love God) is to love Him beyond measure.* The original Latin reads: *modus (diligendi Deum est), sine modo diligere.* The exact meaning intended by St. Bernard is best preserved it would seem, by translating *modus,* in the first instance, as "way"; and in the second, as "manner", according to the double meaning of the word. St. Thomas Aquinas cites these words of St. Bernard in his treatment of the question, "whether in loving God we ought to observe any measure."

"The end of all human actions and affections is the love of God, whereby principally we attain to our last end. Wherefore the mode in the love of God, must not be taken as in a thing measured where we find too much or too little, but as in the measure itself where there cannot be excess and where the more the rule is attained the better it is, so that the more we love God the better our love is". (*Summa Theologica* II. ii, q. 27, art. 6.)

"An affection whose object is subject to reason's judgment should be measured by reason. But the object of the Divine love which is God surpasses the judgment of reason, wherefore it is not measured by reason but transcends it. Nor is there parity between the interior act and external acts of charity. For the interior act of charity has the character of an end, since man's ultimate good consists in his soul cleaving to God, according to *Psalm* LXXII, 28: *It is good for me to adhere to my God;* whereas the exterior acts are as means to the end and so have to be measured both according to charity and according to reason." (*Ibid.* ad 3.)

P. 7, l. 23. This same idea concerning *vain* glory is found in St. Thomas:

"That which we receive from God is not vain but true glory: it is this glory that is promised as a reward for good works, and of which it is written (2 *Corinthians* X, 17-18): *He that glorieth let him glory in the Lord, for not he who commendeth himself is approved, but he whom God commendeth.* It is true that some are heartened to do works of virtue through desire for human glory, as also through the desire for other earthly goods. Yet he is not truly virtuous who does virtuous deeds for the sake of human glory." (*Summa Theologica,* II. ii, q. 132, art. 1, ad 2.)

P. 8, ll. 1-3. In similar strain St. Thomas says:

"It is requisite for man's perfection that he should know himself; but not that he should be known by others, wherefore it is not to be desired in itself. It may, however, be desired as being useful for something, either in order that God may be glorified by men, or that men may become better by reason of the good they know to be in another man, or in order that man, knowing by the testimony of others' praise the good which is in him, may himself strive to persevere therein and to become better. In this sense it is praiseworthy that a man should *take care of his good name,* and that he should *provide good things in the sight of God and men:* but not that he should take an empty pleasure in human praise." (*Summa Theologica,* II, ii, q. 132, art. 1, ad 3.)

P. 8, ll. 8-11. "When it is said that *man lives,* it must be understood that man uses his reason, which is especially his life and the actuality of his noblest part. Therefore whoever parts from his reason and uses only his sensitive part lives not as man but as beast, as the most excellent Boethius affirms when he says that *he lives the life of an ass.* I speak unequivocally, because thought is the act peculiar to the reason; wherefore animals do not think for they have no reason. I do not mean merely the lower animals but those which have the appearance of a man with the spirit of a sheep or of some other loathsome beast." (Dante, *Convivio* II, viii.)

P. 12, ll. 10-11. Saint Bernard gives a different interpretation of this text in his "Sermons on the *Canticle of Canticles,*" Sermon LI, § 2:

"Let us now endeavor under the guidance of the Spirit of truth, to extract the mystical meaning which lies underneath the rind of the letter. If we suppose the speaker in this place to be the universal Church of the saints, the flowers and the fruits must be understood as representing ourselves, and not us only, but all others, equally, throughout the whole earth who have been converted from a worldly life. By the flowers are designated the young and tender virtues of those who are still in their spiritual beginnings, whilst the fruit is meant to symbolize the strength and maturity of the perfect. Stayed up, therefore, with such flowers and compassed about with such apples, holy mother Church, fruitful even in her exile, to whom *to live is Christ and to die is gain* (Philippians I, 21), supports doubtless with equanimity the bitterness of her banishment; because according to Holy Scripture, there is given her *of the fruit of her hands,* as of the first-fruits of the Spirit, and *her works praise her in the gates.* (Proverbs XXXI, 31.)

Another interpretation giving the moral sense, follows immediately and is one of the passages included in our translation. (Cf. chap. XXXIII.) Saint Bernard's justification of this exegetical method is given in the same sermon and is also included in our translation. It has more recently been recommended by Pope Leo XIII in his encyclical *Providentissimus Deus,* on the study of Holy Scripture:

"Let him (the interpreter of Holy Scripture) likewise beware of neglecting what has been applied by these same Fathers to an allegorical or similar meaning, especially when such a meaning flows from the literal sense and is supported by the authority of many. For the Church has received such a method of interpretation from the Apostles, and has approved of it by her own example, as is clear from the liturgy. It is not that the Fathers aimed at demonstrating the dogmas of faith directly thereby, but that they knew from experience that this method was very fruitful in fostering virtue and piety."

P. 15, l. 21. A different interpretation in the "Sermons on the *Canticle of Canticles*" reads:

"Since by *right* and *left* are wont to be designated prosperity and adversity, it seems to me that the Left Hand of the Word may be understood here as signifying His threatenings of chastisement, and His

Right as representing the promise of the kingdom. There are times, my brethren, when the servile fear of punishment weighs heavy upon the soul. While this is the case, the Left Hand of the Beloved should be described rather as over than as under her head; for so long as she is thus affected she certainly cannot say with truth, *His Left Hand is under my head.* But if she mounts higher and exchanges the spirit of servitude for the more worthy disposition which makes obedience spontaneous, so that she is now more drawn by the hope of heaven than driven by the terror of hell, or better still, makes the love of the good for its own sake the motive of her actions, then without doubt she will be able to say, *His Left Hand is under my head.* For she has now lifted her head above the slavish fear of chastisement, which is in the Left Hand, and has attained to a better and nobler disposition of mind. Nay, by the force of her worthy desires she is even drawing near to the Right Hand, which holds the promises, as the Psalmist says, speaking to the Lord, *At Thy Right Hand are delights even to the end.* (Psalm XV, 11.) Therefore she has conceived an assured hope which she expresses in the confident anticipation, *And His Right Hand shall embrace me.*" (Sermon LI, § 8.)

P. 20, l. 3. The exegesis of this text given in the "Sermons on the *Canticle of Canticles*" is this:

"*If you sleep among the midst of lots,* says holy David, *you shall be as the wings of a dove covered with silver.* (Psalm LXVII, 14.) By these words, as I think, he designs to teach us that the intervening space between fear and assurance is occupied by hope, wherein the mind or the conscience most sweetly reposes, reclining at ease on the soft couch of charity. And possibly there is another reference to this intermediate place in a subsequent verse of this Canticle of Canticles, where in the description of Solomon's litter we read, amongst other things, *The midst he covered with charity for the daughters of Jerusalem.* (III, 10.) For the soul which feels herself to be *singularly settled in hope,* can no longer serve in fear, but thenceforward reposes in charity. So the Spouse rests and slumbers, since it is said with regard to her, *I adjure you, O ye daughters of Jerusalem, by the roes and the harts of the fields, that you stir not up nor make the beloved to wake till she please.* (II, 7.) O marvellous and unspeakable condescension! That the Word of God should make the contemplative soul rest upon His own Bosom, and, not content with this, should deign to defend her against the incursions of care, to protect her from the disquiet of her natural activities, and from the weariness of worldly distractions, and should even take precautions to prevent her being awakened until she herself pleases!" (Sermon LI, § 10.)

P. 21, ll. 4-6. In St. Augustine we read: "I did not abide to enjoy my God; but I was caught up unto Thee by Thy beauty, and soon dragged from Thee by mine own weight, and sank down with sighing into these lower things. This weight was carnal custom; but with me was still the memory of Thee." ("Confessions" VII, xvii.)

P. 27, ll. 6-9. In Dante we read:

"For Good, so far as good, when comprehended
Doth straight enkindle love, and so much greater
As more of goodness in itself it holds;
Then to that Essence (whose is such advantage
That every good which out of it is found
Is nothing but a ray of its own light)
More than elsewhither must the mind be moved
Of every one, in loving, who discerns
The truth [1] in which this evidence [2] is founded."
(*Paradiso,* xxvi, 28-36.)

Similarly in Saint Thomas we find: "The cause of the increase of charity, *viz.* God, is possessed of infinite power. Furthermore, on the part of its subject, no limit to this increase can be determined, because whenever charity increases, there is a corresponding increased ability to receive a further increase. It is therefore evident that it is not possible to fix any limits to the increase of charity in this life." (*Summa Theologica,* II. ii, q. 24, art. 7.)

[1] *The truth,* that God is the Supreme *Good.*

[2] *this evidence,* that God is the supreme object of love.

P. 30, l. 20, *etc.* The best commentary upon this paragraph and the following, is Dante's. Speaking of riches he writes:

"These false traitresses ever promise that, if amassed in a certain quantity, they will fill him who amasses them full of every satisfaction; and by this promise they lead the will of man to the vice of avarice. And for this reason Boethius in his book *On Consolation* calls them dangerous, saying, 'Ah me! who was it that first dug up the masses of hidden gold and the stones that desired to be hid, precious dangers?' These false traitresses promise if any one rightly regards them, that they will take away all thirst and deficiency, and will bring satiety and sufficiency. And this they hold out to every man at the outset, guaranteeing the fulfilment of this promise when they have increased up to a certain measure; and after they are amassed to that extent, in place of satiety and refreshment, they produce and set up feverish and intolerable thirst within the breast; and instead of satisfying a man, they set before him a fresh goal, that is to say, a greater amount to be desired, and, coupled with this, fear and anxiety for what is already gained; so that in truth 'they cannot give rest, but bring more care', which before, in their absence, was not felt. . . . Let us turn our attention merely to the life of those who go in pursuit of them, and see how little anxious are the lives of men when they have amassed them, how satisfied, how restful they are! And what else daily endangers and kills cities, country-sides, and individuals so much as the fresh accumulation of wealth by any one man? Such an accumulation of wealth brings to light fresh desires which cannot be consummated without wrong to some one. And what else were the two branches of Law, I mean Canon and Civil Law, designed to remedy so much as that cupidity which grows by the amassing of riches? . . .

"The loftiest desire of each thing, and the earliest implanted by Nature, is the desire of returning to its first cause. And since God is the first cause of our souls, and has created them like unto Himself (as it is written, 'let us make man in our own image and likeness'), the soul desires most of all to return to Him. And just as a pilgrim who travels by a road on which he never went before thinks that every house which he sees from afar is an inn, and on finding that it is not fixes his trust on some other, and so from house to house until he comes to the inn; so our soul as soon as ever she enters on this new and hitherto untrodden path of life bends her gaze on the highest good as the goal, and therefore believes that everything she sees which appears to contain some good in itself is that highest good. And because her knowledge is at first imperfect through inexperience and lack of instruction, small goods appear great to her, and therefore her desires are first directed to these. So we see little children fixing their chief desire on an apple; then as they go farther they desire a small bird; then going farther still fine clothes; after this a horse, then a mistress; after this moderate riches, then great, and afterwards the greatest wealth. And this comes to pass because in none of these things does a man find that of which he is in quest, but thinks to find it farther on. Wherefore it may be seen that one object of desire stands in front of another before the eyes of our soul, as if they were arranged in the form of a pyramid; for the smallest object at first covers them all and is so to speak, the apex over the final object of desire, namely God who is, as it were the base of all. Thus the farther we go from the apex towards the base, the greater the objects of desire appear; and this is the reason why man's desires, as they gain their object, become successively greater." (*Convivio* IV, xii.)

P. 35, l. 20. Scholastic philosophy distinguishes four kinds of causes —the *material* cause, the matter out of which a thing is made; the *formal* cause, which determines the material indeterminate and indifferent of itself, to be the particular thing it is; the *efficient* cause, which actually brings it into existence; the *final* cause, which is the end or purpose for which it is produced.

St. Thomas expresses it thus: "Now there are four kinds of cause, *viz.* final, formal, efficient, and material, to which a material disposition also is to be reduced, though it is not a cause simply but relatively. According to these four different causes one thing is said to be loved for another. In respect of the final cause, we love medicine, for instance, for health; in respect of the formal cause, we love a man for his virtue, because, to wit, by his virtue he is formally good and therefore lovable; in respect of the efficient cause, we love certain men because, for instance, they are the sons of such and such a father; and in respect of the disposition which is reducible to the genus of a material cause, we speak of loving something for that which disposed us to love it, *e.g.* we love a man for the favors received from him, although after we have begun to love our friend, we no longer love him for his favors, but for his virtue.

"Accordingly, as regards the first three ways, we love God, not for anything else, but for Himself. For He is not directed to anything else as to an end, but is Himself the last end of all things; nor does He require to receive any form in order to be good, for His very substance is His goodness, which is itself the exemplar of all other good things; nor again does goodness accrue to Him from aught else, but from Him to all other things.

"In the fourth way, however, He can be loved for something else, because we are disposed by certain things to advance in His love, for instance, by favors bestowed by Him, by the rewards we hope to receive from Him, or even by the punishments which we are minded to avoid through Him." (*Summa Theologica,* II. ii, q. 27, art. 3.)

P. 37, ll. 2-3. This division of man's natural passions into four is of ancient pagan origin. Zeno, founder of the Stoics, looked upon them as evil in themselves and consequently to be crushed in him who would be wise. The same idea is found in Cicero's writings:

"Therefore the man, whoever he is, whose soul is tranquilized by restraint and consistency and who is at peace with himself, so that he neither pines away in distress, nor is broken down by fear, nor consumed with a thirst of longing in pursuit of some ambition, nor maudlin in the exuberance of meaningless eagerness—he is the wise man of whom we are in quest, he is the happy man who can think no human occurrence insupportable to the point of dispiriting him, or unduly delightful to the point of rousing him to ecstasy. For what can seem of moment in human occurrences to a man who keeps all eternity before his eyes and knows the vastness of the universe?" (*Tusculanae Disputationes* IV, xvii.)

According to the christian economy of life these great passions should be properly directed instead of being entirely suppressed. St. Augustine suggests their proper objects:

"With us according to the holy Scriptures and sound doctrine, the citizens of the Holy City of God, while they live according to God in the pilgrimage of this life, fear and desire, grieve and rejoice. And because their love is right, they have all these affections right. They fear eternal punishment, they desire eternal life; they grieve for the present because they still *groan within* themselves, *waiting for the adoption, . . . the redemption of the body.* (Romans VIII, 23.) They rejoice in hope, for *then shall come to pass the saying that is written: Death is swallowed up in victory.* (1 Corinthians XV, 54.) They fear to sin, they desire to persevere; they sorrow for sin, they rejoice in good works." (*De Civitate Dei,* XIV, ix.)

St. Bernard is especially fond of pointing out how these great powers of the soul may be sanctified. For instance, in one of his sermons for the beginning of Lent we read:

"Take diligent heed to what thou lovest, what thou fearest, whereat thou dost rejoice, or art sad; else, under the habit of religion thou shalt find a worldly mind, under the garb of conversion a perverse heart. For the whole heart is in these four affections, and of these I deem is to be understood what is written, that thou shalt be converted to the Lord in thy whole heart. Therefore let thy love be converted, so that thou mayest love nought save Him or, at least, for His sake. Let thy fear, too, be converted to Him; for all fear is perverse, by which thou fearest aught save Him or not for sake of Him. So, too, let thy joy and thy sorrow in like wise be converted to Him. But this will come to pass if thou dost neither grieve nor rejoice save as He doth. For what is more perverse than to be glad when thou hast done evil, and to exult in things that are wicked? But that sorrow too, which is according to the flesh, *worketh death.* If thou sorrowest for thine own sin or that of thy neighbour, thou dost well, and this sorrow *is unto salvation.* (2 Corinthians VII, 10.) If thou dost rejoice at the gifts of grace, this joy is holy, and a secure joy in the Holy Spirit. Thou shouldst rejoice, too, in the love of Christ with thy brother in his prosperity, and grieve with him in his adversity, as it is written: *Rejoice with them that rejoice; weep with them that weep.* (Romans XII, 15.)" (*In Capite Jejunii,* Sermo II, § 3.)

In another passage St. Bernard clearly distinguishes these passions when uncontrolled and consequently sinful, from the same powers when controlled and virtuous:

"Go forth, O ye daughters of Sion, pleasure-seeking souls, from sense of flesh to understanding of mind, from servitude of carnal concupiscence to liberty of spiritual discernment, *and see King Solomon in the diadem wherewith his mother crowned him* (*Canticle* III, 11). Others, indeed, are crowned as imitators of Him, but by labor aided with grace. He alone was crowned by His mother for He alone came forth from his mother's womb with ordered affections *as a bridegroom coming out of his bride-chamber.* (*Psalm* XVIII, 6.) These four affections are well known: love and joy, fear and sorrow. Without them the human soul does not subsist. But to some they are as a crown, to some unto confusion. For when purified and set in order they make the soul worthy of a crown of virtues; when inordinate they cause it to be cast down and shameful through confusion. Now they are purified thus. If those things are loved which should be loved, if those are loved more which are more to be loved, if those are not loved which are not to be loved, love will be purified. In the beginning fear, then joy, afterwards sorrow and finally love in consummation. The composition of these is in this wise. From fear and joy is born prudence. Fear is the cause of prudence, joy the fruit. From joy and sorrow is born temperance of which sorrow is the cause, joy the fruit. From sorrow and love is born fortitude and sorrow is the cause of fortitude, love its fruit. The circle of the crown is closed. From love and fear is born justice, and fear is the cause of justice, love the fruit.

"Consider, then, how these affections, cultivated in their proper order are virtues, but when this order is violated they become sources of disquiet. If sorrow follows fear it engenders despair. If joy follows love it issues in dissolution. Therefore let joy follow fear, for fear guards against the future. Joy rejoices in the present and possesses the objective of prudent caution. Therefore let joy test fear. Tested fear is nothing else than prudence. Let sorrow accompany joy, for he who remembers sad things embraces glad ones with moderation. Therefore let sorrow temper joy. Tempered joy is nothing else than temperance. Let love be joined to sorrow, for he who through love, longs for the things that should be loved, bears sorrow bravely. Therefore let love strengthen sorrow. But strengthened sorrow is nothing else than fortitude. Let love be joined to fear, for he who does not neglect things to be feared, will cleave ordinately to those which are to be loved. Love, then, sets fear in order. Fear set in order is nought else save justice. Two affections, joy and sorrow, do not extend to other things; for in ourselves we rejoice, and in ourselves we sorrow. Love and fear extend elsewhere. For fear is a natural affection which joins us to our superior on the lower side and is related to God alone. Love is an affection which joins us to our superior and to our inferior and to our equal, and is related to God and to our neighbor. Now in these two consists perfect justice, that we fear God for His power, love Him for His goodness and love our neighbor for the fellowship of nature." (*Sermones de diversis,* Sermo L, §§ 2-3.)

P. 37, ll. 11-12. *No man ever hated his own flesh.* St. Thomas has commented upon this same text as follows:

"Properly speaking, it is impossible for a man to hate himself. For everything naturally desires good, nor can anyone desire anything for himself, save under the aspect of good: for *evil is outside the scope of the will,* as Dionysius says (*Div. Nom.* iv.). Now to love a man is to will good to him, as stated above (Q. XXVI, A. 4). Consequently, a man must, of necessity, love himself; and it is impossible for a man to hate himself, properly speaking.

"But accidentally it happens that a man hates himself: and this in two ways. First, on the part of the good which a man wills to himself. For it happens sometimes that what is desired as good in some particular respect, is simply evil; and in this way, a man accidentally wills evil to himself; and thus hates himself. Secondly in regard to himself, to whom he wills good. For each thing is that which is predominant in it; wherefore the state is said to do what the king does, as if the king were the whole state. Now it is clear that man is principally the mind of man. And it happens that some men account themselves as being principally that which they are in their material and sensitive nature. Wherefore they love themselves according to what they take themselves to be, while they hate that which they really are, by desiring what is contrary to reason.—And in both these ways, *he that loveth iniquity hateth not only his own soul,* but also himself." (*Summa Theologica,* II. i, q. 29, art. 4.)

P. 47, l. 1. A detailed discussion of the quality of glorified bodies is found in St. Thomas:

"Just as the soul that enjoys the sight of God will be filled with spiritual brightness, so by a kind of overflow from the soul to the body, the latter will be, in its own way, clothed with the brightness of glory. Hence the Apostle says (1 Corinthians, XV, 18): *It is sown,* namely the body, *in dishonour, it shall rise in glory:* because now this body of ours is impervious to light, whereas then it will be full of light, according to Saint Matthew XIII, 43: *Then shall the just shine like the sun in the kingdom of their Father.*

"Again, the soul which, united to its last end, will enjoy the sight of God, will find its every desire fulfilled: and since the body moves in obedience to the soul's desire, the result will be that the body's movements will be in perfect obedience to the spirit. Hence the bodies of the blessed, after the resurrection, will be agile: and this is indicated by the Apostle (1 Corinthians XV, 43): *It is sown in weakness, it shall rise in power.* For we feel the body's weakness when we find it unable to satisfy the soul's desire in the movements and actions commanded by the soul. This weakness will then be wholly removed, because the body will receive an overflow of power from the soul united to God: wherefore again it is said of the just (Wisdom III, 7) that they *shall run to and fro, like sparks among the reeds.* Their movements, however, will not be occasioned by need, since those who possess God need nothing, but they will be exhibitions of power.

"Moreover, just as the soul that enjoys God will have its desire fulfilled through having obtained possession of all good, so also will its desire be fulfilled as to the removal of all evil, since there can be no evil where the sovereign good is. Accordingly, the body that is perfected by that soul will, in conformity with it, be free from all evil both in act and in potentiality. In act, since in it there will be neither corruption nor deformity, nor defect of any kind: in potentiality, because nothing will be able to do it any harm; so that it will be impassible. This impassibility, however, does not imply insensibility: for they will use their senses for such pleasures as are not incompatible with a state of incorruption. The Apostle indicates this state of impassibility, when he says (1 Corinthians, XV, 42): *It is sown in corruption, it shall rise in incorruption.*

"Again, the soul that enjoys God will adhere to Him most completely and will participate in His goodness in the highest degree possible that is consistent with its mode of being. Wherefore both the body will be perfectly subject to the soul and it will share in the soul's properties, as far as possible, in acuteness of sense, in the orderliness of the bodily appetite, and in the superlative perfection of its nature. For a thing is so much the more perfect in nature, as its matter is more completely subject to its form. Hence the Apostle says (I Corinthians XV, 44): *It is sown a natural* (*animal*) *body; it shall rise a spiritual body.* In the resurrection, the body will be spiritual. Not that it will be a spirit, as some wrongly understood (whether *spirit* means a spiritual substance, or air or wind), but because it will be completely subject to the spirit. Even so, we speak of the *animal* body, not that it is an animal but because it is subject to animal passions and needs food.

"From the foregoing it follows that just as man's soul will be raised to the glory of the heavenly spirits by seeing God in His essence, as above stated, (Bk. III, ch. li.), so will his body be uplifted to the properties of the heavenly bodies, in brightness, impassibility, easy and unwearying movement, and in being perfected by its most perfect form. This is what the Apostle meant when he said that man will rise again with a celestial body, celestial indeed not in nature, but in glory. Hence, after saying that *there are bodies celestial, and bodies terrestrial,* he adds that *one is the glory of the celestial, and another the glory of the terrestrial.* (1 Corinthians XV, 40.) And just as the glory to which the human soul is uplifted surpasses the natural power of the heavenly spirits, as we have proved (Bk. III, ch. liii.), so does the glory of risen bodies surpass the natural perfection of heavenly bodies in greater brightness, more changeless impassibility, and more perfect agility and dignity of nature." (*Contra Gentiles* Bk. IV, ch. lxxxvi.)

Pp. 47-48. St. Thomas reconciles the soul's beatitude with its yearning for its body, in this wise:

"Since hope is a theological virtue having God for its object, its principal object is the glory of the soul, which consists in the enjoyment of God and not the glory of the body. Moreover, although the glory of the body is something arduous in comparison with human nature yet it is not so for one who has the glory of the soul, both because the glory of the body is a very small thing as compared with the glory of the soul and because one who has the glory of the soul has already the sufficient cause of the glory of the body." (*Summa Theologica* II. ii, q. 18, art. 2, ad 4.)

Pp. 47-49. According to St. Thomas, since it is impossible to set any definite limit to the perfection of charity in this life, it always remains only relatively perfect:

"The perfection of charity may be understood in two ways: first with regard to the object loved, secondly with regard to the person who loves. With regard to the object loved, charity is perfect if the object be loved as much as it is lovable. Now God is as lovable as He is good and His goodness is infinite, wherefore He is infinitely lovable. But no creature can love Him infinitely since all created power is finite. Consequently no creature's charity can be perfect in this way; the charity of God alone can, whereby He loves Himself.

"On the part of the person who loves, charity is perfect when he loves as much as he can. This happens in three ways. First, so that a man's whole heart is always actually borne towards God: this is the perfection of the charity of heaven and is not possible in this life, wherein, by reason of the weakness of human life, it is impossible to think always actually of God and to be moved by love towards Him. Secondly, so that man makes an earnest endeavour to give his time to God and Divine things, while scorning other things except in so far as the needs of the present life demand. This is the perfection of charity that is possible to a wayfarer; but it is not common to all who have charity. Thirdly so that a man gives his whole heart to God habitually, *viz.* by neither thinking nor desiring anything contrary to the love of God; and this perfection is common to all who have charity." (*Summa Theologica,* II. ii, q. 24, art. 8.)

P. 53, ll. 11-13. This comprehensive meaning of *chaste love,* so common in medieval times has been narrowed to a much more restricted application in our day. Medieval usage is well illustrated in the anonymous fourteenth-century "Epistle of Prayer:"

"Chaste love is that when thou askest of God neither releasing of pain, nor increasing of meed, nor yet sweetness in His love in this life; but if it be any certain time that thou covetest sweetness as for a refreshing of thy ghostly mights, that they fail not in the way; but thou askest of God naught but Himself, and neither thou reckest nor lookest after whether thou shalt be in pain or bliss, so that thou have Him that thou lovest—this is chaste love, this is perfect love." (Cf. "The Cell of Self-Knowledge", Gardner, ed. p. 86.)

P. 55, l. 14. According to the terminology of Scholastic philosophy, an *accident* is a note which is neither an essential constituent of a given species, nor a necessary concomitant of its essence, but may be absent or present in individuals without affecting their essence. A *substance* is a being that exists in itself, and not in any other being as in a subject of inhesion. Charity as it exists in a human soul is an *accident.* As it exists in God it is identical with the Divine Substance and is the Divine Essence.

In his "Sermons on the *Canticle of Canticles*" Saint Bernard writes:

"If anything at all can be rightly predicated of God, it will be more correct and more proper to say: God is Greatness, God is Goodness, God is Justice, God is Wisdom, than: God is great, God is good, God is just, God is wise. . . . In the pure and perfect simplicity of the Divine Substance nothing can be found that is not Itself, nor is Itself anything distinct from God—Heaven forbid that the Catholic Church should ever admit either a substance or anything else by which God is and which is not itself God." (Sermon LXXX, §§ 7-8.)

A modern authority speaking of these two modes of predication says:

"Predication by abstract substantives expresses the absolute perfection of the divine simplicity; whereas that by concrete adjectives, such as good, just, wise, always imports some composition, as signifying a quality superadded and inherent. For he who is good *is possessed* of goodness: but he who is said to possess goodness seems to be distinct from goodness, is not goodness itself, and therefore, in order to be good, must be informed by goodness; but information presupposes composition. Again, the former mode of predication expresses the infinity of the divine perfections, for what goodness can be wanting to One who is goodness itself? . . . Lastly, it expresses perfection not as a quality inhering in the substance, but as identical with the substance or essence." But he adds, "Since such substantival predicates signify abstract perfection, lest it be thought that God has only an abstract and ideal existence, *viz.* in the minds of men, it is well to combine the concrete with the abstract, and to speak of Him, not only as goodness, wisdom, justice, *etc.* but also as good, wise, and just, because this latter manner of expression indicates His objective existence." ("Dogmatic Theology," Hurter, vol. II. p. 29.)

P. 61. This same thought is thus expressed by St. Augustine ("The City of God" XV, xxii):

"Every creature, since it is good, can be loved well and badly: well, that is, when order is preserved; badly, when order is disturbed. If the Creator be loved truly, that is, if He Himself, not aught else instead of Him which is not He, be loved, He cannot be loved badly. . . . Therefore it seems to me that a brief and true definition of virtue is the *Order of Love;* on account of which in the holy canticle the Bride of Christ, the City of God, sings; *He set in order charity in me.* (Canticle of Canticles II, 4: Cf. Jacopone da Todi, *Lauda* xc.)

P. 63, ll. 7-20. In Saint Augustine we read:

"If to any the tumult of the flesh were hushed, hushed the phantasies of earth and waters and air; hushed too, the heavens; and the very soul hushed unto herself, and passed beyond herself by not thinking of self; hushed all dreams and imaginary revelations, every language and every sign, and utterly hushed whatever exists only to pass away: since, if any should hear, all these are saying, *We made not ourselves, but He made us that abideth for ever;* if, having said this, they then were to be silent, having roused our ears to Him who made them, and He alone were to speak, not by them but by Himself, that we might hear His word not through tongue of flesh nor through voice of Angel nor through sound of thunder nor in the dark riddle of a similitude, but were to hear Him whom in these we love, His very self without these; and even as we now stretch out ourselves, and, in rapid thought, touch that Eternal Wisdom that abideth over all, if this could be continued, and other visions of kind far unlike be withdrawn, and this one catch up and absorb and bury its beholder amidst inward joys, so that our unending life might be such as was that moment of understanding for which we sighed: would not this be to *enter into the joy of thy Lord?*" ("Confessions," IX. x.)

P. 65, ll. 4-6. This concluding sentence illustrates how austere is the Christian ideal of the love of God. St. Thomas expresses it very briefly: "The blessed in glory will have no compassion upon the damned." (*Summa Theologica,* III Suppl. q. 94, art. 2.) And this is the explanation in Beatrice's words to Virgil:

> "God made me such, so far avails His grace,
> Your sorrow may not touch me where I stay
> Nor yet the burning flames of that low place."
> (*Inferno,* ii, 91-92. Eleanor Vinton Murray, translator.)

NOTES ON SERMONS ON THE *CANTICLE OF CANTICLES*

P. 96, ll. 1-3. This sentence may, possibly, be rhetorical. But as it reads, it is a clear statement of the teaching of those modern psychologists who hold with Scotus that there is no *real* distinction between the faculties of the soul and the soul itself. "It is admitted by all," writes Gutberlet, "that a faculty is not a force distinct from and independent of the essence of the soul, but it is the soul itself, which operates in and through the faculty." ("Die Psychologie," p. 4.)

P. 96, ll. 6-7. Cf. *"De Diligendo Deo,"* chapter VIII, § 1 and notes.

P. 102, ll. 17-18. There is some uncertainty concerning the authorship of Psalm CXXXI. Saint Robert Bellarmine writes: "Either it was composed by Solomon after the building of the Temple when the ark of the Lord was brought into the place prepared for it, or, at any rate, it was then sung by him, although David may have written it for that occasion and given it to his son." In either case, the Saint's allusion is a forceful one.

P. 105, ll. 10-11. There is special significance in these words as spoken by Saint Bernard who had refused such important bishoprics as Rheims, Genoa and Milan.

P. 110, ll. 11-14. Saint Augustine writes in a similar strain. Speaking of the writings of Hortensius he says: "There was only one thing in all that eloquent language which distressed me. The name of Christ was not to be found there. . . . And any writing in which that Name was wanting, however learned, polished and true it might be, could not wholly satisfy me." ("Confessions", Book III, chapter iv.)

P. 110, ll. 14-15. There is a striking similarity between this passage and the hymn, *"Jubilus Rhythmicus de Nomine Jesu,"* some stanzas of which compose the Vesper-hymn for the feast of the Holy Name. If the hymn was not written by Saint Bernard, as some scholars maintain, the twenty-second stanza, alone, proves it an amazing instance of literary parallelism:

"Jesu decus angelicum
In aure dulce canticum
In ore mel mirificum
In corde nectar cœlicum."

Archbishop Goodier has edited the complete Latin text of the hymn with a translation into English verse.

P. 113, ll. 9-18. This passage reminds us of the Preface of the Christmas Masses: "By the Mystery of the Word made Flesh, a new ray of Thy glory has shone upon the eyes of our minds; that while we know our God visibly, we may by Him be drawn to the love of things invisible."

P. 117, ll. 18-19. In the "Imitation of Christ" we read: "Jesus has now many lovers of His heavenly kingdom, but few are willing to bear His cross; He has many that are desirous of comfort, few of tribulation. All desire to rejoice with Him, few to suffer with Him." (Book II, chapter xi.)

P. 124, l. 22. "Know thyself," the Greek inscription over the portico of the Temple of Apollo at Delphi, is of doubtful origin. It has been attributed to Thales, one of the Seven Wise Men of Greece and to many other ancient Greeks, and even to Phemonoe, a mythological Greek poetess, daughter of Apollo. Hence, Juvenal's line in Satire XI:

E caelo descendit γνῶθι σεαυτὸν.

But the saying is popularly associated with Socrates, as a brief expression of his ideal of wisdom.

P. 125, ll. 3-5. The Saint refrains here from expressing an opinion as to whether Mary, who anointed our Lord and Mary, the sister of Martha, were the same. But in Sermon III *in Assumptione,* §2, he identifies them as the same person.

Commenting upon this passage, the priest of Mount Melleray who is translating Saint Bernard's works, writes: "Another matter in dispute is the number of anointings. Is the anointing of the Savior's Feet by the sinful woman spoken of in St. Luke VII, the same as that mentioned in St. John XII? St. Bernard evidently thinks so, and hence identifies Mary the sister of Martha, with the *woman who was a sinner.* But it is now generally believed that, although performed by the same person, the anointings were really distinct. As a matter of fact, there is much more reason for identifying the anointing described in St. Mark XIV with that of St. John XII, which, however, St. Bernard assumes to be different, if not by different persons. Both took place at Bethany, the native village of Mary, Martha and Lazarus; on both occasions the disciples complained of the waste; and on both our Lord answered them in the same words. True, St. Mark tells us it was the Head that was anointed, whilst according to St. John it was the Feet. But these statements are easily reconciled by supposing both narratives to be but partial accounts of the same event, and supplementary of each other."

P. 129, ll. 18-19. In Hebrew, *Kedar* means "black skin" or "black-skinned man." In the latter sense it was sometimes used as a patronymic to designate the Arabs. Hence, in the present context, referred to *black* in the fourth verse, it would seem to be in more literal agreement than the Saint implies.

P. 130, ll. 17-18. Saint Bernard here translates *pellis* as *curtain,* instead of *pavillion,* as the Douay Version renders it in this Psalm although it uses *curtain* in the translation of the Canticle.

P. 135, ll. 8-10. In a later passage (Sermon XXXIII, §6.) the Saint expresses a different opinion: "Jacob, still abiding in his mortal body, saw the Lord face to face, and his soul was saved. (Cf. Genesis XXXII, 30.) Moses beheld Him, not in types and figures, nor in dreams, as did other prophets, but in a way transcendent and known to none but God and himself. (Cf. Numbers XII, 6-8.) Isaias, after the eyes of his heart had been opened, saw the Lord high upon His throne and lifted up. (Cf. Isaias VI, 1.) Saint Paul was caught up into Paradise and heard unutterable words and with his own eyes saw Jesus Christ his Lord." (Cf. 2 Corinthians XII, 4.) This same opinion was expressed earlier by Saint Augustine in one of his letters (Cf. *Epistolarum Classis III, Epistola CXLVII, "De Videndo Deo."*), and later by Saint Thomas. (Cf. *"Summa Theologica"*, II. ii, q. clxxv, art. 3.)

P. 152, ll. 15-16. The allusion here is to profane knowledge considered in itself. In the case of one whose vocation demands such learning, it is obviously no longer *indifferent*.

P. 163, ll. 3-17. Saint Teresa gives this description of ecstatic revelation: "While the soul is in this ecstasy, our Lord favors it by discovering to it secrets, such as heavenly mysteries and imaginary visions." ("Interior Castle," Sixth Mansion, chapter IV, §5.) Again: "In an instant the mind learns so many things at once that if the imagination and intellect spent years in striving to enumerate them, it could not recall a thousandth part of them." (*Ibid.,* chapter V, §8.)

St. John of the Cross says: "It is as if God drew back some of the many veils and coverings that are before it [the soul], so that it might see what He is: then indeed—but still dimly, because all the veils are not drawn back, that of faith remaining—the divine face full of grace bursts through and shines." ("The Living Flame," stanza IV, §7.)

Similar descriptions of spiritual ecstasy will be found in Father Poulain's, "The Graces of Interior Prayer," pp. 262-282.

P. 170, ll. 21-25. In 1795 the Abbey of Clairvaux where Saint Bernard was buried was sold at auction by the republican government of France. Subsequently the remains of the Saint were disinterred when the purchaser, Pierre-Claude Canson, began to convert the abbey into a glass factory.

In 1855 Count de Montalembert, in examining the Saint's relics, found among his bones a piece of wood covered with parchment. On it were written the words, *Fasciculus myrrhae dilectus meus mihi, inter ubera mea commorabitur.* A wooden link nailed to the board has led to the conjecture that the inscription hung in the Saint's cell. As Count de Montalembert expresses it: "The inference is surely not a violent one that the Saint had practiced his own precept, and that this text was written out, it may be by his own hand, to hang upon the wall of his cell, to be literally, *always before his eyes.* Then his disciples, after his lamented death, would carry out the precept so dear to their master, a step further. They would lay it upon his breast in his tomb, and thus his devout aspiration would be accomplished: *inter ubera mea commorabitur.*"

P. 177, ll. 23-24. Saint John of the Cross makes this same distinction between ecstasy of the will and of the intellect. In "The Dark Night of the Soul," he writes: "Occasionally, amid the darkness, the soul receives light—*light shineth in darkness* (St. John I, 5.)—the mystical inflowing streaming directly into the understanding, and the will in some measure partaking of it, with calmness and pureness so exquisite and so delicious to the soul as to be utterly indescribable: now God is felt to be present in one way, and again in another. Sometimes, too, it wounds the will at the same time, and enkindles love deeply, tenderly, and strongly. For, as I have said, the more the understanding is purified the more perfectly and delicate, at times, is the union of the understanding and the will. But, before the soul attains to this state, it is more common for the touch of the fire of love to be felt in the will than for the touch of the perfect intelligence to be felt in the understanding." (Bk. I, Chapter XIII, §§ 1-2.) (Cf. also, St. Thomas, "Summa Theologica," II, ii q. clxxv.)

P. 178, ll. 10-12. In his sermon *"De Domo Spirituali,"* the Saint describes discretion as, "the virtue by which we distinguish true virtues from those which are disguised as such, and counterfeits."

P. 179, l. 1. Saint Francis of Sales distinguishes these two kinds of charity in great detail: "There are two ways of exercising our love for God, one affective, the other effective or active. By the first we place our affections in God, and all that He loves becomes interesting to us. By the second we serve God and accomplish what He ordains. The former unites us to the goodness of God, the latter makes us submissive to His holy will. By the one a kind of correspondence is established between us and God, by the communication of His Spirit to our souls and hence arise sentiments of complacency, of benevolence, ecstasies and spiritual ardors. The other imparts solidity to our resolutions, and an inviolable fidelity to our obedience. . . . Affective love conceives the work, effective love brings it forth, if I may so speak. By the first our happiness and delight are centred in God. By the second we serve and obey Him." ("Love of God," Book VI, chapter i.)

P. 179, ll. 14-16. This same subject is treated in greater detail in *"De Diligendo Deo,"* chapter X. In speaking of charity in which "a man's whole heart is always actually borne towards God," Saint Thomas Aquinas calls it, "the perfection of the charity of heaven." Then the Angelic Doctor concludes: "It is not possible in this life; wherein, by reason of the weakness of human life, it is impossible to think always actually of God and to be moved by love towards Him." (*Summa Theologica,* II. ii, q. 24, art. 8.)

P. 180, l. 6. It is evident that here and elsewhere, when the Saint speaks of "charity of action" as distinguished from "charity of affection," he includes a degree of the latter as an essential of the former. The opening sentence of the next paragraph is: "I do not say that we should be without affection, and that with dry heart we should employ our hands only in the performance of external deeds." And later in the same paragraph, speaking of "charity of action" the Saint says: "Although it does not as yet refresh the soul with that sweet love just mentioned, yet it inflames our hearts with an intense love of that love itself. *Let us not love in word,* it says, *nor in tongue, but in deed and in truth.*" (1 St. John III, 18.)

P. 182, ll. 18-20. "Every act should be proportionate both to its object and to the agent. But from its object it takes its species, while, from the power of the agent it takes the mode of its intensity: thus movement has its species from the term to which it tends, while the intensity of its speed arises from the disposition of the thing moved and the power of the mover. Accordingly love takes its species from its object, but its intensity is due to the lover.

"Now the object of charity's love is God, and man is the lover. Therefore the specific diversity of the love which is in accordance with charity, as regards the love of our neighbour, depends on his relation to God, so that, out of charity, we should wish a greater good to one who is nearer to God; for though the good which charity wishes to all, *viz.* everlasting happiness, is one in itself, yet it has various degrees according to various shares of happiness, and it belongs to charity to wish God's justice to be maintained, in accordance with which better men have a fuller share of happiness. And this regards the species of love; for there are different species of love according to the different goods that we wish for those whom we love.

"On the other hand, the intensity of love is measured with regard to the man who loves, and accordingly man loves those who are more closely united to him, with more intense affection as to the good he wishes for them, than he loves those who are better as to the greater good he wishes for them." (*"Summa Theologica,"* II, ii, q. 26, art. 7.)

P. 187, ll. 8-10. Saint Augustine's description of ingratitude is very similar: "Ingratitude . . . is the root of all spiritual evil. It is a wind that dries up and consumes everything that is good. It cuts off at their source, the waters of divine love for man." (*"Liber Soliloquiorum Animae ad Deum,"* XVIII.)

P. 190, ll. 1-2. It is difficult to reconcile with one another Saint Bernard's various descriptions of contemplation. Here he seems to stress the importance of the intellectual element. And in this Saint Thomas agrees when he says: "Contemplation regards the simple act of gazing on the truth. Wherefore Richard of Saint Victor says (*"De Contem-*

platione" i, 4.): 'Contemplation is the soul's clear and free dwelling upon the object of its gaze; meditation is the survey of the mind while occupied in searching for the truth: and cogitation is the mind's glance which is prone to wander.' " (*"Summa Theologica,"* II, ii, q. clxxx, a. 3.)

In *"Scala Claustralium"* the Saint like Saint Augustine, stresses the importance of the will and tells us that contemplation is, "an elevation of the soul, held suspended in God and tasting the joys of His eternal sweetness." Again, he says: "the first and highest contemplation is admiration of majesty." (*"De Consideratione,"* Book V.) And earlier in the same work we read: "Contemplation may be defined as the true and certain intuition of any object, or the certain apprehension of truth." (Book II.)

P. 190, ll. 6-8. The two spiritual states here described are alike in dispensing with sense activity. One makes use of the imagination and memory. The other transcends these activities, and is the result of the activity only of the spiritual faculties of intellect and will.

P. 193, ll. 9-13. There are in Christ three kinds of knowledge. 1) The knowledge which pertains to the Beatific Vision which was His as God. 2) The supernatural knowledge infused into His human soul in the Incarnation. 3) The experimental knowledge acquired by the use of His bodily senses. The last, only, can be said to have increased. Not that our Lord by the use of His bodily senses acquired any new knowledge. But some of the knowledge he already had, He thus acquired in a new way. That is, He acquired experimentally what He already knew by virtue of His Beatific Vision and the knowledge infused into His human soul.

Perhaps an example will make this clearer. It is not an original one, but I have no record of where I read it many years ago. An astronomer, let us say, computes with mathematical certainty, the location of a certain heavenly body that can not be detected by the naked eye. Then, looking through a telescope, he sees that very body in the position he had calculated. His actual knowledge, after he has looked through the telescope, is unchanged. By that use of the sense of sight no new knowledge was acquired. But the knowledge already acquired by mathematical computation, was acquired in a new way.

P. 214, l. 20. The quotations from the Prophet Osee (XIV, 6.) is not the exact wording of the text. It may be, as one commentator suggests, that the Saint made this quotation from memory.

P. 228, ll. 14-17. The Saint is here giving his monks practical instructions concerning the disposition of soul required for the reception of special graces. He is not attempting to describe what transpires in the soul when it has attained to the perfection of spiritual marriage as revealed by Saint John of the Cross and Saint Teresa in such passages as those cited below. Cf. notes on the last paragraph of this translation.

P. 229, ll. 16-17. The distinction between the mode of predication peculiar to God, and the predication used in speaking of creatures is given in the notes on page 247.

P. 230, l. 28. These are the opening words of the "Imitation of Christ," Book III, chapter V: "Love is a great thing."

P. 230, ll. 28-29. The hierarchy of human love ranging from servants to bride is beautifully described by the late Abbot Marmion, O.S.B. in his little volume, *"Sponsa Verbi,"* pp. 13-15.

P. 232. In the words of Saint John of the Cross: "The spiritual marriage of the soul and Son of God is, beyond all comparison, a far higher state than that of espousals, because it is a complete transformation of the soul into the Beloved, and because each of them surrenders to the other the entire possession of themselves in the perfect union of love, wherein the soul becomes divine, and by participation, God, as far as it is possible in this life." ("Spiritual Canticle" XXII, §3.)

Again: "As by natural marriage there are *two in one flesh* (Genesis II, 24.), so also in the spiritual marriage between God and the soul, there are two natures in one spirit and love, as we learn from Saint Paul who makes use of the same metaphor, saying: *He who is joined to the Lord is one spirit.* So when the light of a star, or of a burning candle, is united to that of the sun, the light is not that of a star or of a burning candle, but of the sun itself, which absorbs all other light in its own." (*Ibid,* XXII, §3.)

Saint Teresa, also has left us a description of this same spiritual experience. In "The Interior Castle" we read: "As far as I can understand, the soul, I mean the spirit of this soul, is made one with God." (Seventh Mansion II, §3.) Again: "Spiritual marriage is like rain falling from heaven into a river or stream, becoming one and the same liquid, so that the river and rain-water cannot be divided; or it resembles a streamlet flowing into the ocean, which cannot afterwards be disunited from it. This marriage may also be likened to a room into which a bright light enters through two windows—though divided when it enters, the light becomes one and the same." (*Ibid.* §5.)

The spiritual phenomenon here described and found in the writings of other Catholic mystics must not be confused with the literal "deification" of such false mysticism as the pantheistic quietism of the Beghards. It is briefly stated in one of Eckhardt's propositions condemned by Pope John XXII, March 27, 1329: "We are completely transformed into God and changed into Him. As, in the Sacrament, bread is changed into the Body of Christ, so I am changed into Him." (Cf. *"Enchiridion Symbolorum,* Denziger, §510.)